UNDERSTANDING
MEDIA STUDIES

TONY **SCHIRATO**   ANGI **BUETTNER**
THIERRY **JUTEL**   GEOFF **STAHL**

OXFORD
UNIVERSITY PRESS
AUSTRALIA & NEW ZEALAND

OXFORD
UNIVERSITY PRESS
AUSTRALIA & NEW ZEALAND

253 Normanby Road, South Melbourne, Victoria 3205, Australia

Oxford University Press is a department of the University of Oxford.
It furthers the University's objective of excellence in research,
scholarship and education by publishing worldwide in

Oxford New York

Auckland Cape Town Dar es Salaam Hong Kong Karachi
Kuala Lumpur Madrid Melbourne Mexico City Nairobi
New Delhi Shanghai Taipei Toronto

With offices in

Argentina Austria Brazil Chile Czech Republic France Greece
Guatemala Hungary Italy Japan Poland Portugal Singapore
South Korea Switzerland Thailand Turkey Ukraine Vietnam

OXFORD is a trademark of Oxford University Press
in the UK and in certain other countries

National Library of Australia Cataloguing-in-Publication entry

Understanding media studies / Tony Schirato ... [et al.]

9780195565492 (pbk)
Includes index.
Bibliography.

Mass media—Study and teaching.
Media literacy.

Schirato, Tony.

302.23

Cover design by Future Classic
Text design by Sarah Hazell
Typeset by Kerry Cooke, eggplant communications
Indexed by Tony Schirato
Printed in China by Sheck Wah Tong Printing Press Ltd

CONTENTS

2 Analysing the Media: Theories, Concepts and Techniques 27

3 Subjectivity and the Media 50

4 The Field of the Media 68

5 Media Audiences   92

6 Media and the Public Sphere   110

7 The Media as Spectacle   136

8 Networks and Data 156

9 Media Literacy and Everyday Life 173

GUIDED TOUR

Text, intertext and context

When we use the term **text** we usually refer to a conventional cultural 'package'—such as a book, film, television show, music video, CD and the like—which signals, in a number of easily recognisable ways, that it should be read and treated as a collection or unit. These conventional signals include authorship (the name of a writer, director or band), materiality (some books have hard covers, with softer pages in between), title (*Jaws* and *Jaws 2* would not be shown as the same text in cinemas) and certain kinds of boundary markers (a film often opens with the name of the production company and a musical score, and ends with credits). It also includes lists or inventories (a web page will open with the home page and then name or number all associated pages) and forms of address (a television current affairs, news, arts or sports show might start with a welcome from the host, and end with 'goodnight'). What all these conventions have in common is that they function as a frame that includes, arranges, and confers a unity and/or sense of homogeneity with regard to, various signs. At the same time, acts of inclusion are always simultaneously acts of exclusion; with paintings, for instance, a wooden frame literally demarcates the extent of the text, just as a camera frame works to omit and select content. Moreover, textual production—and the stitching together of a group of signs as a text—is dynamic, rather than set in stone:

> Texts are produced or created; this process … is an ongoing one; and the status of signs and texts is always relational and contingent … there are no natural units of signs within cultures—or anywhere in nature… Every time we treat something as if it were a text, we create a unit out of an infinite number of potential signs (Schirato & Webb 2004:23).

Let us return to the issue of what constitutes the community of the town of Rock Ridge in *Blazing Saddles*. There are a number of signs in the first half of the film that function, collectively, to define and authorise membership of the community. Skin colour is clearly one of these, but there are others such as names (all the people in the town appear to have the surname 'Johnson'), language (everyone speaks English) and religion (they all attend a Christian church service). There is both continuity and similarity across this collection—to the extent that it constitutes what the Russian theorist Mikhail Bakhtin calls a 'coherent complex of signs' (1986:103). That makes it, potentially at least, a text; and the ongoing process of negotiation and renegotiation between Cleavon Little and the townspeople (which moves, initially, from the outright rejection of 'Up yours, nigger' to the qualified 'I've baked a pie for you, but please don't tell anyone') is really about widening frames, and processes of selection and omission.

The identification, production, negotiation & interpretation of texts are tied with two other concepts: intertext and context. John Frow defines **intertextuality** as:

> the range of processes by which a text invokes another, but also the way texts are constituted as such by their relationships with other texts. No text is unique; we could not recognise it if it were. All texts are relevantly similar to some texts

Text Refers to conventional cultural 'packages' such as books, films, television shows, music videos, CDs and the like: they signal, in a number of easily recognisable ways, that they should be read and treated as a collection or unit.

Intertextuality The process through which individual texts relate to other texts and, in part, draw their meaning from that relation. Implies the systems of visible or invisible references that shape an individual text. All texts refer to other texts.

Margin notes: Glossary terms are highlighted in bold and explained in the margin to help students understand the meaning of important concepts.

---

dot com boom
The 1990s saw a surge in business interest in the Web. Thousands of start-up companies used the Web and the Internet as a business resource, with much speculation and venture capital invested in companies and individuals. By the end of the millennium most of them had collapsed.

doxa
A common and unquestioned statement that stands as self-evident truth.

emergent games
Games that offer an environment and sets of rules, without directing the way in which a player must proceed.

epistemology
The means by which we come to know and understand the world.

ethos
The fundamental disposition and beliefs in a field which guide and inform its participants' practices. This might not be codified in rules but it should be shared by all participants.

everyday life
Constitutes the social conditions within which the field of the media operates. Everyday life is also the main site of our productive and consumptive media activity.

fan fiction
A subgenre of writing wherein the readers of an established genre expand upon its possibilities, usually by writing new fiction about the characters within that genre.

fanzine
A small, often hand-printed magazine, dedicated to a specialised topic or cultural phenomenon.

fascism
A political ideology and system of government in which individual fate and actions are subordinated to the interest of the state embodied in the figure of an authoritarian leader. Relies on a strong sense of a common, and usually racial, identity to the exclusion of others to the point of violence, destruction, and even genocide. Example: Nazism in Germany (1933–1945).

field
See cultural field.

flâneur
An urban explorer and meanderer whose walk through a city, its streets, its shops, and its back alleys, constitutes a form of sensory immersion in the logic of consumer culture. The flâneur does not see himself or herself as a direct participant.

flash mob
Temporary gathering of people, called together for a collective prank, usually alerted through email or text messages.

fourth estate
Refers to the institutional status of the press. The first three estates are executive, legislative and judicial powers. The expression raises the status of the press to that of a pillar of democracy.

franchise
See media franchise.

Glossary: A full glossary appears at the end of the book.

window' of desires and performances, and a selection of subjectivities from which viewers can theoretically 'pick and choose'. The reality, of course, is somewhat more complex. As Judith Butler points out, the forms of subjectivity that are made available in the media, and the provision of the role models and exemplars that do a great deal of the work of commoditising those performances, are always bound up with various kinds of sociocultural authorisation: Is this normal? Is this fashionable? Is this desirable?

Go online
The Miley Cyrus 'scandal'

How does the commercial media deal with the question of the newly sexualised, desiring child? Let us look at the situation involving **Miley Cyrus**, the daughter of American country singer Billy Ray Cyrus. In 2007, when she was under 16 years of age, she took part in a series of media events (a *Vanity Fair* shoot by Annie Leibowitz, also involving her father; and music clips for songs such as '7 Things' and 'Start All Over' where she was represented as sexually desiring and desirable. Moreover, these texts simultaneously emphasised her status as a child and a sexual commodity, without any sense of contradiction or ambiguity. This all drew a considerable amount of media attention—in newspapers, talkback radio, television news reports, Internet blogs and YouTube clips—about whether or not her behaviour in the media was appropriate. More specifically, it called into question her status as a role model for young girls.

The *Vanity Fair* photographs were read as sexual (and sexualising) for a variety of reasons: Cyrus was naked from the waist up (but with her breasts covered) in one shot, and in others the way her body was arranged (shots of her breasts from the side, held tightly in a black top; lying back staring knowingly at the camera) suggested sexual availability and knowledge. This sexual and sexualised reading was generally privileged over other explanations (Leibowitz is a photographer whose work is associated with, and part of the field of, art and aesthetics; draping the daughter's body over the father connoted familial affection) because of various intertexts, specifically photographs on the Internet showing her pulling down a top to reveal her bra, and another of her naked in a shower (behind frosted glass). The simultaneous combination of the insistence and denial of overt sexuality gave rise to a parody, also on YouTube, featuring a fake scenario of Annie Leibowitz urging Billy Ray to put his hand on his daughter's breast, while in the foreground a Disney executive explains that he is at the shoot to ensure that Miley Cyrus's 'family image' is not being damaged. What made all this particularly scandalous was precisely this insistence that the subject of desire and desirability was a child. In the *Vanity Fair* shots she is presented as a little girl—kissing and cuddling daddy. In the clip for 'Start All Over' she is initially presented as cuddling under the sheets of a doll-like bed.

Go online
Pavement magazine

The Miley Cyrus example is becoming increasingly commonplace, even as it generates moral denunciation, ridicule and scandal. A similarly blatant example can be found in the Spring 2006 issue of the glossy fashion magazine *Pavement*, which was published in New Zealand (it stopped publishing in 2007). The cover of this 'special teen issue' shows a prepubescent girl in a short, off-the-shoulder dress with one half-formed breast partly visible. Regardless of the girl's age, she is made to look like she is 13 or so. The idea is clearly to refer to the idea of, and desire associated with, paedophilia. Most of the images in the issue are presented

---

Go online: Directs students to go online at www.oup.com.au/orc/ums to access a range of online resources that are integrated with the book—including annotated web links to articles, videos, photographic material and interviews, together with case studies and questions.

Additional reading: Annotated lists of key references (grouped as introductory or advanced reading) offer guidance to students about how to delve deeper to find further information and to research topics of particular interest.

Conclusion

The iPod, as a cultural icon of the empowered listener, is a provocative example on which to close this discussion of the audience. There are, as we have outlined in this chapter, a variety of ways in which we engage with media texts, as individuals and as part of a broader social community or network. There is space, as we have seen, for the audience to be active, to use the media as a tool, either for themselves or against the media itself. However, this is not to suggest that power and ideology have disappeared. We are still caught up in larger and more expansive networks of economic, political and social control, as the YouTube example illustrates. The manner in which media are produced and consumed has changed in a way that suggests that power is not simply coming from the top down, as Horkheimer and Adorno (1972) otherwise suggest. Power can be distributed in different kinds of ways, through different channels, and analysing it requires an acute awareness of the complexity of the contemporary audience, as many of the models outlined here demonstrate. Increasingly, media texts are produced for narrower and more specific audience types, with regard to lifestyle, age, gender, sexuality, race and ethnicity. In the last few decades, we have moved away from broadcasting as the preferred model to narrowcasting, with programming increasingly tailored to different tastes. The audience as entity and concept is constantly changing, subject to ever finer gradations of marketing techniques as well as sociological study. The individual and collective experience of the media in this shift is caught up in technological changes and economic imperatives as well as the emergence of new media in ways that the following chapters will consider in more detail.

Additional reading

Introductory

Gauntlett, D. (ed.) (2000). *Web Studies: Rewiring Media Studies for the Digital Age*. London: Arnold.
  A useful consideration of the Internet and related culture.

Jermyn, D. and Brooker, W. (eds) (2003). *The Audience Studies Reader*. London: Routledge.
  This collection provides an overview of key writings on audiences.

Advanced

Adorno, T. (1990). *The Culture Industry: Selected Essays on Mass Culture*. New York: Routledge.
  The best known critical theory account of culture.

Bourdieu, P. (1989). *Distinction*. London: Routledge.
  A highly influential book on the relation between culture and audiences.

HISTORY OF MEDIA AND TECHNOLOGY

Introduction

From the late nineteenth century onward, the mass media and popular culture have, by and large, mediated the world for us: they have provided the images, information, stories, templates and categories that we use to see and understand everything around us, including our bodies, identities, interests, desires and fantasies. This has not always been the case: the period of the last 200 years has been marked by significant changes in the ways in which human perception is organised, and the media and their technologies have been central to this development. These changes are not attributable to technology alone, since technology is always produced out of, and determined by, historical circumstances. However, the way we see the world cannot be understood or explained without taking into account different forms of technology, such as the camera, motion pictures and, more generally, the electronic and digital media.

In explaining the relationship between technological changes, human perception and history, we can turn to the ideas of the German cultural theorist Walter Benjamin, particularly those expressed in his essay 'The Work of Art in the Age of Mechanical Reproduction' (1979). Benjamin draws a line from woodcuts, the printing press, etchings, lithographs and photography to sound film in order to show how high culture, which had been considered original, authentic and specific to a time and place, gradually began to 'lose its aura' (Benjamin 1979). This had come about, Benjamin suggested, once high cultural texts could be reproduced in mass quantities. There may be just one, original painting of the *Mona Lisa* hanging in the Louvre in Paris, but with mass reproduction anyone could obtain a cheap and relatively authentic-looking copy for their home or office—or an electronic version for the computer wallpaper.

The ramifications of this development reach out much further than giving people the opportunity to own copies of famous paintings. The technology that facilitates and drives the activities of the mass media has effectively changed our everyday lives. Benjamin quotes the French poet Paul Valéry to the effect that:

> Just as water, gas, and electricity are brought into our houses from far off to satisfy our needs in response to a minimal effort, so we shall be supplied with visual or auditory images, which will appear and disappear at a simple movement of the hand (1979:221).

Valéry's prediction is now, of course, a reality of the twenty-first century, mass-mediated age. As Jean Baudrillard writes, our dealings are not predominantly with other human beings, but rather 'with the reception and manipulation of goods and messages' (2003:25). The printing press and the camera, for instance, enabled various media (newspapers, magazines and books) to reproduce cultural texts mechanically and disseminate them to mass audiences. This has had a number of consequences, one of which Benjamin characterises as 'the adjustment of reality to the masses and of the masses to reality' (1979:225). What he means is that, because capitalism has been at the forefront of the mechanical reproduction of culture, and since it always seeks out new and larger markets to sell its goods and services, cultural texts are usually orientated towards the widest possible demographic. This transition to a world of mass-produced (and commercially orientated) culture has had what we could refer to as a 'democratising effect' on perception. At a very basic level, the fact that these cultural texts are now directed at mass markets has influenced the kinds of stories that circulate within a culture. Heroes, for instance, had usually been represented, in high culture, as aristocratic, distant and above the people, while the ordinary people themselves were usually childlike and submissive, humble and knew their place, troublesome and threatening, sang and danced a lot, the salt of the earth, and/or comic. The idea of the hero as everyman, a notion that we are comfortably familiar with today, is largely a twentieth-century invention.

We have divided this book into nine chapters. Each one of the chapters introduces key concepts, contexts, debates, theorists and schools of thought. The chapters should first be read on their own terms. At the end of each chapter, and on the companion website, we provide additional resources that will help readers to pursue further study and research. There are also continuities in the book across chapters, especially through the discussion of recurring examples, a focus on the social and historical nature of the media, and theories regarding the relation between media and society. So rather than having a dedicated chapter on digital media, readers will find that a discussion of digital media is integrated into all the chapters.

We do not offer a single perspective or a unified theory of the media. The book reflects the debates taking place in the scholarly study of media studies, and does not try to resolve them: debates are what makes fields of intellectual inquiry interesting and productive. As we will discuss in chapter 9, we want this book to be a tool that helps readers acquire a wide media literacy. Part of this process involves readers gaining an informed and practical understanding of key ideas and concepts, and major schools of thought.

This chapter deals with the history of media and technology, and identifies the relevant social, cultural and economic factors that have had an impact upon their development and use. Drawing upon a selection of media and technologies, this chapter will explore in detail how they are used to organise systems of communication and social relations, outline their institutionalisation and consider how space, time and notions of power, control and resistance are bound up in media practices and technological forms. Chapter 2 introduces students to what we call 'techniques of media analysis'. In this book we will be making use of theoretical concepts, categories and ideas generally used both in media studies and in related disciplines, such as communication studies, cultural studies and sociology. Central concepts will be introduced and exemplified, and we will show how they can help students to do the work of media analysis. We will look at how media texts function, both in a technical (how they work as communication practices) and contextual (what are their sociocultural functions, what are they trying to do) sense.

We have suggested that the media have become central to determining what we are, how we behave and how we see and understand ourselves. The term that media scholars use to capture these activities is subjectivity. Chapter 3 will describe and exemplify influential ideas about subjectivity, derived from the work of theorists such as Michel Foucault, Pierre Bourdieu, Judith Butler and Arjun Appadurai. We will explain how subjectivities are created, maintained and authorised, and analyse the role the media play in these processes.

In order to make sense of the relationship between the media and wider society and culture, we need to understand the kinds of ideas, logics, values and practices that characterise the cultural field of the media. The concept of the cultural field, drawn from the work of the French sociologist Pierre Bourdieu, provides the basis for an analysis of the principles and practices of the media. In chapter 4 we look at the legal, industrial, economic, institutional and regulatory characteristics of the media and its institutions, and their organisational and discursive logics. We discuss media ownership and control; the roles of public and industry; and their implications for media practices and professions.

Any discussion of the relation between the media and its publics raises the question of the extent to which media texts not only produce and act upon, but are also negotiated by, different types of audiences. Chapter 5 looks at how definitions of the audience have changed over time, and at related questions, such as how an audience is constituted through and across different media and genres. We will look at the nature of contemporary audiences, which are increasingly mobile, diverse and disparate in terms of their 'rules of behaviour'.

One of the main roles of the contemporary media is to provide the sites where a society and its members can get information about, debate and discuss what it is, where it is going and what its values are. Our hyper-mediatised world is dominated by rapidly changing new media technologies, and characterised by the proliferation and fragmentation of publics, spheres and information. At the same time the concept of the (mediated) public sphere as a democratic social space in which public opinion is formed is one of the central discourses or myths through which the field of the media recognises and represents itself. Chapter 6 will provide an overview, evaluation and exemplifications of these issues and debates.

In chapter 7 we look at the way the media interacts with, and influences, society and everyday social life, predominantly through the ideas of French cultural theorists Guy Debord, and his notion of the society of the spectacle (2006). For Debord, the media direct and facilitate the management of attention and consumerism, while simulating the illusion of consumer choice and interactivity. This chapter demonstrates how, at a technical level, our attention is captured and maintained through the production of fantasies that stand in for and surpass everyday realities.

In chapter 8 we discuss the advent of networks as the dominant form of economic and social interaction. Through the writings of Castells and Mattelart, we look at processes that have transformed modern capitalistic societies into post-industrial societies driven by the production and circulation of information. We also explore the transformation of information into digital data, which facilitates the logics of networks, especially through interface, software and databases. Finally, we look at how the flow of information operates through navigation, management and control, and raises the possibility of surveillance.

Such cultural and technological changes are tied up with other significant developments, such as the emergence and diffusion of new information technologies, the globalisation of the media and the internationalisation of culture. This requires subjects (in their various roles as citizens, workers and professionals, consumers and audiences) to be media literate: that is, to have both a knowledge of the rules by which the media-as-field operates, and the competencies to keep pace with rapidly changing technologies. Chapter 9 will define and exemplify what is meant by the term media literacy, and show how it informs everyday cultural practices and issues, from the challenges of participatory culture posed by new media forms and a new conception of citizenship, to a consideration of the difference between media effects and a productive and effective consumption of the media.

This book will analyse and evaluate these developments, and explain how and why the field of the media has taken on such a central role in contemporary society and culture. We are aiming to provide students with two related forms of knowledge-as-literacy. The first is an understanding of the cultural field of the media, along with its history, different technologies, institutions, logics and discourses. The second, which is equally important, is a set of techniques that can be used for analysing how media texts work. In other words, the main aim of this book is to make students more media literate.

History of media and technology

We begin this task by looking at the history of media and technology. What do we mean when we use the word **technology**? We often understand it to refer to the use of devices or tools, but the origin of the term suggests a wider and more flexible definition. The word itself is rooted in two Greek words *techne* (craft) and *logia* (saying). In one sense, we can think of technology as referring to objects that we as humans produce (from the wheel to the iPod). It is also a term that captures the ways in which we manipulate and transform the world around us (such as the use of fire to keep us warm, to see, or or to prepare food). Technology is also the manner through which we extend ourselves into the world. This takes place through various modes of **communication**, such as speech and art, the elaboration of vast networks (from ancient sea routes to the Internet) and certain techniques we use to make sense of the world (from astronomy to GPS). These include the gathering and accumulation of knowledge, and its organisation into systems that allow us to store, retrieve and transfer content. Therefore, technology refers not only to physical artefacts or tools, but also to the ways in which these objects become a vital part of social **networks**, as well as mechanisms of power. Technology is bound up in a range of practices and artefacts that have become embedded in daily life through their functionality, as well as their political and economic utility. As they have appeared over millennia, technologies and media can be seen as products of particular contexts and histories, and become phenomena through which a culture comes to understand itself.

Communication in the twenty-first century is strongly characterised by technologies that commentators refer to as new media. However, all media and technologies were 'new' at some point, surrounded with the thrill of novelty and promise when they first appeared. Carolyn Marvin has suggested that, with the appearance of any technology and media on the public stage, there remains a 'tendency of every age to read the future as a fancier version of the present' (1998:190). As Marvin also states, 'new' and 'old' media and technologies share this in common: they are often taken up as though they appeared from nowhere, and promise to lead us out of the darkness into a new and better social order. There is a range of discourses attached to the appearance of new technologies and media, both past and present: what was said about the Internet at the end of the twentieth century echoes what was said about electricity in the middle of the nineteenth century, for example. As a counterpoint to this, the development of media and technologies most often proceeds first and foremost incrementally, bit by bit out of what came before, rather than appearing out of nothing. New media and new technologies sit alongside old media and technologies; rather than having been rendered obsolete (though this is certainly true in some cases), earlier media and technologies often recede into the background of everyday life. They maintain a certain utility, but the aura surrounding their initial appearance fades. For instance, we still use pencils and paper for a number of daily tasks: technologies and media that once were new but are now millennia old, looking somewhat dated and dull next to our glossy computers.

Technology (1) Tools that humans produce. (2) The ways in which humans manipulate and transform the world around them (for example, the use of fire to keep them warm, to see or to prepare food). (3) The way in which humans extend themselves into the world: various modes of communication, such as speech and art.

Communication The production, exchange and negotiation of meanings. The word originally referred to 'making common to many, imparting', but also refers to transport lines as 'lines of communication', and now also to the media and other forms used to disseminate information.

Network A system of interconnected machines, computers, means of communication, places, and/or people. The term is used to denote a system of remote, channelled, organised, structured, expandable and more or less instantaneous and multidirectional connections.

The history of media and technology highlights a number of key ideas that have been, and remain, central to the field of media studies. This chapter will outline a number of these issues in relation to the emergence of media forms and related technologies. The emphasis will be on social, cultural and economic factors that have an impact upon media and technologies, their development and their use. Drawing on a selection of media and technologies, we will explore in more detail how they are used to organise systems of communication and social relations. We will also outline their institutionalisation, as well as consider how space, time, and notions of power, control and resistance are bound up in media practices, institutions and technological forms.

Preliterate technology and media

Go online

Preliterate technology and media

The use of tools has been part of human history for more than two million years. People have employed them for hunting, agriculture, clothing and transport, among many other practical applications. It is estimated that humans began making use of technologies and media in the form of painting, carving, illustration and early record-keeping approximately 50 000 years ago. These early forms of communication took shape through the application of tools, often made of bone or stone, which were put to use in a range of symbol-making practices. Archaeological evidence in Europe and elsewhere suggests that this period of technological development and early media practice began during the last Ice Age. Traces of image and symbol-making, along with various tool fragments, have been found in caves in Lascaux, France, estimated to be 16 000 years old. Painting and ochre residue have been found in caves and around sheltered rock faces in northern parts of Australia, mainly around Kakadu, but also at Uluru, and in South Australia, with some of the images dating back more than 40 000 years. These images indicate that symbol-making was an important part of these early cultures, and was a form of visual communication through which daily life, including its varied rituals and sacred beliefs, could be represented.

At the same time as these expressive visual forms were appearing, early humankind was also developing language skills. The organisation of noisy vocalisations into rudimentary language slowly formed into basic language systems complete with syntax. The communications historian Walter Ong (1988) has suggested that we understand the appearance of organised vocal sounds in the form of speech and language as 'primary orality', by which he means they are acts that require a degree of intimacy (distance is an enemy to sound), and are situational and not abstract (here and now, rather than there and later). This has much to do with the ephemeral nature of the spoken word, which disappears at the exact moment it is uttered. This transience has profound consequences in terms of its role as a mode of communication, as it affects how and what kind of knowledge is transferred between individuals and groups. It would be some millennia before sound could be captured and preserved, in a form that Ong calls 'secondary orality'. However, other techniques developed among preliterate communities for recording and collecting ideas. As Ong suggests, a range of mnemonic devices, such as song, music and poetry, were often used as memory aids. Writing would be another.

Writing and the alphabet

Go online

Writing and the alphabet

Archaeological evidence suggests that early writing (and also numeracy) developed around the practice of accounting. As trade became an increasingly central part of early human cultures and their economies, there was a need for better record-keeping. Much of this early writing was in the form of keeping tallies of livestock and foodstuffs. These forms of writing, or what is sometimes called 'proto-writing', evolved into styles such as cuneiform, which was developed by the Sumerians (located near modern Iraq), in approximately 3000 BCE. Not much earlier, the Egyptians also used an early form of writing, in the shape of hieroglyphics. These were forms of pictographic inscription, usually done on clay tablets or soft stone surfaces, which were slowly systematised into an elaborate set of characters. Only a limited number of scribes could read and write with these forms.

An extension of these early symbol systems, the Western alphabet, as we recognise it, emerged through Greek culture. The imported Phoenician alphabet was modified by the Greeks, and was standardised by the fourth century BCE. It eventually made its way to Europe through Italy, where it would later give way to the Roman (Latin) alphabet. Over the ensuing centuries, through colonial and Christian missionary activities, the use of Latin expanded throughout, as well as beyond, Europe.

Writing is derived from orality. However, writing in the form of a standardised alphabet differs from orality, in that it allows thought to be objectified, with sound made visible through inscription. It is, as Ong suggests, the literal dissection and fixing of sound flows into individuated visual markings. In materialising the word, representing something that is said, a cognitive shift occurs, making a different kind of intellectual life possible. As part of this shift, the appearance of writing in a standardised form such as the alphabet is often credited with giving birth to subjectivity, with the ability to think about, and reflect upon, an individuated 'self'.

Beyond the individual, at a social and cultural level, the standardised alphabet also allowed the organisation of information into systems. The ability to catalogue information according to an accepted code, such as the alphabet, was an important step in not only accumulating data, but also knowledge through story-telling, myths, epic poems and histories. It functioned as the externalisation of collective memory. Institutions began to emerge through this new ability to systematise, catalogue and retrieve information. The alphabet facilitated, for example, the growth and success of early libraries, such as the Library of Alexandria, which at its peak is said to have housed nearly 1 000 000 scrolls. Made up mainly of papyrus scrolls, drawn from works in mathematics, physics and literature, its success had much to do with Egypt's role as a hub between the East and West, but was also a result of its ready access to a steady supply of papyrus.

Many centuries later, the written word had a profound impact on indigenous cultures in both Australia and New Zealand in the eighteenth and nineteenth centuries. In describing the arrival of the written word with European colonisation of Australia, Penny van Toorn (2006) notes that the rich culture that evolved over many thousands of years among Aboriginal groups involved a range of media and tools for expression. This took the form of painting on bodies, bark and rock faces, and songs, dance rituals and bodily gestures, with oral culture as a central communicative tool. The British arrived in the late eighteenth century; van Toorn suggests that this did not signal the end of Aboriginal oral culture; rather, it meant the 'entanglement of two sets of reading and writing practices' (20). The politics of cultural dominance in this instance has been literarily inscribed with, and through, the written word.

In New Zealand, oral culture was also a central part of Māori life. They too had to deal with the imposition of another language and form of organising knowledge. After the colonisation of New Zealand by the British in the mid-nineteenth century, and their colonial emissaries in the form of missionaries who brought with them the Bible, Māori were forced to conform to the dominance of the written word. They learned, however, to also use the written word to find a political voice to counter government policies and initiatives (later using newspapers and newsletters to articulate their concerns). The preference for the written and printed word presented a number of challenges to the Māori language, many of which have been overcome through the recent proliferation of Māori-focused television, radio and education programs. Oral culture has remained a vital part of life on the modern *marae*, from the *whakapapa* to the *takai* to the *powhiri*, and is a privileged form of communication that continues to supersede the written word.

Early new media: Papyrus, parchment, paper

Go online

Early new media:
Papyrus, parchment, paper

Palimpsest The practice of scratching a text off a parchment (made of animal skins) and writing the new text over the top. This practice and the way in which the earlier text leaves a trace or residue are referred to as palimpsests.

Writing requires a medium for inscription. Clay tablets provided just such a surface, but their weight and non-portability proved limiting. An alternative, more lightweight medium was found in the form of papyrus, a reed-like plant that flourished along the Nile River in Ancient Egypt. The particular qualities of papyrus were useful in arid regions such as Egypt, but in humid climates, such as those found in Europe, it had a tendency to crack and split.

Between the first century BCE and the first century ACE, parchment became more prevalent. Made from the skin of goats or calves, it lasted longer than papyrus, and was more flexible. Parchment eventually became the preferred medium for the production of religious texts throughout Europe, and was used well into the fifteenth century. It could be recycled, which was another of its useful qualities. From approximately 400 ACE, monks throughout Europe were given the task of putting together illuminated manuscripts on reused old parchment. Previous texts were scrubbed away, and new texts written over the top (the result is called a **palimpsest**, which refers to the way in which the earlier text leaves a trace or residue that a keen eye can spot). Many of these illuminated manuscripts were collected and bound into codices (which have a history extending back to the third century BCE, and were also included at the Library of Alexandria). These were put together in a form that looks very much like that everyday technology, the book, as we know it today.

While parchment never entirely disappeared, the expanding trade routes and empires of Europe facilitated the appearance of its eventual replacement, paper. Further European contact with the East, and in particular Chinese technology, often via Arab traders and merchants in the Middle East, led to the incorporation of paper into the manufacture of religious manuscripts and a variety of other documents. While paper first appeared in Europe in approximately the twelfth century, replacing parchment as the preferred medium by the sixteenth century, the technology behind paper has been dated as appearing in China in 2 ACE, where it was prized for its lightness and portability. Cities such as Baghdad became centres for papermaking in the Arabic world—where people had begun using paper as early as the eighth century BCE.

Media such as papyrus, parchment and paper also functioned as container technologies, carrying not only information but also documenting history and culture. They were vehicles that served the interests of those in power, taking on the form of proclamations, decrees and laws that could then be widely disseminated. However, given the limited capacity of lay people during these periods to read and write, scribes and others with the necessary expertise and skills transcribed and translated the texts (often publicly announcing proclamations). The political economist Harold Innis linked this kind of specialised know-how to what he calls monopolies of knowledge. By this he means the connection between social hierarchies and the role that media play in the production and distribution of knowledge, factors that can determine a civilisation's social organisation, particularly with the centralisation of power, skills and expertise among cultural and political elites.

These monopolies of knowledge demonstrate a link between power and the media in relation to communication technologies in ancient civilisations. With this in mind, Innis formulates three questions we can ask about the media and their relation to power, not only historically, but also in terms of the present:

1   How do specific communication technologies operate?
2   What assumptions do they take from and contribute to society?
3   What forms of power do they encourage? (quoted in Soules 2007).

Describing the relationship between media, power and the accumulation of knowledge in ancient civilisations, Innis (1951) outlines the ways in which many of these early media display what he would call a bias. By biased media, Innis means the way in which a particular medium is either time-biased or space-biased. According to Innis, their specific qualities, such as weight or permanence, determined the geographic reach of empires as well as the duration of kingdoms.

A **time-biased medium**, such as speech or clay tablets, is typically tied to civilisations that may have long life spans, but are not interested in territorial expansion. According to Innis, these civilisations are religious in nature, with

Time-biased media
Term used by Harold Innis to describe media used in civilisations that may have long life spans, but are not interested in territorial expansion. The media found here were marked by durability, such as clay tablets.

their relative lifespan tied to theocracies which emphasise divinely ordained social hierarchies. The media found here were marked by durability, which means a civilisation (and, more importantly, its leaders) could leave a legacy literally inscribed in stone, the pyramids in Egypt being a good example.

By **space-biased media**, Innis is referring to a particular medium's specific limits in its ability to transcend space. Papyrus and paper exemplify this quality, in that they could travel far and wide (though they did not often last long). Civilisations that used these media were secular, interested in empire building, and were reliant upon a military to serve as a vehicle for dissemination as well as a vanguard for territorial expansion. The media in this case were portable, such as paper, and able to be carried across vast distances with ease in order to convey information from the centre of power to its farthest margins.

Space-based media
Term used by Harold Innis to describe highly portable media, such as paper, used by civilisations engaged in empire building.

Print, the printing press and literacy

Go online

Print, the printing press and literacy

Like many of the phenomena we discuss here, the incorporation of new technologies and media into various religious and secular practices was based in large part on modifications made to existing forms that had begun to reveal their limits. As the weightiness of the clay tablet and the fragility of papyrus demonstrated, the limits of media and technologies are often born out of a realisation that certain social needs, as well as political or economic demands, can no longer be met. Paper seemed to serve many of these demands, particularly because of its capacity to be easily transported and produced in abundance. The printing press, which came to rely heavily on paper, also has a long history.

Early versions of printing presses have been traced back to eighth-century Japan and China, where they were used in block printing large canvases. These presses were reliant on large carved woodblocks for printing. The printing press was suitable for ideographic languages such as Chinese, Japanese and Korean, which rely upon characters or symbols that represent a thing or concept. However, for languages with smaller numbers of characters used to make up words, in the form of the alphabet, for example, block printing was much less practical. The appearance of effective and workable woodblock printing in Europe would need modifications to meet the demands of the Western alphabet.

The printing press associated with the German Johannes Gütenberg (1400–1468) offered a novel modification of these earlier presses. Modelling, in part, his device on olive oil and wine presses, which were quite common in his area of Germany, Gütenberg's wooden press also incorporated a version of a moveable type printing press developed by the Koreans. In this system, each letter was etched into its own piece of metal. These pieces of metal could then by rearranged into any number of words and sentences in long lines of type across a page. All the lines of type on a page were then pushed together by blocks of wood, forming pages. Gütenberg also introduced an oil-based ink, which was much more suited to the absorption capacities of paper, and tended not to fade over time. In its mechanised reproduction of hundreds of exact copies, the printing press also anticipates, as Marshall McLuhan suggests (1962), Henry Ford's automobile assembly line in the early twentieth century. This combination of modifications proved highly productive, and led to what is called the 'print revolution', which began to unfold in earnest during the fifteenth century.

The success of Gütenberg's press, and in particular the publication of the Gütenberg Bible (in approximately 1455), led to a proliferation of presses around Europe. Their rapid spread and their ability to mass-produce texts at low cost resulted in a publishing boom in both religious and secular texts. It is estimated that by 1500 nearly 20 million books had been published in Europe. The expansion of printing presses beyond Central Europe, however, was uneven. In Muslim countries, religious proscriptions against the reproduction of Islamic icons and the printing of religious texts generally resulted in the late appearance of presses (as late as the eighteenth century in some countries). The overall effect of the printing press in Europe was a general rise in literacy levels, along with declarations that, with the spread of knowledge attached to the ability to read, new kinds of democratic orders would emerge, with the enlightened masses no longer willing to tolerate oppressive regimes (Briggs & Burke 2007:14).

However, the appearance of the press did have some negative long-term social consequences. New kinds of elites began to emerge. Knowledge and expertise were no longer limited to monasteries and their scribes; intellectual life was moving beyond the Church, with universities emerging as new sites of learning. Along with the ascent of new institutions such as universities, and the creation of a reading public, the printing press is often credited with playing a central role in the rise of the Renaissance (fourteenth to seventeenth centuries), a period of expansive scientific, artistic, religious and philosophical thought throughout Europe. This was an era marked also by a rediscovery of ancient classical texts, many of which were now reprinted and widely disseminated. The printing press, through its medium the book, would be one of the prevailing technologies during this period.

Toward the end of the Renaissance, large and small presses, turning out their many pamphlets and booklets, continued to flourish in Europe and elsewhere. Space for dissent did exist, and challenges to governments of the day took many different forms. Through cartoons, or in many cases through obscene, often pornographic, representations, numerous publications sought to satirise well-known political figures, heads of state and royalty. In this way, as a technology, the printing press and its literary product complemented a longstanding oral culture of public debate and discussion that took place in a variety of spaces, such as cafés, pubs and public squares. In certain respects, the printing press contributed to the appearance of the public sphere through which ideas, both for and against states, individuals, governments and monarchies could be further elaborated (see chapter 6).

There was also an anxiety held by those in power, in religious and political positions, that with the appearance of mass-produced books, and the increasing ability of lay people to learn for themselves, there would be a questioning of authority, and challenges mounted to their monopolies of knowledge. There were various strategies used to control or stifle the publishing boom. Publications were monitored through the introduction of various taxes, and early forms of censorship were common. In England, laws were introduced to ensure that nothing seditious would be said against the country, or anything libellous about the monarchy.

Capitalism The dominant economic system in the West since the advent of the industrial revolution in the eighteenth century. Based on the ever-expanding logic of private ownership of capital, investment, production, the organisation and control of human labour, consumption and the accumulation of more private capital.

The English presses were also controlled through the introduction of the *Licensing Act* of 1662, which limited the number of publishers allowed to publish (consolidating publications among a few select guilds); required entry on a registry of all publications; and allowed the government to censor books or pamphlets prior to publication.

While its contribution to the shaping of the public sphere is an important part of its legacy, the printing press also introduced a notion of ownership and intellectual property that we still contend with today. The appearance of the printing press and the expanding market for production and consumption of literary goods raised for the first time the issue of copyright, and the notion of the 'author', with which we are familiar today. As befitted European economies in which **capitalism** was slowly being entrenched as an economic system, with its emphasis on private property and ownership, the relationship of publishing to its producers was also changing. Copyright, for instance, first appears in England in the Statute of Anne (1710), and in the US through its Constitution (1787). During this same period, France had developed another system, *droit d'auteur* (right of the author), a concept that influenced the Berne Convention, where a globally agreed upon idea of copyright was established. (Australia's copyright law, introduced first in 1911, borrows from both the Berne Convention and British copyright law.)

The emergence of newspapers, journalism and the nation

Go online

The emergence of newspapers, journalism and the nation

As John B. Thompson (1996) points out, the patterns of communication upon which early periodicals depended set up frameworks that anticipated the appearance of newspapers. Newspapers further solidified existing communication networks, rendered others obsolete and created new ones. Thomson notes that before the invention of the printing press, for example, there were four pre-print types of networks that allowed information to be distributed:

1 a network controlled by the Catholic Church, which allowed the papacy based in Rome to maintain contact with a geographically dispersed clergy
2 networks of communication which political authorities set up to ensure the administration of distant territories as part of maintaining a coherent state
3 networks tied to commercial activity (sea and land), which linked banking houses, merchants and trading partners (local and non-local)
4 networks of pedlars, merchants, travellers and entertainers, who brought stories from distant places.

The fifteenth and sixteenth centuries saw these formal and informal networks transformed, and new infrastructures developed, with the role of local and international postal services becoming central to the getting and sending of information across vast distances. Over time, the broad international reach of the postal service proved an effective tool for maintaining the imperial scope of a number of countries and their colonies. During the eighteenth and nineteenth centuries in Australia, and not long afterward in New Zealand, the postal service proved to be a vital link that served to maintain those countries' colonial connections to England, as well as underwrite the latter's global imperial interests. Beyond this, the evolution of a postal service in a number of countries, regularised and quickly institutionalised, was a development that laid the foundation for the emergence of newspapers.

Another development that underpinned the growth of newspapers was the role the printing press played in the regularised dissemination of information, both local and global. As we have already seen, the printing press allowed a range of media to be mass produced, from handbills to books. This ability on a large scale to reproduce the same text was also tied to an increasing interest in and demand for information from elsewhere, linked in no small part to the colonial expansion of numerous European empires. Throughout the eighteenth and nineteenth centuries, newspapers solidified their role as a tool that could be used to bind people together, not just globally, but more importantly, locally. Benedict Anderson (2006), for example, has linked the emergence of the printing press, newspapers and what he refers to as 'print capitalism' during this period as forces that became vital in shaping a new political entity, the nation. He calls the nation an 'imagined community'. Anderson suggests that the nation had certain qualities, namely that it was a free, limited, independent and self-determining entity. These characteristics of the nation were imagined as essential to its formation, and print media a necessary element to its success, because:

- the size and scope of a nation is such that no one can ever meet all the other citizens
- it is limited because even the largest nation has borders, beyond which lie other nations
- it is free and self-determining because it emerged during the Enlightenment and was tied to a number of revolutions—a period of secularisation where divinely chosen hierarchical monarchies saw their legitimacy challenged or destroyed.

As they matured over the following centuries, newspapers become vehicles that transformed time and space in such a way that people were bound to this new political entity called 'the nation'. Newspapers created a shared space, but also allowed shared time through rituals of simultaneity. By this, Anderson (2006) means that the reader imagines him or herself to be participating in 'the nation' with regularity—daily or weekly sharing the same stories in the form of national events with thousands of other readers as part of the project of nation building.

Print capitalism spread through the eighteenth century and became increasingly industrialised in the nineteenth century. The possibilities for advertising were enhanced by engraved illustrations, then photography, which increased the ability of newspapers to generate revenue. During this period, a new cultural field appeared, that of journalism, especially the reporter. Journalism at the time was a practice marked by a certain ideology, one meant to distinguish itself from the penny presses, which placed an emphasis on the spectacular storytelling. The 'new journalism', as Michael Schudson (1984) calls it, relied upon principles of objectivity, fairness and dispassion. Throughout the century, there was a distinction made between the storytelling emphasis of certain newspapers (what we might recognise today as tabloids) and the information that these new journalists were distilling (Schudson uses the example of *The New York Times*). Borrowing from Walter Benjamin, Schudson notes that this idea of information is a 'novel form of communication'. Benjamin calls it a 'product' of fully developed capitalism, in that it 'lays claim to prompt verifiability … [is] understandable in itself … [and must] sound plausible' (in Schudson 1984:139). Detachment and objectivity become the language, and more so the code and ethos, of this new professional, the reporter.

Newspapers were a vital part of the information network in many of England's colonies, in which a tension between a burgeoning nationalism and lingering imperialism began to emerge. Newspapers flourished in Australia (in 1803, *The Sydney Gazette and New South Wales Advertiser* began regular publication) and New Zealand (the first was *The New Zealand Gazette*, appearing in 1840, with the first Māori-language paper appearing not long after, in 1842). These publications served not only as vehicles for stories from overseas, particularly England, but were also an important part of how these fledgling countries worked to create a sense of a locally imagined community. The sheer distance of the colonies from England often meant a delay of many weeks in news coming from overseas, so the majority of the content in these early publications was primarily local news, information, poetry, short stories, religious advice and details of cargo on recently arrived ships.

Industrialisation: New forms of power and communication

Go online

Industrialisation: New forms of power and communication

As a source of power and sustenance, water is one of civilisation's primordial media forms. For thousands of years, it has been harnessed for use in agriculture in the form of pumps, mills, aqueducts and irrigation canals, and has been used for travel and transport for even longer. These early forms of water-powered mechanics would evolve by the seventeenth century, quite literally, into a fully fledged motor for the industrialisation of Europe, and not long after, the rest of the world. The use of steam engines to drive not only industry but also transport networks, in the form of steamboats and trains, the domestication of electricity through steam turbines, and a range of other applications, reached its peak in the late eighteenth and mid-nineteenth centuries. Steam power would slowly give way to a new form of power, electricity, but, as with many of those earlier technologies discussed here, it has never entirely disappeared (steam turbines are still the primary tool used for the generation of electricity even today).

The steam railway was a medium of communication as much as a form of transport. It delivered people and goods as well as newspapers, forming a national and then international land-based distribution network. As rail lines began to crisscross entire countries, they served to further bind people together in the idea of the nation, another way in which a large-scale community could be imagined (and then actually experienced as rail tourism developed). Tales of frontiers being breached by further extensions of the rail into previously 'unknown' territory are part of the mythology (and ideology) that surround steam travel throughout the nineteenth century. The link between progress, expansion and the railway are an important part of the way in which the nation was symbolised throughout the nineteenth century. In Australia, for example, the idea of federating the states depended on the steam railway, as well as other factors. Ken Livingston (1996:23) suggests that there were three technological developments at work in constructing the idea of the nation in Australia (and, by extension, New Zealand) during the nineteenth century: the appearance of steamships, which replaced sail vessels; the extension of the electric telegraph and the laying of submarine cable; and the development of railways. In New Zealand, the country's topography proved a challenge to unification. The first main trunk lines appeared on the South Island in 1879, and the first line connecting Auckland to Wellington was completed in 1908 after nearly two decades of construction.

As railway networks formed a dense latticework across and between nations around the world, they were often accompanied by a new medium of electrical communication: telegraphy. In many countries, these two networks emerged simultaneously (Australia was one exception, as the various states had adopted different rail gauges, which prevented the easy linkages between them). Electrical telegraphy (which Tom Standage (1998) has called 'the Victorian Internet'), and its system of Morse code made up of dots and dashes, replaced a complex semaphore system developed in France at the end of the eighteenth century, which had been employed primarily for military and maritime purposes. The use of cable and electricity in the form of telegraphy became the preferred communication medium of the military. It was also preferred by the financial and maritime sectors throughout the latter half of the nineteenth century, with wired telecommunications eventually expanding to create a global financial and information network that connected much of the world. In 1839, the first lines connected points in England, and then beyond its borders, further consolidating its imperial role as a global economic and long-distance communication hub. In the US, it would be 1844 before contact was made between cities. The first telegraph lines were laid in Australia between Williamstown and Melbourne in 1854. The British Empire's imperial reach was strengthened in 1902, with Australia and New Zealand connected to England via Pacific submarine cable, land cable through Canada, and eventually through Atlantic submarine cable.

In New Zealand, telegraphy was inaugurated in 1862 in Canterbury, but its development would be ensured by the gold rush in Otago in 1869, and the need for financial information and mine statuses to be updated as quickly as possible in the interest of prospectors, speculators and investors. It was also becoming more important for the hinterlands to be connected with urban centres, or, at the very least, with larger transportation hubs such as Christchurch and Dunedin. Increasingly, as with other forms of communication, economic demands required a more robust and efficient infrastructure to allow the flow of information between the various parties involved in New Zealand's fledgling role as 'the Empire's Dairy Farm'. New Zealand was an export-orientated colonial economy, based mainly around agriculture, that at the time still serviced the needs of England.

As James Carey (1989) notes, the telegraph (much like past, present and future communication technologies) had its greatest impact upon the way in which businesses, governments and the military operated. The telegraph's ability to transfer information almost instantaneously across vast distances transformed time and space; it 'compressed' them, to use Stephen Kern's term (2000). However, its largest and most significant transformation happened at the level of the market. Carey suggests that 'the effect of the telegraph is a simple one: it evens out markets in space. The telegraph puts everyone in the same place for purposes of trade; it makes geography irrelevant' (1989:54).

The space and time biases of telegraphy soon led to the national and international distribution of news. News agencies such as Reuters (founded in 1851), which first used the telegraph for sending and receiving market information, later began doing the same for news stories. These agencies, some of which had colluded not long after their founding to divide the global market up in the interest of avoiding competition (Mattelart 2000), would soon be sending news stories to telegraphers and newspapers around the world. Many of these same agencies are still functioning in that capacity today, supplying content not only for hard-copy newspapers, but also for many online news providers.

The telegraph office was most often situated at postal stations, where telegrams would be printed and then mailed, and were thus tied to postal services and their well-entrenched networks. Telegraph transmission and translation required training, as telegraphers had to display an expertise in reading Morse code (deciphering skills not unlike the scribes of old). This meant that private citizens who wished to send messages had to rely upon an intermediary. The advent of the telephone, and the development of microphone technology in the late 1870s, would soon change this monopoly of knowledge and expertise, and allow people to speak to one another over long distances through phones in their homes (the first telephone exchange in Australia was established in Brisbane in 1880). The process was initially quite complicated, and power and sound were issues. However, as the technology developed, and as local and then national networks were established in various countries, along with efficient operator exchanges, the domestication of telecommunications in many countries was well established by the end of the nineteenth century.

Electrification as ideology

Go online

Electrification as ideology

The success of the telegraph, and later the telephone, are important indicators of the way electricity was generally perceived in the nineteenth century. If the eighteenth-century imagination was dominated by the power of steam, the late nineteenth-century imagination was seduced by the power of electricity. The harnessing of electricity was another instance of a technology rendered as a tool for communication, rhetorically framed as a vehicle for liberation and enlightenment, but also signalling the consolidation of expertise and economic power. Armand Mattelart (2000) has suggested that the discursive power given to electricity allowed even critics of the dehumanising effects of heavy industry to extol its emancipatory virtues:

> Electric energy was the means for returning to this history of community logic that brought human beings into solidarity with one another. By casting off the weight of the 'era of paleo-technics' characterised by mechanics, industrial and

urban concentrations, and expansionist empires, this new stage in human history would spawn a horizontal and transparent society. Only the model inspired by industrial ideology could hinder the development of the liberating potential of electricity (2000:21).

The electric incandescent light bulb (successfully patented by Thomas Edison in 1880) became an icon of this new power source. Marshall McLuhan has said of the light bulb that **'the medium is the message'**. It is not simply that a light bulb might be used to spell out in a sign on the side of a building, for instance, but rather that the electrified bulb is itself a message. Like the promise associated with the printing press as a revolutionary tool, this can be understood to suggest that electricity generated not only light, but also a range of discourses about what this new medium would come to mean. The light bulb symbolises what David Nye (1996) has referred to as the 'technological sublime', the pinnacle of an idea that captures the many ways in which electricity was understood as a transformative force during the late nineteenth century.

Medium is the message
A phrase coined by Marshall McLuhan. Refers to the notion of a range of discourses that surround the appearance of a new technology.

This fascination with the spectacle of electricity took hold most tellingly in cities, which became grand showcases for electricity's potential. Throughout the nineteenth century, cities were being transformed by transportation networks, an increasing migration of people from rural regions and other countries into urban centres, an expanding middle class, the rise of industry, as well as their illumination initially by gas light and then by electrical light (Schivelbusch 1988). Urban electrical lighting would first appear in Australia in Tamworth in 1884 (with Melbourne having most of its streets lit by 1894, and Sydney by 1904), and in New Zealand in Wellington in 1889. Cities like these, and others around the globe, were slowly becoming sites for a new kind of consumerism, as the day could now be extended well into the night, and where a range of activities could now take place at any time of day. Nowhere was the nexus of urban life, mass consumption, progress and electricity better embodied than in the first department stores, such as Bon Marché in Paris (opened in 1852), in what Rosalynd Williams has called 'dream worlds of consumption' (1982).

Photography and cinema: Still and moving images

Go online

Photography and cinema: Still and moving images

Electricity helped illuminate a new kind of sensibility in the nineteenth century, one fascinated with public displays of the links made between progress, science and technology. Part of this fascination included a renewed emphasis on visual spectacles deeply invested in the appearance and elaboration of new technologies and related media, of which electricity was but one. Electric lighting formed a line of continuity that extended back to an earlier technological fascination with an ability to render the world knowable. The advent of photography, and later cinema, were extensions of an increasingly popular desire to capture and reproduce the world accurately through technology.

As Robert Legatt (2000) suggests, the appearance of photography depended on the merger of two elements: the camera obscura and a chemical process. Both of these existed long before photography came about, but it took the work of a number of individuals, each with their own approaches, to produce photographic practice and the photographic medium as we know it today. The camera obscura (from the Latin 'dark chamber') was a device with a long history, extending back to the Greeks, Chinese, Arabs and Europeans. Leonardo da Vinci and other artists often used it as a drawing aid, as it was a device that could be used to capture accurate images. In its variations, it has usually taken the form of a darkened box, which has a tiny pinhole where light can enter. As light passes through this tiny opening, an image is projected on the wall opposite, upside down, but with a great deal of detail. Some of these boxes were portable, and camera obscuras often took the shape of tents, which allowed more flexibility. Early experiments with photography borrowed many of these tools when they were first made. Daguerre, giving us his daguerreotypes (1839), and Henry Fox Talbot (1835), made use of these tools in their early photographic experiments.

The chemical process that made photography possible evolved over the course of the nineteenth century, moving from the very messy and somewhat impractical wet plate process to the dry plate process, which was popularised by George Eastman, who had founded the Eastman Kodak Company. Not long afterwards, Eastman found a way to create an emulsion on paper, which allowed a user to generate many images without having to remove cumbersome glass plates for each new photo. By the end of the century, Eastman and Kodak had created a portable camera, which non-experts could use with relative ease, and popular photography was born.

The technologies and media involved in photography informed a new kind of visual culture that was also tied to emerging social sciences such as psychiatry, psychology, sociology and anthropology. The links made between photography and these new sciences drew upon the camera's ability to 'capture' images that had more verisimilitude and relied on less human interference than earlier forms of rendering (such as painting, sculpture and sketches), and thus made them appear more objective. The photographic medium became a vital part of this desire to identify, classify and, ultimately, contain social difference and deviance. The use of photography, alongside new identification techniques such as fingerprinting in the emerging field of criminology, formed part of an arsenal of techniques designed to render the 'truth' of individuals, as well as producing a social typology in the form of an image-based database that might then be used to 'predict' criminal dispositions as evidenced through physiognomy.

Photography's ability to capture a fleeting moment in time also led a number of scientists, physiologists, neurologists and amateurs to explore other ways to document movement, the results of which anticipated the appearance of early cinema. Etienne Jules-Marey's motion studies in France were an important first step. In 1882, Marey's chronophotographic gun was first put to use. It could take twelve consecutive frames a second, with all of them appearing as part of the same picture. He documented birds in flight, dogs, people walking and other activities in a series of motion studies. The appeal of this and other early cameras is that they had the ability to make something visible that was otherwise invisible to the naked eye (through individual frames, or through slow-motion photography). As its etymology suggests, photography ('light writing'), like writing, dissects by providing detailed and accurate snapshots abstracted from the flow of time, which made it a useful scientific tool.

This ability of photography to abstract and objectify a moment in time led to another series of motion studies, this time in the US, which got even closer to moving pictures. In 1888, the American Eadweard Muybridge was asked to settle a wager about the nature of a horse in motion: did all four hooves ever leave the ground at once? Muybridge created a photographic device that saw a number of cameras attached to trip wires, which would then capture the movement of the horse in stride. The sequence of individual still images were then run together and analysed, in a way that looks remarkably like a sequence of film frames, to reveal that all four hooves did indeed leave the ground. Muybridge's technique was used most recently in the creation of 'bullet time' in *The Matrix* (1999). Using a circle of independent cameras, with each taking a shot in sequence, the frames could be stitched together to produce a seamless 360-degree pan of the well-known and often-copied scene.

Thomas Edison had also begun making extensive use of this new tool, using film and a number of measurement techniques in his own motion studies (the band U2 recently quoted these early films in the music video for 'Lemon'). Edison, and even more so his employee William Kennedy Laurie Dickson, built upon Muybridge's and Jules-Marey's ideas and translated them into the kinetoscope, first publicly shown in 1884. This was a device that made motion pictures available for individual viewing, looking at film loops through a tiny peephole, for a small fee. The idea of mass consumption of projected film would be picked up across the Atlantic, in France. Borrowing Eastman's idea of roll film and Edison's kinetoscope, the Lumière brothers and other early filmmakers began to make motion pictures and projection devices (with the brothers' first public screening with an admission price held in Paris in 1895). Georges Méliès, a contemporary of the Lumières, was an early pioneer of narrative filmmaking. His short *Trip to the Moon* (1902) is a fantastical tale that has inspired many contemporary music videos (for example, Daft Punk's 'Around the World' or the Smashing Pumpkins' 'Tonight, Tonight'). Similar experiments in public screenings and filmmaking happened in other countries not long afterwards. Australia, for example, contributed to this burgeoning world of cinema by producing the first feature-length film, *The Story of the Kelly Gang*, in 1906. Gaston Méliès, brother of Georges, produced the first feature film in New Zealand, *Hinemoa*, in 1913, and in 1914, a film of the same name, shot by New Zealander George Tarr, was shown in Auckland.

Shortly after this brief flurry of independent and idiosyncratic moviemaking in numerous countries, various parties began consolidating their interests and forming large-scale film companies. Pathé and Gaumont, for example, bought up Méliès' films, many of which were later lost. Recognising the vast commercial potential of cinema, companies like these were soon to take root in most countries that had a nascent cinema culture. This had notable consequences for the emergence of national cinemas around the globe. In Australia and New Zealand, the high cost of producing local films, for example, far outweighed the cheaper alternative of importing foreign, mainly American, movies. Only later would government-created funding bodies step in, such as the Australian Film Corporation (1972), the Australian Film Commission (1975), and in New Zealand, in 1941, the National Film Unit (NFU), and later the New Zealand Film Commission (1978). Much like their counterparts in radio and television, these were organisations interested in supporting and further developing regional content, funding locally produced movies, as well as aiding their distribution and exhibition both nationally and, more importantly, internationally.

Recorded sound

Go online

Recorded sound

The ability to capture sound, record it and later mass produce it in a readily consumable form comes rather late in the history of reproductive technologies. Music was of course consumed in various live forms, and performances could be reproduced through the purchase of sheet music, provided you had the expertise to both read music and play an instrument, or, at the very least, hire musicians. This was not an experience available to many people, other than those with high incomes. The industrialisation and mass production that characterised much of the nineteenth century—which made things such as photography cheaper and more accessible—developed (in relation to sound) around the convergence of various experiments into information transfer. This included the movement of messages that the telegraph made possible.

The most notable of these developments happened in 1877. While trying to devise a new way of transcribing telegraphic messages and converting them into sound, Thomas Edison developed the tinfoil phonograph, literally a 'sound writer'. The ability of this device to allow a recording to be played back endlessly was seen by Edison as just one of its many virtues. The uses to which Edison wanted his new phonograph put were many, including letter writing and all kinds of dictation, phonographic books (which would speak to blind people, for example), the teaching of elocution, the reproduction of music, recording the last words of dying persons, the preservation of languages, educational purposes (spelling or other lessons) and connection with the telephone so that it might record conversations (*North American Review* 1878). That the reproduction of music would become the dominant function of the phonograph illustrates the point that the intentions of the creator may in fact be undermined by the way in which listeners and consumers actually domesticate a new technology.

There were other attempts at recording sound. Alexander Graham Bell introduced the wax cylinder model not long after Edison, but, as each cylinder had to be recorded individually, its limitations were soon realised. Notable among these new additions to early sound recording, and more long lasting, was the work of Emile Berliner. Berliner, a German emigré to the US and a contemporary of Edison, worked on recording sound as well, and had improved telephone communication by developing the first microphone (he was briefly hired by Bell as a result). In 1887, Berliner created the phonograph, which, like Edison's, could both record and play. In 1888, he moved away from cylinder recordings and developed the flat discs that we recognise as records today. Using this system, he then devised a way to press countless records, in the form of zinc plates, from the same original plate. However, his attempts to trademark a number of devices were undone by patents put together by rival companies, combined with his having given away the rights to the gramophone to a number of different US interests. It became impossible for Berliner to sell his gramophone in the US, so Berliner eventually moved his operation to Montreal, Canada, where he soon formed the Victor Talking Machine Company. One of the first record labels, it was on Berliner's recordings of Enrico Caruso and others that the image of Nipper the dog, and the slogan, 'His Master's Voice', first appeared (RCA would purchase the company from Berliner in 1929).

Broadcasting: Radio and television

Go online

Broadcasting:
Radio and television

During the late nineteenth century, Edison's desire to create a sound-based telegraph would appear in a number of different forms, many of these designed by others. Of the various devices that emerged, Guiglielmo Marconi is generally credited with developing the technology that would lead to radio. However, it is important to remember that Marconi's work was the result of earlier experiments into electromagnetic waves conducted by Nikola Tesla, Oliver Lodge, New Zealander Ernest Rutherford, and others. Like Edison, his contemporary, Marconi successfully lodged a patent (and a number of other patents that were later overturned), which credits him with the invention of the wireless technology that would eventually lead to the birth of radio. Not long after this significant moment, the corporation British Marconi was founded, a company designed to develop technology to maintain contact between ships at sea and the mainland. (In the 1920s, the company would eventually become the British Broadcasting Corporation, the BBC.) As Lynn Spigel (1992) notes, the use by the navy of ship-to-shore communication is one of the primary functions of radio waves as a communication tool (most famously used as a distress call from the ill-fated *Titanic* in 1912). However, wireless technology was also used by numerous businesses to contact overseas markets and business interests, which required technical improvements to increase the speed of messaging. While these two uses anticipated the rise of radio, it was up to a subculture of radio amateurs, who believed this to be an ideal new democratic form of mass communication, to develop and help push radio technology to its maturity.

The experiments of amateur radio operators, both successes and failures, were vital to the emergence of radio as a mass medium in the early part of the twentieth century. Radio amateurs were experimenting with wireless technology, devising transmitters and receivers, and forming early radio stations wherever possible. In New Zealand, the first radio amateurs, often called 'Zedders', set up a wireless transmitter and receiver in Dunedin in 1908. Not long afterwards, the technology and expertise to establish a transmitter became more readily available, and amateur radio took off throughout the country. These initial messages still relied on Morse code, but by the early 1920s, sound was being broadcast. Eventually, the New Zealand government stepped in and made it mandatory for the Zedders to have a licence to broadcast, with amateurs relegated to the lower end of the frequency spectrum, and eventually marginalised all together, as a nationalised radio network owned and operated by the government began to take over many small stations (Dougherty 1997).

It was only in the 1920s that various corporate interests recognised radio as a viable commercial pursuit, leading it to become the medium we recognise today. The first publicly licensed radio broadcast in the US happened in 1920, in Pittsburgh, Pennsylvania. In New Zealand the first broadcast would be done at Otago University, in Dunedin in 1921; Australia heard its first broadcast in Sydney, in 1923. The blossoming of private broadcasting experiments all but disappeared in the 1930s in New Zealand, as the government set about regulating the industry through licence fees. Regulation was imposed in Australia as well, where there were two classes of licenses, A and B, with the former subsidised through licence fees, and the latter funded through advertising.

The ability of radio to communicate across vast distances, and to reach thousands of people with the same message, from one point to many, is its strength as a medium. It can bind people together as a national audience, an 'imagined community' and a market. In North America, as advertising had become the primary source of revenue for newspapers by the end of the nineteenth century, it was not long before advertising also dictated the shape of radio broadcasting. Given its broadcasting reach, radio became an important medium for the creation and maintenance of national and local markets for consumer goods, and advertisers capitalised on this. In countries like Canada, the United Kingdom, Australia and New Zealand, however, a hybrid system made up of private and public broadcasters, funded by commercial revenues and taxation schemes, would become the preferred model for radio (as it would for television). To this end, these countries created models of public broadcasting that would serve a national audience, based on principles put forward by John Reith, who had worked to found the BBC in the 1920s. The Australian Broadcasting Corporation (ABC) appeared in 1932, and the New Zealand equivalent, the government-run New Zealand Broadcasting Service (NZBS) emerged in 1937 (it would become the New Zealand Broadcasting Corporation in 1962). Both governments recognised the power of radio to act as a national binding medium, offering a public service in the form of education, information and highbrow entertainment, and saw its role as an important tool in constructing a sense of an imagined community. In New Zealand, radio was dominated on a national scale by government-owned stations, forming a broadcasting network throughout the country that would slowly absorb a number of private broadcasters over the course of the 1930s and 1940s. Commercial radio appeared in the early 1970s, emerging out of a culture of pirate radio (broadcasting offshore), playing mainly popular music of the day, which appealed to audiences. Public demand saw a selection of pirate broadcasters become private broadcasters, eventually recognised by the government and given licences to air their programming legally (pirate station Radio Hauraki, which began broadcasting in 1965, is the best known of these, and still exists today, although in commercial form).

Many of these regulatory concerns would be raised again with the appearance of television. The changing economic fortunes of Western countries after the Second World War had a profound effect on the spread of television, which had first appeared as a novelty item in the US in 1939. Post-war rebuilding, the advent of satellite technology, suburbanisation, an affluent and expanding middle class and a new kind of consumerism drove television to become the preferred mass medium throughout the 1950s in the US, and many European countries. Australia would have its first television broadcast in 1956. Television appears relatively late in New Zealand, with the first airings happening in 1960, and shown through regional networks (some of these were amalgamated as one national network in 1969). Colour transmissions aired in New Zealand for the first time in 1973.

Roger Horrocks (2004) suggests that there were a number of factors that needed to be in place in order for television to become a viable medium in New Zealand (Australia was not much different):

1   an infrastructure had to be developed
2   technology had to be used efficiently, economically and effectively
3   a national audience had to be built
4   local programs had to be produced
5   the country's diversity had to be represented
6   management and regulatory systems had to emerge.

Television in New Zealand originally looked to radio as a model of public service, but the expense of producing and airing programs could not be met with simple licence fees. Not long after its appearance, television in New Zealand moved towards a hybrid model of commercial and public broadcasting, not unlike what had happened with radio, but on a larger scale. As new private commercial channels appeared in the mid-1970s, this became the preferred funding model. Deregulation throughout the 1980s and 1990s saw the appearance of more commercial broadcasters and more foreign ownership, not the least of which was Rupert Murdoch's SKY-TV and the Canadian-owned CanWest.

Computer-mediated communication: The Internet, the Web and digital media

Go online

Computer-mediated communication: The Internet, the Web and digital media

The evolution of the modern computer from the early accounting methods dealt with at the start of this chapter is part of a long history of calculation. A desire for speed, efficiency and accuracy in the ability to quantify information or data has been a hallmark of computer development, but this step was initially taken by the military.

Over the last half of the twentieth century, however, their role as oversized calculators to pocket-sized (or lap-sized) everyday communication devices relied on a number of developments in technology that moved computers beyond being just tools for the military and business.

The modern computer marks a shift in how information is translated into data. Previous computer systems relied on analogue information, in the form of punch cards and later magnetic tape. Their practical use lay in the ability to process massive amounts of data very quickly; however, they were large, cumbersome and expensive to house and maintain. Military interests in the UK and the US developed the first electronic digital computers after the Second World War. It was with the appearance of the integrated circuit in the early 1960s, and later the silicon chip, that information would move away from being bound by physical limitations as a material thing to an immaterial signal, or binary code (using two symbols, 0 and 1, not unlike that earlier binary of Morse code, which used dots and dashes). The advent of microchip technology reduced the size of computers substantially, and their use became more practical for information processing outside of military areas. They were initially used by business, but as their size and cost was reduced, computers slowly made their way into homes through the late 1960s and 1970s. Their domestic communication potential was in the beginning somewhat limited, though it was possible to send messages to other computers through telephone lines using a modem. It would be with the maturation of the **Internet**, beyond its military use, and the advent of the **World Wide Web**, that telecommunications would enter a different phase.

The Internet is a vast regulated network composed of other networks, including military, business and personal networks, and the Web is its hypertext and linked interface. Their history is tied to computer development, with the advent of the Internet linked explicitly to the strengthening of military infrastructures. The forging of a national military network in the US after the Second World War required a strong and efficient means of communicating information and data. Academics, technicians and military experts throughout the country worked to create tools that would allow them to transfer data quickly. The first system was called ARPANET, and emerged in the late 1960s. It would be almost two decades later, in the late 1980s, that its public and commercial applications would be realised, with email being one of its initial primary functions.

The World Wide Web, an interface created in 1989 by Tim Berners-Lee, relied on a browser that enabled users to access documents in the form of links (through **hypertext mark-up language (HTML)** relayed via the Internet and typically read through an application such as Internet Explorer, Safari, Firefox, or another user-friendly interface. In 1993, it was opened to the public, and by the mid-1990s, the load on the Web had expanded exponentially, as users, in the form of 'surfers', and businesses began to utilise its services. This led to what is commonly known as the '**dot com boom**', or 'dot com bubble', where thousands of start-up companies began to use the Web and the Internet as a business resource. It was a period in which the market once again determined the shape of the technology's development, with a great deal of speculation and venture capital invested in companies and individuals. This surge in business interest in the Web was substantially tempered by the collapse of thousands of start-ups by the end of the millennium.

Internet A vast regulated network composed of other networks, including military, business and personal networks.

World Wide Web The hypertext and linked interface of the Internet. Whereas the Internet is the infrastructure supporting the Web, the Web is one of its interfaces. It relies on Web browsers (Firefox, Internet Explorer, Safari) and on HTML to create links.

Hypertext mark-up language (HTML) A computer language with a set of annotations and instructions which provides the basis for the structure and behaviour of web pages.

Dot com boom The 1990s saw a surge in business interest in the web. Thousands of start-up companies used the Web and the Internet as a business resource, with much speculation and venture capital invested in companies and individuals. By the end of the millennium most of them had collapsed.

The Web's initial success, both for business and the public, relied in no small part on the kind of rhetoric we have seen attached to the appearance of a number of older media. It was imagined as a democratising force and formed, as Vincent Mosco (2004) understands it, part of the 'digital sublime', a computer-mediated fantasy echoing the 'technological sublime' that Nye found in the nineteenth-century fascination with electricity (1996). Its advocates framed the Web as promising a more open, creative, egalitarian and progressive vision of the future. However, much like the social consequences of writing, the printing press, and other media and technologies described throughout this chapter, certain hierarchies and monopolies of knowledge emerged with the introduction of the Internet and the Web that undermined this myth. The **digital divide**, as it was often referred to, indicated that there were questions around access and availability, where the image of a borderless 'global village' was challenged by matters of infrastructure within national borders, but also in developing countries. Issues of copyright, censorship and corporate control also served to moderate many of the early enthusiastic and utopian claims made about the power of the Web to transform the world.

Digital divide The technological inequality between those who can and those who cannot afford computer technologies (hardware and software) and broadband access.

More recently, the World Wide Web has entered into what is sometimes referred to as Web 2.0, with an emphasis on social networks and user-generated content. The social consequences of this, as Manuell Castells (2001) suggests, are notable for being both positive and negative. For Castells, the Internet, through the Web, chat rooms, social network sites (such as Facebook, YouTube, MySpace and Bebo) and peer-to-peer networks (such as Limewire, Soulseek and Bit Torrent) can decrease, increase or supplement notions of community, drawing attention to tension between this and what he calls 'networked individuality'.

The Web and the Internet call attention to the way in which our experience of time and space is once again mediated through technology. Much like those earlier media, such as paper and the long-playing record, technologies such as the Internet and the Web allow us to think about time and space again, in ways that return us to Innis's concern with the particular bias of a given media. Today, for example, there is a tendency to speak of a culture that is always and forever speeding up, accelerating at a delirious pace. As a counterpoint to this, Will Straw (2007) has suggested that the proliferation of new online spaces, such as blogs, websites, peer-to-peer networks and bulletin boards, offer points to where the flow of information is decelerated, 'thickened up', around a different kind of monopoly of knowledge. Fan websites and blog sites, for instance, lovingly annotating a particular musician's career, or charting the finer points of a cult film genre, offer spaces where the flow of information is gradually fixed, accumulating and layering over time. Time and space can be seen to both expand and contract online.

The recent introduction of the iPhone is a useful way to revisit some of the main points raised in this chapter. An icon of the convergence of existing media and technologies (camera, phone, mail, maps, Web browser, the Internet), as well as discourses of convenience, mobility and design, the iPhone reveals much about the way in which the media has an impact upon our understanding and experience of time and space, ourselves and one another. The iPhone crystallises the seductive relationship between power, social relations and the role and value of technology in our everyday lives. As a tool, the iPhone might be said to draw attention to the concern some people have with the ability of technology and media to fragment cultures and atomise individuals. As a status object, it highlights the distinction between the haves and have-nots. This is nothing new, as various moments in media history discussed here demonstrate. Nor is the power of the iPhone to keep dispersed people in touch, to bind people together across time and space, novel either. In the end, the way in which media and technology have been imagined at various historical epochs, as Carolyn Marvin suggests (1988), says a great deal about who we would like to be and how we would prefer to see the world unfold.

Conclusion

In this chapter we have outlined how technology and media have unfolded over many millennia. We have placed emphasis on a number of dimensions of technological and media development: how power is embedded in technologies and media, how they are used as vehicles for particular interests, how social hierarchies are reproduced through a discourse attached to the media and technology, particularly those of 'newness' and 'novelty'. The way in which media and technologies are bound up in our relationships to time and place has also been a central focus of this chapter, noting the ways in which they serve to mediate our experience of place and one another. Many of the points discussed here will be taken up in various forms in the chapters that follow. In chapter 2, we look at the techniques of media analysis, and how they allow us to understand how media texts function.

Additional reading

Introductory

Briggs, A. and Burke, P. (2007). *A Social History of the Media: From Gutenberg to the Internet.* Cambridge: Polity Press.
  A useful overview of the emergence of a range of media forms around the globe.

McLuhan, M. (1973). *Understanding Media.* Cambridge: MIT Press.
  A good primary text, written by a highly influential media theorist.

Advanced

Mattelart, A. (2000). *Networking the World: 1794–2000.* (L. Carey-Libbrecht and J. Cohen trans.) Minneapolis: University of Minnesota Press.
  An in-depth analysis of the political economy of the media and globalisation.

Marvin, C. (1988). *When Old Technologies Were New: Thinking about Technologies in the Late Nineteenth Century.* Oxford: Oxford University Press.
  A thorough consideration of the discourses of 'new media' from the nineteenth century.

ANALYSING THE MEDIA: THEORIES, CONCEPTS AND TECHNIQUES

Introduction

The aim of this chapter is to introduce, explain and exemplify the concepts, techniques and theories that are generally used by media studies scholars (and scholars in various related disciplines, such as communication studies, cultural studies, sociology, literature and linguistics). Certain central concepts will be used and referred to throughout this book: they include mediation, communication, sign and meaning, ideology, discourse, text, context, intertext, genre and narrative. (Another important concept, subjectivity, will be dealt with in a separate chapter.) We will look at how media texts function, both in a technical (how they work as communication practices) and a contextual sense (what their sociocultural functions are; what they are trying to do). More specifically, we will consider the ways in which they mediate and represent the world; how they communicate and produce or inflect meanings; how they are organised; how readers and audiences recognise, read and negotiate them; what they want from, and how they attempt to relate to, their readers and audiences; and finally, what are the contexts, rules and logics that influence and govern their production.

The organisation of perception

In Michel Chion's book *Audio-Vision*, he relates what happens in the opening scene of Ingmar Bergman's art film *Persona* (1966):

> The house lights go down and the movie begins. Brutal and enigmatic images appear on the screen: a film projector running, a close-up of the film going through it, terrifying glimpses of animal sacrifices, a nail being driven through a hand. Then, in more 'normal' time, a mortuary. Here we see a young boy we take at first to be a corpse like the others, but who turns out to be alive—he moves, he reads a book, he reaches toward the screen surface (1994:30).

Chion then 'rewinds' this scene, but this time without the sound:

> Now we see something quite different. First, the shot of the nail impaling the hand: played silent, it turns out to have consisted of three separate shots where we had seen one, because they had been linked by sound. What's more, the nailed hand in silence is abstract, whereas with sound, it is terrifying, real. As for the shots in the mortuary, without the sound of dripping water that connected them together we discover in them a series of stills, parts of isolated human bodies … And the boy's right hand, without the vibrating tone that accompanies and structures its exploring gestures … just wanders aimlessly. The entire sequence has lost its rhythm and unity (1994:4).

Audiovisual illusion
In film, television and other audiovisual texts, sound is used to naturalise, inflect or produce certain readings, meanings, narratives, responses and moods.

Chion is dealing here with what he refers to as the **audiovisual illusion** of filmic texts. He means several things by this. The first and most obvious point is that in film and television texts sound is used to naturalise, inflect or produce certain readings, meanings, responses and moods. Chion makes reference to examples from the horror genre, where noises (screams, crushing sounds, thuds) or music (sharp notes, rapid edgy violin playing) announce or speak the horror, violence, pain, fear or terror that we then transpose onto what is happening on the screen. Perhaps the best-known example of this phenomenon is the music from the first *Jaws* film, where a droning double bass announces, tracks and stands in for the approach of the shark, as well as presages its attack: it has become so well known that humming the music is almost universally taken as a reference to the horror of an impending shark attack.

Another audiovisual genre that makes similar obvious use of sound and music is comedy. The Mel Brooks film *Blazing Saddles* (1974), for instance, opens with conventional soaring strings and horns playing over a typical Western landscape (wide open spaces, saltbush, desert and distant hills), the idea being to approximate the heroic milieu and deeds performed by brave, courageous men of the frontier. Then the mood 'turns sour': the sound sharply falls down and away and dies out, providing a point of musical bathos. All thoughts of heroism are banished from the screen. It immediately returns in the form of the title song performed by the popular country and western ballad singer Frankie Lane, but again what is given is quickly taken away by something inappropriate: in this instance, the voice and music are overlaid by the loud and constant repetition of the sound of a whip, which drowns out the voice at times. The sound of the whip is particularly and peculiarly effective in breaking the mood. Normally it would be heard in the background, and would complement the song-as-mood, but here it is just too loud, too close to us, and sounds as if it is being delivered with a little bit too much enthusiasm, relish and perverse pleasure—what the cultural theorist Slavoj Zizek (1992) calls 'enjoyment'. It is clear that we are dealing with a deliberate over-performance of sounds and music associated with the Western. When we hear the ludicrously loud cracking of the whip, we know that the world appearing on the screen is comic rather than heroic, dramatic or serious.

As well as facilitating and naturalising meanings, sound in audiovisual texts also acts as a **narrative** device; in other words, it helps to move the story along. Let us stay with *Blazing Saddles*. There is a scene early in the film where the townspeople are expecting their new sheriff. While dignitaries wait in welcome, a marching band plays a lively tune dominated by trombones and bass drums. The mood is festive and friendly. One person, equipped with a telescope, notices that the sheriff is an African-American, but he can't alert the others because the music and the pealing church bells are too loud. Finally the sheriff (played by Cleavon Little) rides into town. Nothing is said, but the reaction of the crowd, and by extension the filmic story, is entirely given in a few sounds (and absences of sounds). The band abruptly stops playing, the last notes from the trombone sounding like a discordant quack from a cartoon duck. This produces one of the few scenes in the film where the Western is played 'straight'. For a brief moment nobody says anything, and all we are left with is the weirdly disembodied sound of the horse's hooves clopping on the hard dirt road, played over the camera scanning across the stunned and hostile faces of the townspeople. In terms of pure content and mood (not to mention affective response), we could be watching *High Noon* (1952) or *Shane* (1953) or any other classic Western. In other words the story, which at this point moves from friendliness, welcome and a sense of community to rejection and racism, is contained and played out by and through the activities (playing enthusiastically, ceasing to play) of the band, and by the isolation of the sound associated with the sheriff (which mirrors his social isolation). What moves the film back to comedy is the sudden and highly inappropriate voice of the chairman of the welcoming committee who, because he has not seen anything yet, starts to deliver his speech about 'extending a laurel and hardy handshake'. The chairman then stares at the figure on the horse, pauses distractedly at 'new', and finishes, not with 'sheriff', but 'nigger'.

Different sounds can be used in a variety of ways, and mean different things, across audiovisual texts and genres. As Chion (1994:24) notes, the gargling sound that suggests the horror of torture (boiling oil being poured down a victim's throat in Tarkovsky's 1966 film *Andrei Rublov*) can just as easily function as a sign of comic social incompetence when performed by Peter Sellers playing Inspector Clouseau in *The Pink Panther* (1964). Moreover, as long as there is a convincing immediate connection made between the two spheres, audio does not even have to be, and in fact is usually not, authentic or organic in relation to the visual activity or phenomenon with which it is paired. Audiovisual texts are generally the products

Narrative The organisation of a story into a sequence of causally and/or temporally connected elements.

of intensive editing, involving selections, additions, deletions and other choices about technology (such as the placement of microphones and soundproofing techniques). As Chion points out, 'reality is one thing, and its transposition into audiovisual two-dimensionality (a flat image and usually a monaural soundtrack) … is another' (1994:96). What he finds amazing is that audiovisual texts carry any conviction of verisimilitude whatsoever:

> Indeed, we tend to forget that the audiovisual tableau of reality the cinema furnishes us with, however refined it may seem, remains strictly (on the level of reproduction) that which a sketched representation of a human, with a circle for the head and sticks for the arms and legs, is to an anatomical drawing … There is really no reason for audiovisual relationships … to appear the same to us as they are in reality (1994:96).

Mediation

Mediation The idea of a representation or medium of some kind that reproduces or gives us access to reality. There are many forms of mediation (such as paintings or photographs), with many technologies of representation (such as a brush or a camera).

Go online

Raymond Williams

The quote from Chion, and the other quotes and filmic texts we have been describing and analysing, serve as a departure point for a wider and more detailed consideration of questions and issues concerning media texts. The examples taken from Chion, and our own analysis of scenes from *Blazing Saddles*, are all tied in with questions of **mediation**. The concept of mediation, like all words and signs, has a history. In his book *Keywords*, **Raymond Williams** points out that the term came into the English language in the fourteenth century, and originally meant 'to divide in half, to occupy a middle position, to act as an intermediary' (1983:204); in other words, to mediate was to come between two things. This has gradually been developed to encompass the idea of a representation or medium of some kind (television, a painting, photograph, film, stick drawing) reproducing or giving us access to reality. Its modern usage, however, has focused on mediation as a form of interaction that is 'in itself substantial … it is not the neutral process of the interaction of separate forms, but an active process in which the form of the mediation alters the things mediated' (205).

This usage has a basis in, and is confirmed by, physiology. Consider Richard Gregory's description of the physiological mechanics and processes of seeing:

> We are given tiny distorted upside-down images in the eyes … From the patterns of stimulation on the retinas we perceive the world of objects … The task of eye and brain is quite different from either a photographic or television camera converting objects merely into images … What the eyes do is to feed the brain with information coded into neural activity—chains of electrical impulses—which by their code and pattern of brain activity, represent objects … When we look at something, the pattern of neural activity represents the object and to the brain is the object … The seeing of objects involves many sources of information … knowledge of the object derived from previous experience, and this experience is not limited to vision but may include the other senses; touch, taste, smell, hearing and perhaps also temperature and pain (1967:7–8).

At the very basic level of physiology, the world we perceive is in fact something we put together or make, rather than a straightforward replication of what is around us. Seeing (and by extension, all forms of representation) is thus an activity or practice. What is more, it is an activity that is framed by, dependent on and produced out of the particular mechanism or technology being employed, whether physiological or technological. This is partly what **Marshall McLuhan** (1973) meant by his famous statement that 'the medium is the message' (15): every medium of perception and representation 'shapes and controls the scale and form of human association and action' (16). Television, for instance, produces an entirely different relationship between spectators and sporting events compared to the mediated experience of being at the game itself. The use of multiple (and mobile) cameras means not only that we see a great deal more than an 'in situ' spectator, but we see it more than once (replays), in slow motion, from a variety of angles—and all this is accompanied by constant commentary, analysis, statistical updates, projections, computer graphics and profiles, while constantly being interrupted by commercial breaks. Some television coverage provides split screens, which allow us to choose what part of the game we see, what we frame and where we focus. Various forms of cameras-as-participants (driver-cam in Formula One racing, stump-cam in cricket) have also been developed, not just to emulate the experience of spectator 'at the game' (early television coverage of sport, with its static cameras, made for a very detached and comparatively limited experience), but to put viewers into the thick of things, and thus give them a sense of participating in the action, rather than simply watching it.

Go online

Marshall McLuhan and 'the medium is the message'

Visual regimes

The visual theorist Jonathan Crary (1998) refers to this historically specific and technologically based organisation of vision and representation as a **visual regime**. The ways in which we see, understand and mediate the contemporary world are strongly influenced by technological change, particularly as regards the mass media, which developed out of the logics and imperatives of capitalism. Precapitalist societies and cultures, on the other hand, saw a different world. To Ancient Egyptians, Greeks of the classical age, or Chinese from the Han dynasty, the idea of the value and meaning of things being determined by the marketplace would be unthinkable. Perception and value were organised around such things as the Pharaoh and the gods, civil and religious responsibilities, and Confucian ethics, respectively. To draw us a little out of our own naturalised way of mediating and making sense of the world, consider the following extract taken from the work of Michel Foucault, in which he discusses the work of the Argentine writer Jorge Luis Borges:

> **Visual regime** The way in which contemporary media and media technologies vision is arranged and organised. Vision is not just a biological function; it is also a cultural practice, with codes, conventions and rules (often specific to particular cultures).

(it shattered) all the familiar landmarks of my thought—our thought, the thought that bears the stamp of our age and our geography—breaking up all the ordered surfaces and all the planes with which we are accustomed to tame the wild profusion of existing things ... The passage quotes a 'certain

> Chinese encyclopaedia' in which it is written that 'animals are divided into: (a) belonging to the Emperor, (b) embalmed, (c) tame, (d) sucking pigs, (e) sirens, (f) fabulous, (g) stray dogs, (h) included in the present classification, (i) frenzied, (j) innumerable, (k) drawn with a very fine camelhair brush, (l) et cetera, (m) having just broken the water pitcher, (n) from a long way off look like flies' (1973:xv).

This (fictional) example shows us three things: first, how mediation is specific to time and place; second, how perception is organised by particular kinds of visual regimes; and third, how the visual regimes of other times and cultures can seem utterly alien, unrealistic and even comically ludicrous. The classificatory system above, which is based on specific logics, rationales, technological factors and forms of cultural differentiation (for instance, the position and status of the Emperor is clearly one of the 'organising principles' of perception; this system is not commensurate with Western science; the camelhair brush is a significant technology of representation), divides the world into distinct categories. When people from this culture look at animals, these are the means or frames through which they recognise and see things.

To this point we have introduced the notion that rather than simply 'take in' reality, we produce and read the world by way of different forms of mediation: everything from our optical physiology to various representations and texts (such as paintings, photographs and books). The forms these mediations take are dependent on, and tied in with, available technologies. Technological change is always the result of historical circumstances, forces and developments. This combination of technology and different ways of seeing (such as the feudal system, capitalism, communism, nationalism and Buddhism) works to organise and influence our perceptions.

Perception and knowledge

Forms and patterns of mediation and perception are not set in stone; cultures are usually both plural and dynamic. A culture is always marked by negotiations across, and struggles between, different groups with separate and sometimes antithetical values, agendas and imperatives. How we see and think is in flux, to some extent, because every day of our lives we are addressed by representations with their different stories, ideas, questions, demands, threats and fantasies. The French sociologist Pierre Bourdieu (1990) makes the point that subjects are capable of 'thinking against' dominant or habitual ways of seeing. There are, for Bourdieu, two principal forms of **epistemology**: practical and reflexive knowledge. The practical sense or the logic of practice constitutes an ability to comprehend and negotiate what Bourdieu and Loic Wacquant (1992) refer to as the 'games' that characterise cultural fields. Knowledge of how to play these games—especially the unwritten rules—is a form within which we operate. Such knowledge allows subjects to make sense of what is happening around them, and to decide how the game should be played; in other words, to determine which practices, discourses, moves or tactics are appropriate to the moment.

Epistemology The means by which we come to know and understand the world.

Bourdieu's second epistemological form—reflexive knowledge—can be understood as the set of dispositions that allow thought space outside 'the limitations of thought'; that is, it encourages us to look beyond the habitual frames through which we see the world. **Reflexivity** is orientated towards challenging two main sets of limitations: first, our social and cultural origins and categories (generation, class, religion, gender, ethnicity); and second, our position within whatever field(s) we are located (as anthropologist, bus driver, journalist, politician, accountant). Bourdieu associates a disposition towards reflexivity with a variety of fields and groups, including intellectuals (Bourdieu 1993:44), literature and the sciences (Bourdieu & Wacquant 1992:175), history (Bourdieu & Wacquant 1992:90) and art (Bourdieu & Haacke 1995:1). Reflexivity is therefore not, for Bourdieu, associated with one privileged field, but rather is potentially available within any field that disposes its subjects towards 'the systematic exploration of the unthought categories of thought which delimit the thinkable and predetermine the thought' (Bourdieu & Wacquant 1992:40). This is what the scientist Thomas Kuhn (1970) was dealing with in his influential book *The Structure of Scientific Revolutions*: a shift from one scientific paradigm to another (from a Newtonian conceptualisation of the universe as a giant, self-regulating machine, to Einstein's notion of relativity, to contemporary quantum mechanics and chaos theory) occurs precisely because one of the defining characteristics of the scientific field is that its members are disposed to think about and beyond their habitual ways of seeing.

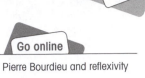

Go online

Pierre Bourdieu and reflexivity

Reflexivity In Bourdieu's work, the set of dispositions that allow thought space outside 'the limitations of thought'; that is, it encourages us to look beyond the habitual frames through which we see the world.

Communication and cultural literacy

This brings us to our next significant point: it is an apparent contradiction, but cultures can only exist because people can communicate with each other. People can communicate with each other because they share stable meaning systems (spoken language, writing, body language); but when people communicate with each other, those systems are altered and 'destabilised', to some extent. Like the concept of mediation, **communication** can be read and understood in different ways; and like mediation, its meanings have a history. Raymond Williams points out that communication came into the English language in the fifteenth century, and originally meant 'to make common to many, impart' (1983:72). This has remained its primary meaning, but from the seventeenth century onward the term came to refer to transport or 'lines of communication' (roads, canals, train lines); and in the twentieth century to the media and other forms and technologies used to disseminate information: hence the notion of a communications industry (72).

Williams posits the question of whether communication simply involves the sending and receiving of messages and information, or whether it is something that is negotiated by and between different people in a culture. The issue is really about how communication works at the level of everyday practice. When we represent something—by writing a letter, typing an email, making a film or drawing

Communication
The production, exchange and negotiation of meanings. The word originally referred to 'making common to many, imparting', but also refers to transport lines as 'lines of communication', and now also to the media and other forms used to disseminate information.

a stick figure—we are potentially involved in an act of communication. Works of representation are always 'orientated towards the response of the other' (Bakhtin 1986:75), even if the other I am communicating with is myself. I can write myself a note, think something to myself, produce a drawing that only I get to see. In all these cases I am positing another me toward which communication is orientated.

Communication means that we are addressing, or want to share something with, or want something from, another. Put simply, it is a kind of work. In order to get this work done we must, at the very least, share a meaning system of some kind with our potential audience(s); or, to use V. N. Volosinov's expression, communication must 'be placed into the social atmosphere' (1986:46). This does not have to be too sophisticated. In 2008, at an Australian Rules Football (AFL) game between Hawthorn and Port Adelaide, a Hawthorn player **Mark Williams** kicked the winning goal, and then ran towards the part of the ground holding the opposition's spectators with his hand held tightly around his throat. He was using at least two generally recognisable meaning systems. First, his body language, in this case the arrangement of hand and throat, referred to the act of stopping someone from breathing. Second, the usual English word for this act is choking. So Mark Williams was making a sign that referred to choking. This, of course, tells us little or nothing—except perhaps that there is a story here, that this story is tied up with football, and that it probably involves the relations between Williams, his team and their opponents.

What is the first thing at stake in this communication practice as a piece of work? The answer is **meaning**. Williams was producing, or at least trying to produce, a meaning for both himself and for an audience; in this case, the audience consisted of rival players, coaches and fans (not to mention the various media telecasting and reporting on the game). We wrote that the first part of his work, and the first context or social atmosphere in which it took place, involved using common meaning systems to produce the idea or concept of choking. To get to the next level of meaning, however, we have to delve more deeply into that social atmosphere: at a general level the cultural field of sport, and more specifically, the AFL and its recent history.

Within the field of sport, choking is a highly derogatory notion that refers to a player, team or coach losing their nerve at a moment of intense pressure; in other words, when things get tough, they are simply not up to the challenge. This is the equivalent of cowardice in battle for soldiers, or erectile dysfunction for ultra-machismo men. In sport it is the ultimate insult: it questions one's character and right to membership of the field. If we were familiar with recent AFL history, we would know that the Port Adelaide coach had very famously and histrionically 'hung himself'—that is, pulled his tie tightly round his neck and poked out his tongue—in front of the crowd and television cameras after his club had won the premiership in 2004. The point then was that there was an idea or feeling, widely disseminated in the media and across fan groups, that Port Adelaide was a talented team that could not win close games—they were chokers. The coach—coincidentally also named Mark Williams—was communicating his own rejection of this charge. When they lost the game to Hawthorn in 2008 (after holding the lead for most of the game), the Hawthorn player was clearly intent on putting the issue 'back on the agenda', so to speak.

Go online

Communication and Mark Williams' 'choking gesture'

Meaning The significance that is read into and from a sign.

We made the point that the first thing at stake in communication is meaning: this example of 'meaning in action' can help us to address the theoretical issue, articulated by Raymond Williams, as to whether communication involves the transmission or sharing of meaning. When Mark Williams put his hand around his throat, he was sending a relatively unambiguous message: the Port Adelaide players were chokers. We can read it as unambiguous because of the close, reinforcing connection between the body language, the context in which it took place, and the relevant history of communication practices and meanings (there were numerous newspaper articles, computer, and radio and television discussions devoted to the issue).

What is interesting is what the various audiences did with it; in other words, the way they negotiated it, and the meanings they made of Williams' attempt at making meaning. Port Adelaide players and fans read it as an indictment of the Hawthorn player: the relevant context here was the ethos of the field of sport, which militates against the idea of humiliating a beaten rival. In the National Football League (NFL) and in American College Football games, for instance, it is considered extraordinarily poor form to continue to try and score points once a game has effectively been decided. For Port Adelaide, what the hand-round-the-throat gesture meant, first and foremost, was that the Hawthorn player was a bad sport. The media made something else of it: a dramatic, controversial story. Here was a fairly uneventful game in an uneventful weekend of AFL coming to an end, when suddenly controversy flared, passions were aroused, and arguments, accusations, denials and apologies all ensued. Television ratings soared, newspapers were purchased, and Internet forums and talk shows were flooded with people giving their opinion. For the AFL hierarchy there were two, more or less antithetical, ways to read events: on the one hand (officially) they deplored the gesture as unsporting, while on the other hand (unofficially) they welcomed it because it helped sell tickets and provided the game with valuable publicity.

There was clearly an intention, on the part of Mark Williams the player, to send (transmit, to use Raymond Williams' term) a clear message. For communication to be possible, however, there must be (a) an orientation towards someone else; (b) a shared code; and (c) a relevant 'social atmosphere'. Once an act of communication enters into this process of circulating within the social atmosphere, the meanings that are made cannot be controlled or delimited. Why? Because the position from which the communication originated is always unique, to some extent: it comes from, and is tied up with, a particular time, place, identity and set of intentions or imperatives that are never exactly replicated anywhere else. To take things to their most extreme position, Mark Williams himself did not (in the end) read the message the way he intended: once he realised 'what he had done' (that is, he became aware of how unpopular he was, most significantly with his own coach) he apologised and retracted his gesture. His ownership of the meaning of the gesture was contested by himself: a self defined by another time and place.

There is another important reason why people don't 'get', accept or even understand what seem like straightforward or unambiguous communication practices: they may share the same social atmosphere, but that does not mean

that they share the same cultural literacies. We can define **cultural literacy** as
'a familiarity with, and an ability to read and make use of, the various meaning
systems (and the practices that inhabit them) that characterise the cultural fields
of a society' (Schirato 2005:26). We pointed out that we could make something
out of the gesture of a player holding his throat even if we knew nothing about
the AFL: there is enough of a shared code (body language) for us to make some
perfectly reasonable guesses about what is going on. But that is a world away from
the highly detailed reading available to someone who is AFL-literate. The same
situation applies to every field of culture: someone watching, for the first time and
with 'illiterate eyes', a film directed by David Lynch, a Japanese tea ceremony, an
exhibition of contemporary abstract art or a Norwegian fish-slapping dance will
see little or nothing that makes sense. We only see and understand something
because we have a close familiarity with certain codes of movement and expression,
rules and rituals, and histories; everything else is more or less chaos. We literally
recognise things; that is, we see, understand and follow expressions, movements,
stories, gestures and meanings because we have seen and understood them, and
know the meanings that they are making available.

Signs, meanings and ideologies

Communication is signification-as-work. It involves the production and negotiation of meanings that effectively 'make the world' around us. So what are the
terms and concepts that allow us to recognise, describe, analyse and explain, at
a technical level, these communication practices and processes? Let us start with
the basic unit of meaning—the **sign**. There are many different definitions of a sign,
but one that is frequently used, probably because it is very practical, comes from
the American semiotician C. S. Peirce, who suggested that a sign is 'something
which stands to somebody for something in some respect or capacity' (Hawkes
1977:126). In other words, a sign is anything that is read or treated as if it were
meaningful (Schirato & Webb 2004:28). What do we mean by **signification**? If a
sign is anything that is read as meaningful, signification is the process of turning
something (the clothes someone is wearing, skin colour, bodily movements) into
a sign. Things or events are never significant 'in themselves'; rather, they become
so when someone recognises and works them to produce meaning: to one's self,
or to others.

If we return to the scene in the film *Blazing Saddles* where Cleavon Little rides
into town as the new sheriff, we find it awash with potential signs that, if we are
literate enough, can be read to give us the story. The scene starts with an obvious
sign: the music, which is loud, upbeat and festive, indicating both a happy occasion
and perhaps a welcome of some kind. The clothes worn by the townspeople are
signs: they tell us that they are a mixture of men and women, formally dressed and
probably from the nineteenth century. Then a bell tolls: it is time; something is going
to happen. The lookout uses a telescope to pick out the approaching sheriff. He
sees something that he clearly thinks is an important sign and calls out a message,

but the townspeople cannot hear him; they just think that the sheriff is getting nearer. A stranger rides in on a white horse; that is the kind of sign you would expect to be associated with a new sheriff. Then we have two more important signs: silence (something is wrong) and Cleavon Little's face (he is African-American). We shift to the townspeople. The camera pans slowly across their faces, which are no longer characterised by smiles; instead, they have expressions that can be read as puzzlement, shock, disbelief, horror and disgust. Then we get the final sign, the one little word that sums up the whole scene: 'nigger'. In this context it is clearly a derogatory term, indicating the townspeople are racist and clearly were not expecting, and want nothing to do with, an African-American sheriff.

We defined a sign, following C. S. Peirce, as something that is read as meaningful, and clearly from this perspective the colour of Little's skin is an important sign, just as the word 'nigger' is read as a sign by Little and the film audience. But this scene directs us to three further aspects of the sign. First, meaning is to some extent derived from what a sign is not: so, for instance, Little's skin means something both because it is black and not white (we could also suggest that in the context of the film, 'nigger' means 'not sheriff'). The point here is that meaning is not found in the things that are referred to, so much as in the relation between the sign and a sign system. In other words, and following from the work of the Swiss linguist Ferdinand de Saussure (1989), we can say that meaning is derived from the relationship between signs and sign systems, and that meaning is 'relational'. Second, Saussure also makes the point that when we use words as signs for certain things this relation is always arbitrary; so we can say that there is no natural or organic connection between a sign and the thing or concept it is meant to represent or stand in for. The word 'sheriff', for instance, has no necessary connection with a person wearing a badge and riding a white horse who serves as a law enforcement officer in the American West. We could provide a description of the history of the word in the English language (it originates in Old English, and is possibly derived from an amalgamation of 'shire' and 'reeve', which referred to a town officer; and in the USA it refers specifically to a county or the civil subdivision of a state), but that history only gives us an account of how an arbitrary allocation of the sound and the arrangement of letters to a category or office has been modified across time and place. The obvious way of exemplifying this point is to contrast the ways in which different sign systems (such as national languages) deal with the same object or thing: Saussure's famous example is that the English, French and German language systems use different words (*ox*, *boeuf* and *ochs*, respectively) to refer to the same animal (Schirato & Yell 2000:20).

We have suggested that the relationship between the sign and the concept is both arbitrary and relational. However, we need to qualify this position, which leads to our third point: following on from Volosinov, we can say although meaning may be arbitrary, it is always motivated. All signs are both 'saturated with meanings', and:

> the sites where struggles over the control and naturalization of meanings are fought out. In other words, for Volosinov, the production of a meaning has to be understood as the forgetting of 'meanings'—that is to say, all meaning is ideological (Schirato 1998:397).

Let us see how this idea plays out in *Blazing Saddles*, which is, among other things, about skin colour as a sign, and the struggle over what that sign means to different people at different times. The colour of a person's skin constitutes what we can call a master sign: that is, it is one of the primary markers for organising categories and formulating sociocultural value. In an early scene, the people working on the railway line in the blazing heat are specifically not white; they are mostly black (African-American) or yellow skinned (Chinese). Their overseers, on the other hand, are all white skinned: they carry the guns, give the orders and do not do any manual labour. When their leader (played by Slim Pickens) tells a subordinate that there is quicksand up ahead and to go check it out, this clearly would not involve people with white skin—they are valuable. The subordinate suggests sending horses, but that outrages Slim Pickens—horses are valuable too. Instead, he tells the subordinate 'to send a couple of niggers'. The implication here is straightforward enough: a number of points of differentiation, including the important distinction between the human and the non-human, are predicated on skin colour. This is played out in the initial insistence, on the part of the townspeople, that the sheriff 'can't be a nigger': having black skin not only excludes Cleavon Little from holding any kind of position of power or authority, it also marks him out as being outside the town-as-community.

There is more than one community in the film; there are Chinese, African-Americans, Hispanics, southern Europeans and, famously, the Irish. Each community has their own markers of identity—skin colour, clothes, language, food, names, religion and forms of behaviour—but it is the white-skinned, Anglo-Saxon community that is in a position to assign meanings to, and determine, how those other communities are seen, and what their markers of identity mean. Of course Cleavon Little, and members of other non-dominant groups, first, do not accept the meanings that are assigned to them, and second, have their own set of meanings that they apply to markers of identity, both their own and that of others. But remember our point that mediations make the world, and perform a kind of work: in this case, the mediations, forms of communication and meanings that have the most practical impact—determining who lives or dies, eats or starves, is accepted or rejected as a full citizen—are those associated with the white community, while other meanings are ignored or forgotten. We can say that they have become naturalised or ideologised, which is how we describe a situation where meanings circulating in a culture are treated (sometimes by both dominant and dominated groups) as if they simply reflected reality, do not need to be thought about and are not the product of a group's self-interest.

Ideology Narrative about the forces that organise the world. It disposes people to see things and act in certain ways. It authorises or privileges one group over another. An ideology produces meanings that are naturalised or universalised.

Ideologies are narratives about the world that also effectively organise the world; that is, they dispose people to see things and to act in certain ways, and at the same time they authorise or privilege one group over another. Think of how women have, for thousands of years, been subject to discrimination and other forms of violence. This has been, to some extent, facilitated by, and a consequence of, ideology. Why? Because systematic discrimination against, and violence towards, women has been authorised by what we call 'masculinist' ideologies that tell us that women are, by nature, weak, irrational, stupid and indecisive. Moreover, these accounts of women as being somehow 'less than human' (they are like men, but inferior to men, and therefore incapable of taking on responsibility) are always backed by powerful and authoritative institutions, groups or texts (a church, priests or other religious, the Bible or other holy books). Every group within a society attempts to naturalise meanings that are suited to its own interest; that is, it attempts to naturalise the way signs are read. This is the case with all signs-as-meanings: as Volosinov writes, 'The domain of ideology coincides with the domain of signs. They equate with one another. Whenever a sign is present, ideology is present, too' (1986:10).

How does ideology perform its work? Let us consider, by way of example, the Marxist Claude Lefort's suggestion that the modern Western world has, until very recent times, been dominated by something he calls bourgeois ideology. According to Lefort, in the nineteenth century:

> While it continued to be interlaced with the remnants of religion, bourgeois ideology gradually broke its links with religious discourse and discarded the reference to a spiritual or physical elsewhere. In place of this elsewhere it substituted general, abstract ideas; the text of bourgeois ideology … is written in capital letters: Humanity, Progress, Science, Property, Family, Nation. These ideas … thus give rise to an opposition between the subject who speaks and acts in accordance with the rule, and the 'other' who has no access to the rule and is therefore deprived of the status of subject (1986:17).

The regulation of social practices and subjects through the deployment of these capitalised ideas is one obvious way of loading the dice of the game of power; first, because it acts to literally exclude certain groups (woman, children, non-whites) from the game itself (by designating them as non-human, for example); and second, because even when marginalised groups are included in the game, the effects of bourgeois ideology often predispose those groups to work against their own interest and carry out the work of the dominant classes.

Discourse

Go online

Discourse

The concept of **discourse**, which is closely associated with the work of Michel Foucault, can be defined as a type of language associated with a cultural field and its institution. In Foucault's work, it is used to describe 'language in action' (Danaher et al. 2000:x). Let us consider Lefort's suggestion that, in the nineteenth century, bourgeois ideology succeeded in replacing the once dominant discourse of the field of religion with, among others, that of science. The Church produced much of what counted as authorised knowledge, and that knowledge (in the form of books, pamphlets, lectures, sermons—or even just the capacity to read and write) employed a type of discourse that both reflected their ideas and values, and turned a very specific way of looking at the world (that of the Church) into something universal and beyond disputation. Terms such as faith, belief, heaven, devil, angels, sin, obedience, humility, righteous, repent, suffering, transgression, mercy, soul,

> **Discourse** In Foucault's writings, discourse does the work of both opening up and closing off the world. It disposes us to make sense of and see things from a field-specific perspective.

sacrifice and confession, for instance, produced a particular understanding of, and relation to, the world. They turned everyday practices into a series of experiences based on the denial of the self and the acceptance of God's grand plan, which was administered and translated by his clergy (so the Pope is literally God's representative on earth). Generally speaking, when it comes to deciding what to do, or who to believe, or a question as to whether something is good or true, the only opening that religious discourse allows is predicated on terms such as faith and belief. In other words, the world is God's book, and in order to make our way through the world (and make decisions about the world), we have to forego our arrogance (in the form of thinking that we have the capacity to decide for ourselves) and trust and have faith in God, which means having trust and faith in those appointed to act for him (the Pope, bishops, priests and nuns).

Discourse not only orders our relation to, and explanation of, the world, it also provides what we can call categories of subjectivity; in other words, discourse divides people into typologies that largely correspond to, or follow from, the extent to which they accept and comply with the authority of the Church. So terms such as heretic, blasphemer, unbeliever, infidel, sinner, harlot, apostate and whore of Babylon are examples of discourse 'making something appear'; in these cases, strongly negative typologies that are used to both recognise a person ('Look, there's the whore of Babylon!') and to prescribe one's relation to them (shun her, treat her badly, do not marry her).

Words associated with the field of science, on the other hand, are clearly part of a different order of discourse (to use Foucault's expression). For a start they do not derive their authority from God or a single, holy book. Rather, they are tied with the notion that human reason and rationality is now the measure of all things, and that the only valid knowledge is that produced through the application of various principles, techniques and methodologies (reason, observation, experimentation, critical analysis and quantitative research). This order of discourse privileges proof over faith, argumentation over doctrine, and this world over the next one (heaven), which is not verifiable anyway, and therefore cannot be a subject of analysis or debate. Forms of discourse taken from the older religious discursive regime are here transformed from the positive into the negative, and are disqualified (at least within the field of science) from playing any serious or significant role regarding questions of truth or epistemology. Moreover, people are no longer categorised in terms of their compliance with moral codes, but with regard to their resemblance to descriptive criteria based on observation, proof and the work of experts authorised by the field and its institutions (universities, research centres and prestigious journals). The whore of Babylon we identified in our earlier example would now be described, in scientific discourse, as a female human of indeterminate age, possibly suffering from nymphomania.

If the discourse of the scientific field is based on and tied with rationality, reason and analytical methodologies, how do we make sense of Lefort's suggestion that bourgeois discourse had a political dimension? That is, it gave rise to 'an opposition between the subject who speaks and acts in accordance with the rule, and the "other" who has no access to the rule and is therefore deprived of the status of subject' (1986:17). Foucault famously argued, in the first volume of *The History of Sexuality*, that in the Victorian age (commonly understood as a period in the second half of the nineteenth century characterised by repression regarding sexual matters) there was a tremendous 'incitement to discourse', largely but not exclusively of a scientific nature, about issues of sexuality. There was, he writes, 'a steady proliferation of discourses concerned with sex … a discursive ferment that gathered momentum from the eighteenth century onward' (2008:18). This movement was tied up with the exercising of power—by governments, medical bodies, bureaucracies, the police, educational institutions and the law courts—over populations (workers, students, mothers). Sexuality, specifically scientific discourses of sexuality, was put to work to help identify, analyse, evaluate and categorise which parts of the population were normal and healthy human beings (in both physiological and psychological senses), and which parts were not. This initiative gave rise to a series of scientifically authorised discursive categories—the homosexual, the nymphomaniac, the hysteric, the neurotic—that were, in Lefort's terms, 'deprived of the status of subject' (1986:17).

Discursive categories continue to frame and explain people—and to deprive them of the status of being 'normal'. Crary writes that:

> Over the last few years we have been reminded of the durability of attention as a normative category of institutional power, in the form of the dubious classification of an 'attention deficit disorder' (or ADD) as a label for unmanageable school-children and others … what stands out is how attention continues to be posed as a normative and implicitly natural function whose impairment produces a range of symptoms and behaviors that variously disrupt social cohesion … Even after admitting that there is absolutely no experimental or empirical confirmation of an ADD diagnosis, the authors of a best-selling book on the subject make the claim: 'Remember that what you have is a neurological condition. It is genetically transmitted. It is caused by biology, by how your brain is wired' (1999:35–6).

And this authority of the biological explanation of children's behaviour in school and in other sites continues to influence how children are seen and understood, despite researchers noting the apparent paradox that 'Many, if not most, hyperactive children are apparently able to sustain attention for a substantial period of time in high interest situations, such as watching television shows or playing video games' (Crary 1999:37).

A non-scientific contemporary example of an authorised discourse that (more or less literally) divides people into human and non-human categories is the term 'terrorist'. Those imprisoned in Guantanamo Bay, for instance, who have all been labelled as 'terrorists', were transformed into something without legal rights, available for torture, degradation and indefinite incarceration. Another example of just how productive this form of discourse has been can be seen in what happened in New Zealand (in Tuhoe and elsewhere) in October 2007, when police mounted an 'anti-terrorist operation' and arrested or detained a number of people, most of them Māori. The fact that it was labelled an 'anti-terrorist operation'—by the police, the government, politicians and the media–automatically located it within the wider operations, imperatives and logics of the War on Terror, despite the fact that 'most arrests were made under the *Firearms Act*' (Jackson 2007). As Māori lawyer Moana Jackson points out, 'people are charged nearly every day with breaches of the *Firearms Act*' but here 'the Crown chose to label these particular arrests "terrorist"' (2007). What made this possible was the introduction of a *Terrorism Suppression Act* in 2002, closely following on and resembling similar acts in the United States, Australia and Britain. The Act gave the Prime Minister the right to 'name or designate … individuals or organizations as a terrorist entity', while terrorist activity itself is defined, in a circular manner, as 'terrorizing a population' (2007). Before the Act, people who kept guns illegally in New Zealand were dealt with through the normal processes of the law, which among other things, required proof before someone could be detained. With the enacting of anti-terrorist laws, groups and individuals who are designated as a potential 'terrorist threat' by the government effectively become terrorists, at least in terms of their legal status and representation in the media.

Although ideologies and authorised discourses try to convince 'dehumanised groups' that their status is natural, universal and inescapable (you are sick; you are evil), discursive work can always be undone. Let us return to *Blazing Saddles*. The important and difficult task that falls to Cleavon Little is to 'do the work' that will transform the dominant understanding of what his skin colour means. The personal consequences of his success (he saves the town and arrests the villain) are that he is accepted both as the sheriff and as a member of the (previously all-white) community. The wider consequence is that he is able to re-negotiate, from a position of some strength (as hero, as representative of the law), the terms that define that community. In order to defeat the various roughs, renegades and outlaws (and anachronistically, Nazis and Hell's Angels) that threaten to destroy the town, he enlists the aid of the previously disenfranchised groups (such as the Chinese and African-Americans)—on the understanding that by helping the community, they will become part of the community. The townspeople confer, and initially say that they will accept the 'niggers and the chinks and the spicks, but we won't take the Irish'. However that only moves the meaning of community along a little way, from being very exclusive (whites only) to moderately exclusive (whites and some others, but not the Irish). Cleavon Little wants the community to be inclusive (whites and blacks and the Irish), and for skin colour to lose its status as a master **signifier** (operating to categorise, and by way of extension, exclude). In Volosinov's terms, he wants to re-ideologise the way skin colour functions as a sign.

Signifier A primary marker for organising categories and formulating sociocultural value.

How does ideology, and more generally the process of meaning making, work? How can we analyse these processes and effects at a practical level? There are a number of technical concepts that we can utilise for this purpose, concepts-as-techniques that enable us to see and show how meanings are made, negotiated, transformed, disseminated (predominantly through the media) and naturalised across a culture, to the extent that they permeate the 'social atmosphere' that we breathe in every day of our lives. These concepts-as-techniques, which we will look at in detail in the rest of this chapter, are text, intertext, context, narrative, genre, interpellation and subjectivity.

Text, intertext and context

When we use the term **text** we usually refer to a conventional cultural 'package'—such as a book, film, television show, music video, CD and the like—which signals, in a number of easily recognisable ways, that it should be read and treated as a collection or unit. These conventional signals include authorship (the name of a writer, director or band), materiality (some books have hard covers, with softer pages in between), title (*Jaws* and *Jaws 2* would not be shown as the same text in cinemas) and certain kinds of boundary markers (a film often opens with the name of the production company and a musical score, and ends with credits). It also includes lists or inventories (a web page will open with the home page and then name or number all associated pages) and forms of address (a television current affairs, news, arts or sports show might start with a welcome from the host, and end with 'goodnight'). What all these conventions have in common is that they function as a frame that includes, arranges, and confers a unity and/or sense of homogeneity with regard to, various signs. At the same time, acts of inclusion are always simultaneously acts of exclusion; with paintings, for instance, a wooden frame literally demarcates the extent of the text, just as a camera frame works to omit and select content. Moreover, textual production—and the stitching together of a group of signs as a text—is dynamic, rather than set in stone:

> Texts are produced or created; this process ... is an ongoing one; and the status of signs and texts is always relational and contingent ... there are no natural units of signs within cultures—or anywhere in nature. ... Every time we treat something as if it were a text, we create a unit out of an infinite number of potential signs (Schirato & Webb 2004:23).

Let us return to the issue of what constitutes the community of the town of Rock Ridge in *Blazing Saddles*. There are a number of signs in the first half of the film that function, collectively, to define and authorise membership of the community. Skin colour is clearly one of these, but there are others such as names (all the people in the town appear to have the surname 'Johnson'), language (everyone speaks English) and religion (they all attend a Christian church service). There is both continuity and similarity across this collection—to the extent that it constitutes what the Russian theorist Mikhail Bakhtin calls a 'coherent complex of signs' (1986:103). That makes it, potentially at least, a text; and the ongoing process of negotiation and renegotiation between Cleavon Little and the townspeople (which moves, initially, from the outright rejection of 'Up yours, nigger' to the qualified 'I've baked a pie for you, but please don't tell anyone') is really about widening frames, and processes of selection and omission.

The identification, production, negotiation & interpretation of texts are tied with two other concepts: intertext and context. John Frow defines **intertextuality** as:

> the range of processes by which a text invokes another, but also the way texts are constituted as such by their relationships with other texts. No text is unique; we could not recognise it if it were. All texts are relevantly similar to some texts

Text Refers to conventional cultural 'packages' such as books, films, television shows, music videos, CDs and the like: they signal, in a number of easily recognisable ways, that they should be read and treated as a collection or unit.

Intertextuality The process through which individual texts relate to other texts and, in part, draw their meaning from that relation. Implies the systems of visible or invisible references that shape an individual text. All texts refer to other texts.

and relevantly dissimilar to others. Similarity and difference form one pole of intextextual relations; citation, including implicit or explicit invocation … and even at times the significant absence of reference to a text, forms another. All texts are shaped by the repetition and transformation of other textual structures … Texts may refer to other, quite specific texts; they may refer to a more general form of organization of texts, such as genres … or they may refer to bodies of knowledge which do not have a specifically textual form (2006:48–9).

All texts refer to other texts. Sometimes this is done in a very specific and comprehensive way, as when a sport computer game creates a world based on the positions, logics, rules, categories and players of the NFL, NBL or MLB; or when Hollywood 'updates' old television cartoons and sitcoms (*Superman*, *The Hulk*, *The Flintstones*, *Rocky and Bullwinkle*, *Lost in Space*, *Zorro* and *Batman*). On other occasions, intertextuality draws upon a history of certain types of texts scattered across various media, as is the case, for instance, with the Steven Spielberg–Harrison Ford Indiana Jones films. They clearly and self-consciously utilise the content, forms of characterisation and narrative pace of predecessors from literature (such as Arthur Conan Doyle's *The Lost World*, Jules Verne's *Journey to the Centre of the Earth* and Rider Haggard's *King Solomon's Mines*); radio (American serials from the 1940s, such as *John Steele Adventurer* and *Ports of Call*); television (the 1950s series *Soldiers of Fortune* and *Ramar of the Jungle*); and other Hollywood films (Cary Grant vehicles such as *Gunga Din* and *Only Angels Have Wings*).

Genre and narrative

Go online

Genre and narrative

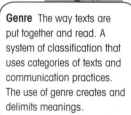

Genre The way texts are put together and read. A system of classification that uses categories of texts and communication practices. The use of genre creates and delimits meanings.

When we walk into a library, or video or music store, for instance, the texts are usually arranged in terms of categories, such as detective, science fiction and romance novel; comedy, horror and adventure film; and jazz, country and punk music. Television guides make use of the same process; we are told that a particular program is reality television, current affairs or a children's show. If we were to visit any major news home page on the Web, we would find links to local, national and international news, weather, sport, lifestyle, the arts, IT, entertainment and business pages. We refer to these forms of categorisation as **genres**. Frow defines genres as:

a set of conventional and highly organised constraints on the production and interpretation of meaning … they shape and guide, in the way that a builder's form gives shape to a pour of concrete, or a sculptor's mould shapes and gives structure to its materials. Generic structure both enables and restricts meanings, and is a basic condition for meaning to take place … That is why genre matters: it is central to human meaning-making and to the social struggle over meanings. No speaking or writing or any other symbolically organised action takes place other than through the shaping of generic codes (2006:10).

Generic categories, first, contribute to the way texts are put together and read; second, create and delimit meanings; and third, function as intertexts. In the Indiana Jones films, we find templates, derived from the long generic history spanning literature, radio, television, film, computers and other media, that tell us what we can expect from the content, characters and narrative. We know that there will be a hero. He (it is usually a 'he') will be a rugged, quick thinking individual, who is brave and tough, and able to endure pain and overcome adversity. The story will be set in some exotic and often primitive location: a jungle, a remote desert or some lost world. The locale will be threatening and difficult (there will be heat, thirst, wild animals and hostile natives), and the hero must endure all this to succeed in his quest (such as find the treasure, rescue the girl and defeat evil). The details of the primitive world, and the relationship between different characters (hero and heroine or romantic interest, hero and buddy, hero and villain) will be painted in broad strokes; that is, it will be relatively superficial, with a few obvious signs (a strong jaw, a snarl) doing a lot of work (indicating that the hero is tough, or that the villain is ruthless). The action will be thick and fast: as one crisis is overcome (the natives are driven off), another is always developing (the group are entering the part of the jungle inhabited by fierce beasts or huge poisonous spiders).

Genre sets out, follows and commits to the way of the world it envisages. It not only gives us a world with its own rules, identities, values, relationships, forms of behaviour and stories, it also naturalises them. In the Hollywood version of Kipling's poem of the same name, *Gunga Din* (1939), directed by George Stevens, the way of life, adventures and brotherhood enjoyed by three soldiers of fortune (played by Cary Grant, Victor McLaglen and Douglas Fairbanks Jr) in the British army in colonial India is threatened when one of them, Fairbanks, plans to marry a well-to-do, respectable, serious and highly attractive young woman (Joan Fontaine) and go into the tea business. If the world of the adventure film is largely a boy's fantasy played out by and for grown men, Fontaine represents its antithesis: responsibility, routine, domesticity and adult life. Marriage will remove Fairbanks from the army and adventuring, and a heterosexual relationship will replace male bonding.

In many genres the move to some form of heterosexual intimacy is a given. It may vary in the way it is played out and manifested—a spiritualised 'more than this world' in romance, frenzied coupling with numerous partners in countless positions in pornography—but heterosexual romance is a dominant narrative that coexists with the narratives found in various non-romance genres (comedy, science fiction, fantasy, the Western and the thriller). In the adventure genre, however, it often constitutes more of a threat to the way of life and the well-being of the hero than all the text's savage natives, fierce beasts and poisonous spiders.

No text ever completely reproduces all the characteristics of a genre, and all uses of generic characteristics are not necessarily straightforward. In *Raiders of the Lost Ark* (Spielberg 1981), the first of the Indiana Jones films, there is a scene where Ford-as-Jones is confronted by an enemy, who performs a series of elaborate, over-the-top tricks with swords and knives, the idea being to emphasise his skill, and to indicate that he poses a serious threat. However, instead of meeting and beating him in fair, one-on-one combat (and therefore demonstrating his superiority), Jones pulls out a pistol and dismissively shoots him dead. To some extent this constitutes something of a subversion of generic expectations (the hero does not fight fairly), but one of the characteristics of the adventure genre is that, precisely because so much of the content and action is ludicrously over the top and unrealistic, it often sends itself up.

This spoofing of genre is also to be found in comedy: a film such as *Blazing Saddles* reproduces the Western film in considerable detail, but in such a way that transforms it from something natural into a series of ludicrously unrealistic conventions. To a certain extent, the film is about what happens when generic conventions run into realities that are normally ignored in the Western (the effects of an all-bean diet on a cowboy's digestive system).

Blazing Saddles is a comic Western that sticks closely to the generic rule that comedy does not show or deal with 'reality'; people are killed, blown up, hanged, beaten, humiliated and subjected to racist taunts and treatment, but because it is a comedy, it 'never really happens', and we are not meant to feel it. In romance pain is overcome, in pornography it is enjoyed, but in comedy it simply disappears. This is what disqualifies *Blazing Saddles* from being considered a 'real Western'; although it carefully and comprehensively (indeed, almost perversely) replicates the generic conventions, and articulates the values, of the classic Western, it does not perform any kind of 'belief in them'. One of the generic imperatives of comedy is to mock and deny naturalised conventions, forms of representation and belief systems; although usually not its own.

So how do we make sense of the fact that texts often mix generic conventions, such as comedy and the Western in *Blazing Saddles*, or the gangster movie and the musical in Francis Ford Coppola's 1984 film *The Cotton Club*? John Frow (2006) points out that texts do not simply replicate one set of generic rules and conventions; there are often comic moments in horror films, and romance pervades and often dominates many genres. Jacques Derrida (1980) refers to the necessary 'contamination' of the laws of genre, since texts always cite and reference, and are thus constituted out of, other texts from across the world of genres. To a certain extent it is more accurate to say that, rather than texts belonging to genres, genres 'inhabit texts'.

We suggested that sign and texts are the sites of struggle over meanings, and when meanings are pervasive and accepted unthinkingly as certain or natural, they have been ideologised. Now given that the concept of genre is critical to the ways in which texts are organised and read, it follows that genre has an ideological function. In *Blazing Saddles*, there is a clear disjuncture between Cleavon Little-as-text and the generic characteristics of the office of sheriff. This is dramatically evident when the governor is introduced, by a scheming Hedley Lamar (he wants to appoint a sheriff that the town will reject), to 'the new sheriff of Rock Ridge'. The governor (Mel Brooks) extends his hand, but at the moment they come face-to-face the look of (presumed) recognition on the governor's face is replaced by a violent reaction of non-recognition: as he says, taking Hedley Lamar by the arm and leading him away, 'Have you gone berserk? Can't you see that that man is a nig?' At this point there is another generic disjuncture (of course, this is a comedy, and comedy makes frequent use of the technique of violation of expectation). The intimacy associated with personal friendship (taking Lamar by the arm, openly using a racist expression) is inappropriate when the interlocutor is not known to you (and is an African-American).

The rest of the film, even if it is obviously played out as comedy, is about Cleavon Little's attempts, not just to re-negotiate the meaning of skin colour, but also to put an end to that disjuncture between content (skin colour) and generic category (the sheriff). What he does, by performing all the other constitutive generic parts (he is brave, resourceful, able to uphold the law and overcome the villain, romance the white heroine, save the community and bring it together), is to draw attention to the way skin colour functions as an anomaly within the genre. Of course the idea, on the part of the community, that there is a necessary continuity between one generic feature (skin colour) and the rest (such as bravery and resourcefulness) is a convenient fiction. It suits the (white) community for this entirely arbitrary and anomalous feature to be seen as essential, precisely because it helps justify the power differential (people of Anglo-Saxon descent are in charge and run things) that is the basis of frontier politics (African-Americans cannot vote or receive the protection of the law).

■ Narrative

Go online

Narrative

How do certain obviously anomalous features end up as continuous with other features of a genre? The answer is that a necessary articulation or link is established between them through the circulation of sociocultural narratives. What do we mean by narrative? Tzvetan Todorov distinguishes two main ways of organising a text, largely differentiated by the extent to which 'causal–temporal relationships exist between the thematic elements' (1981:41). He means that a narrative posits or implies a logic or explanation (causal and/or temporal) about the connection between elements in a text, in contrast to a list or a purely descriptive text, in which all the parts are referred to without an accompanying explanation or account (a 'how and why and when') of their belonging together.

At a practical level, Michel de Certeau helps us link narrative to our point that mediations and texts do some kind of work: he writes that narratives are stories that 'produce effects, not objects' (1988:79). The white community of Rock Ridge, for instance, and by way of extension all the other Anglo-Saxon communities that make up the United States of America at the time the film is set, have emerged out of, and prospered by, various forms of physical and symbolic violence (massacring native American tribes and stealing their land, and enslaving African-Americans). The same sorts of things could be said about all forms of 'colonisation', from the Spanish Conquistadors in Central and South America to the British intrusions in Africa, Australia, New Zealand, Canada and India. What all these colonialist practices have in common is that they were authorised by various stories that enabled them to represent what was clearly the exercising of violence to promote self-interest (the acquisition of land, slaves, power and wealth) as something entirely different: nature running its course, doing God's will, taking on the white man's burden and spreading civilisation. A travestied form of Darwinism was employed, for instance, to justify what was tantamount to genocide in Australia: the story of the ascent of man had no place for Aboriginal peoples, cast as an evolutionary dead end.

Similarly, Michael Adas has demonstrated how Western scientific and technological superiority was often:

> put to questionable use by Europeans and North Americans interested in non-Western peoples and cultures. It has prompted disdain for African and Asian accomplishments, buttressed critiques of non-Western value systems and modes of organisation, and legitimised efforts to demonstrate the innate superiority of the white 'race' over the black, red, brown, and yellow (1990:15).

We referred to the adventure film *Gunga Din*, which exercised a considerable influence over the revival of the genre by Steven Spielberg (the second film in the series, *Indiana Jones and the Temple of Doom*, makes numerous intertextual references to *Gunga Din*). Although the activities of the three soldiers are mostly presented as high rollicking fun, what they in fact do is slaughter Indians and rob their temples. The story of the Indian 'mutiny', from the film's perspective, is that certain people are rational adults (the British), and they have a right to dominate people who are barbaric, pagan, treacherous children (Indians). The events that follow (slaughter, enslavement, humiliation and theft) develop out of this initial story (and the presumptions it is based on). This is how genre emerges, and where it does its work. The genres of the adult and the sheriff, for instance, are formed out of a mix of general or abstract features, ideas and qualities (these would include maturity, rationality, bravery and resourcefulness) and quite specific or particular content (the British, Anglo-Saxons, white people). This is why the governor and the townspeople of Rock Ridge react, initially with the shock of misrecognition ('What I see is not what I see'), and then with indignation and scorn. An African-American sheriff is both a non-sense and an affront to their values.

Conclusion

This chapter has described, analysed and exemplified the relations between the processes, techniques, technologies, contexts and politics of mediation. We defined mediation as a practice or an activity that involves negotiating and producing the visual reality around us. We also made the point that it is dependent on, and influenced and limited by, different media and technologies. This leads to the point that mediation has a history. How people and cultures have seen and represented the world—and the dominant forms of mediation that have served this function—has varied from one historical period to another. The development of writing systems, books, cameras, moving image technology and computers has transformed or changed dominant ways of seeing and representing the world.

We also suggested that the way we read and represent the world is carried out through the production of signs and texts. These are the sites of struggle over meanings. When meanings are pervasive and accepted unthinkingly as certain or natural, we can say that they have been ideologised. Ideologies are articulated and naturalised through the repetition of discourses, genres and narratives, which provide us with the templates that we used to recognise and evaluate the world, and in doing so bring the world into existence.

Finally, we can sum up this chapter by saying that the world we perceive is always mediated: it is something we put together, rather than being a straightforward replication of what is around us.

Additional reading

Introductory

Frow, J. (2006). *Genre.* London: Routledge.
    Explains and exemplifies the concept of genre.

Williams, R. (1983). *Keywords.* London: Fontana.
    Provides a valuable account of history-of-meaning of concepts such as communication and mediation.

Advanced

Chion, M. (1994). *Audio-Vision.* New York: Columbia University Press.
    An excellent, detailed and well exemplified account of the relation between visual texts and sound.

Volosinov, V. (1986). *Marxism and the Philosophy of Language.* Cambridge: Harvard University Press.
    A seminal work on the relation between meaning and ideology.

SUBJECTIVITY AND THE MEDIA

Introduction

In this chapter we will explain the concepts of subjectivity, and show how their related processes, practices and categories are bound up with the texts, technologies, logics and imperatives of the field of the media. We will describe, exemplify and analyse influential ideas about subjectivity, derived from the work of theorists such as Michel Foucault, Pierre Bourdieu, Judith Butler and Arjun Appadurai. We will also contextualise these theories and ideas through consideration of the enhanced role of capitalism and the media (both generally as regards the electronic media age, and more particularly in terms of the advent of global media technologies) in influencing and organising everyday life. The concerns of this chapter are twofold: first, to explain how subjectivities are created, maintained and authorised; and second, to analyse the role the commercial media play in these processes.

Go online

Foucault and the emergence of the human sciences

Subject The notion of cultural identity produced through discourses and ideologies.

Disciplinarity, biopower and normalisation

Michel Foucault argues that the modern **subject** emerges from a set of historical circumstances more or less contemporaneous with the development of scientific forms of knowledge (including the so-called human sciences), and their application, through techniques and regimes of standardisation and quantification, to populations. During the late eighteenth and early nineteenth centuries, disciplinary techniques were developed for administering 'large populations of workers, city dwellers, students, prisoners, hospital patients, and other groups' to turn them into 'manageable subjects' (Crary 1998:15). This coincided with the appearance of 'new technologies for imposing a normative vision on the observer' (16). These changes are tied up with a number of closely related sociohistorical contexts, in particular the development of what Foucault calls the '**reason of state**', the growth of **liberalism** and the increasing influence and pervasiveness of capitalism. The logical extension of economic liberalism is free-market capitalism. We will deal with liberalism and capitalism later in this chapter; it's sufficient to say that they are orientated towards individualism, and are in a sense antithetical to the reason of state and government intervention in the lives of citizens and business.

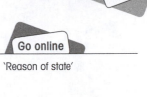

Go online

'Reason of state'

Liberalism A general distrust of, and opposition to, strong state intervention in society, particularly in economic matters.

Foucault locates the beginnings of the reason of state in Western Europe, and dates its initial appearance to the end of the sixteenth and beginning of the seventeenth centuries. He places its apogee of influence in the eighteenth and nineteenth centuries; and he argues that it still remains a significant, if modified, feature of the contemporary world. Its departure point is the question 'What is the art of government?' (2007:237). This question develops out of the transition from sovereignty understood as being overseen and authorised by the Church and God and the divine right of kings, to an expectation that governing and government will be driven by human reason and rational decision-making.

There were two main aspects that, hand in hand, facilitated the reason of state. The first of these was **knowledge**. To govern the state well (that is, productively) and to facilitate its development (in terms of territory, military strength, wealth, skills and communication systems), you need to know what constitutes the state. By way of example, communications systems are crucial to government, military action and commerce, so it makes sense to have inventories of, and statistics about, roads, canals, horses and mail depots. However, along with those inventories, lists and maps, you need information about what state of repair the roads are in, how reliable the barges are, how long it takes for a rider or carriage to transport messages or goods, how goods and people move through and between towns and where populations live. All this requires bodies of knowledge, such as engineering, architecture, geography, town planning and metalwork. Overall, to effect a transformation of communication networks and systems you need to do two things: first, ascertain what is efficient and functional, which largely means coming up with descriptive, numerical and statistical templates that are realistic and reliable; and second, find a way of turning the ideal (exemplary statistical categories) into the real (actual systems, equipment and practices), and keeping things that way.

Knowledge In Foucault, the systematic and disciplinary forms of information gathering that shape the consciousness of subjects and support the objectives and justify the powers of the state.

The same kind of logic applies to your most important resource: the state's population. Forms of knowledge—especially the newly developing human sciences—are put to work to 'act on the consciousness of people' so that 'their opinion is modified … and along with their opinion their way of doing things,

Go online

Disciplinarity

Discipline (also disciplinarity)
In Foucault, refers to a process in the late eighteenth and early nineteenth centuries, whereby people would be disposed to bring their behaviour, thinking and seeing into line with what the state and its various institutions considered to be normal, healthy and productive. This process was meant to train people to lead normal lives without the need to think or reflect on what they were doing.

Normalisation Taken from Foucault's work, refers to the means of managing populations by establishing norms (of behaviour and physicality) against which people are measured.

Panopticon Jeremy Bentham's model for a prison with a central tower from which a guard could observe prisoners. Since the prisoners would never be able to know if they were being scrutinised, they would adjust their behaviour. Foucault, by extension, sees this as providing a model for the ways in which discipline operates in society.

Self-surveillance A social process by which subjects are disposed to make themselves the objects of their own gaze, constantly monitoring and evaluating their bodies, actions and feelings.

their way of acting, their behavior as economic subjects and as political subjects' (Foucault 2007:275). The reason of state-demanded constant state intervention in the lives of subjects-as-populations, dealt with and viewed in terms of principles and techniques of resource management. Populations were, and still are, seen (by the state and its various institutions) as potential resources. For the state to gain the maximum benefit from these resources, people had to be subjected to techniques that regulated and orientated their thinking and general behaviour; in other words, they had to be disciplined.

Being disciplined did not simply mean being punished. Rather, it referred to processes whereby people would be disposed to bring their behaviour, thinking and seeing into line with what the state and its various institutions considered to be normal, healthy and productive. This process was meant to train people to lead normal lives without the need to think or reflect on what they were doing. It started at an early stage in a person's life (a child in a family and at school learned what the rules of society were, the need to respect authority and the consequences of delinquency), and continued until death (manifested, for instance, through the need to consider what were the most appropriate and normal ways to die and how to arrange one's affairs). Just as a soldier is trained to fit in to and comply with military culture instinctively (by saluting an officer, and automatically and unquestioningly following orders), so populations were meant to accept and be directed by a similar, but much wider, disciplinary regime.

Foucault identifies two major stages to this process of **discipline** and **normalisation**. The first stage is best represented by Jeremy Bentham's model of the **panopticon**, which consisted of:

> A tower placed in a central position within the prison. From this tower, the guards would be able to observe every cell and the prisoners inside them, but it was designed in such a way that the prisoners would never know whether they were being observed or not. Prisoners would assume that they could be observed at any moment and would adjust their behaviour accordingly (Danaher et al. 2000:53–4).

The second stage of the process was **self-surveillance**, which was considered to be a more economical and effective form of regulation. Through immersion in, and contact with, various cultural institutions and their discourses, narratives and images, subjects would be disposed to make themselves the objects of their own gaze, constantly monitoring and evaluating their bodies, actions and feelings. As Crary writes, these processes, and the ways that they produced modern subjects, were tied up with:

> the fixing of quantitative and statistical norms of behaviour. The assessment of 'normality' in medicine, psychology, and other fields became an essential part of the shaping of the individual to the requirements of institutional power in the nineteenth century, and it was through these disciplines that the subject in a sense became visible (1998:15–16).

Foucault (2007) refers to these processes and techniques of normalisation as the exercising of **biopower**. His argument is that biopower simultaneously served the ends of the reason of state and contributed to the development of capitalism by providing a healthy, active, hard-working and disciplined population. On an everyday level, people came to see themselves in the context of what has been designated as normal or average. So a person's height or weight, how hard he or she worked, or how many times he or she had sex during the week, was viewed and evaluated in terms of standards and templates derived from, and authorised by, scientific knowledge. Armand Mattelart traces this specific statistical inflection back to 'the last two decades of the nineteenth century', when 'sciences based on the calculation of individual behaviour took off' (2003:37). To a certain extent this merely added to the disciplinary techniques and resources available to the state, helping 'policemen, judges and forensic scientists … in their mission of social hygiene against the dangerous classes' (2003:37). But the development of, say, 'machines for recording the pace of work in factories, stadiums and barracks' (37) meant that knowledge, in the form of exact and specific measurements of normality, were now disseminated for the population to 'use against itself'. It would be much easier, in the light of the production of this kind of information, for workers to see themselves as lazy and unproductive, and to feel the need to work harder and longer, just like a 'normal' person. In the contemporary world there is a plethora of pseudoscientific statistics of normality, constantly articulated in newspaper articles, magazines, television shows and internet websites, that both remind people of what they have to measure themselves against, and offer the means (better toothpaste, Viagra, self-help books, exercise equipment, diets, cars and clothes) for achieving and surpassing such norms.

> **Biopower** In Foucault, the processes by which knowledge, power, administrative and political authorities effect and enforce standards of normality for subjects and serve the interest of the modern state.

Interpellation

> **Go online**
>
> Louis Althusser

How are people turned into compliant, normal subjects in everyday practice? There are two (quite complementary) explanations we can call upon. The first, derived from the work of the French Marxist **Louis Althusser**, stresses the structural and procedural nature of the relationship between the sites and apparatuses of power (the state, capitalism, bureaucracies and the media) and its subjects; the second, based on the theories of Pierre Bourdieu, emphasises how our immersion in time and place (in the form of our sociocultural history) helps us to naturalise and universalise what are effectively arbitrary ideas, dispositions and worldviews.

Althusser (1977), in his essay 'Ideology and Ideological State Apparatuses', provides us with perhaps the best-known explanation of the process of subject production. For Althusser, subjects are **interpellated**. What this means is that they are called or addressed by institutions, texts and discourses that:

> **Interpellation** Interpellation produces subjects. It refers to the way institutions, texts and discourses call (or 'hail') and address subjects in order to 'recruit' them.

> (recruit) subjects among the individuals … or 'transforms' the individuals into subjects … by interpellation or hailing … which can be imagined among the lines of the most commonplace everyday police (or other) hailing: 'Hey, you

> there!' Assuming that the theoretical scene I have imagined takes place in the street, the hailed individual will turn round. By this mere one-hundred-and-eighty-degree physical conversion, he becomes a subject. Why? Because he has recognized that the hail was 'really' addressed to him (163).

The analogy is straightforward enough: in Althusser's example, it is a policeman shouting to someone in the street, but it could be a school teacher talking to a student in a classroom, or even a bureaucratic form that has to be filled out. When any authority addresses us and gets a response, in that moment the departure point or context of the encounter is the right of the authority figure to categorise us, and the validity of the categorisation that's been provided. This formulation is problematic to some extent, because it appears to leave out the possibility of disobedience: as the gender theorist Judith Butler points out, 'The law might not only be refused … it might also be ruptured' and its 'monotheistic force' called into question (1993:122). Althusser's point, however, is that it does not matter so much whether a subject 'believes' in authority and its self-narratives (the state knows best; the police are working in your interest; you should work harder). He refers to the French philosopher Blaise Pascal's famous dictum that if you 'Kneel down, move your lips in prayer … you will believe' (1977:158). What this means is that the ritual of call and response produces compliant subjects. Put simply, by acting as if we believe, we end up believing in what we act.

Go online

Uncle Sam

Consider those old '**Uncle Sam** wants you' posters, which originated in the nineteenth century and were meant to convince people to enlist in the American army in the two World Wars. They are still around, in the United States and elsewhere; but instead of trying to get people to enlist in the US army they are now used to establish a relationship between a group (a political party, a voluntary organisation) and the public, based on the notion that members of the public have a duty to help out, get involved or contribute to the cause. The Uncle Sam figure is a manifestation of the imperatives associated with patriotism, which we are meant to recognise and accept as part of our role as citizens. In the usual images, Uncle Sam addresses us with a severe and intense gaze, and he points at us directly. Even allowing for the over-the-top hat and the goatee beard, he is an imposing and intimidating figure. What is implicit in his facial expression, gaze and gestures is that Uncle Sam is the embodiment, at least in the United States, of the right of authority to speak to, and make demands of, us. Uncle Sam is absolute certainty personified: he knows what a good citizen should do, how he or she should behave, and the sacrifices the good citizen ought to make for their country. It is hard to laugh at, refuse or even negotiate with that particular form of address. If you dismiss or refuse Uncle Sam, you categorise yourself as something other than a good patriotic citizen, which is a very difficult thing to do.

The logic is circular but nonetheless effective, and goes something like this: Uncle Sam knows the good citizen; Uncle Sam has stated that he wants 'you'; he would only want good citizens, therefore you are a good citizen. In other words, you do not have to believe—he believes for you. When groups (such as political parties and non-government organisations) use the Uncle Sam image, they are not just trying to get your attention by referring to a famous figure, or simply attempting to

establish a link between themselves and another just cause (fighting your country's enemies or being a patriot). They are instituting the performance of a 'between us' (the fixing gaze and the pointing of the figure demands a response) with the aim of getting you invested and involved in a form of belief (of course you care about the environment, or want to restore law and order), which is eventually productive (you'll become an activist).

We have identified three important characteristics regarding the production of **subjectivity**. First, it involves work of some kind: a person is an American, a good citizen, a Goth or a woman because an authorised **cultural field**, institution or discourse (in the form of a text, medium, narrative or genre, such as an advertisement, television soap, security camera, bureaucratic form or lecture) has addressed them so as to produce what we can call an effect of subjectivity. This does not presume or require compliance; even a rejection produces a form of identity (such as delinquent, bad father or alcoholic). Moreover, since this work categorises and evaluates people, it inflects or even determines their social trajectories: to be labelled a terrorist, pederast, alcoholic, fat or suffering from ADD is not exactly destiny, but it does influence how someone will be seen and treated.

We can say then, as our second point, that the processes and practices of subject formation are both abstract and material. On the one hand, the category of 'fat' is not a thing; rather it is an idea, category or concept. However, when it is applied to someone, it influences how that person's body will be perceived, and the significances and meanings that are attached to it. The reality of a body-as-materiality is inextricably linked to, and produced out of, the idea of what we understand as a normal, healthy body. So when we see someone's body—or for that matter, look at our own body—we simultaneously recognise and evaluate that person in terms of the different categories of normality.

Our third point is that, while categorising or naming someone does produce certain effects, the processes and practices of subject formation are always predicated on contexts such as time and place. Not only is there no one-to-one relation between a subject category and a person (a normal man, woman or child is always an idea, not a thing), there is also no necessary continuity in terms of how subject categories are interpreted or understood.

This is obvious enough at a cross-cultural level: think of how differently female sexual activity is viewed in the Trobriand Islands of Papua New Guinea (high activity is a sign of maturity and sociability) and Saudi Arabia (adultery is a crime). It is also possible to see how responses to a category or subject trait are played out differently across cultural fields: it might be acceptable to be gay in Hollywood (you might still get work in television or films), but it would in all probability disqualify you from having a political career in California, let alone Alabama or Arkansas. What is harder for us to understand or accept is how a major subject category (such as man, child or homosexual) can vary over time. These forms of subjectivity can be remarkably pervasive and long lasting within specific societies and cultures. Because they are so central to how we organise and arrange our world, we tend not to think about them at all, or to think of them as being natural and universal.

Subjectivity The forms and processes of individuation; that is, how humans are made subjects in relation to culture, place and power. Subjectivity is contextual, in the sense that it relies on the forms of discipline, validation and authorisation in the specific cultural field to which the subject belongs.

Cultural field A social system with institutions, agents, subjects, discourses and practices that structures and reproduces power relations within and without. The field's practices are organised and validated through the habitus.

The habitus and cultural fields

Go online

Pierre Bourdieu

Habitus A concept based on the work of Pierre Bourdieu. Habitus is history naturalised. The values and dispositions gained from our cultural history are part of who we are, how we see the world and how we do things.

We suggested that the way a person was categorised (such as fat or suffering from ADD) could determine his or her social trajectories. As **Pierre Bourdieu** (2000) points out, however, the opposite is also true: sociocultural practices and forms of behaviour take place, are produced in, and are inextricably bound up with, the world. All activities, from the highest form of disinterested scientific or scholarly work to the most tacit (and therefore, virtually unconscious) bodily movements, poses or dispositions, are always informed by a relationship between where the subject has been, and how their history has been incorporated. For Bourdieu, subjectivity is always the result of a coming together of what he calls the **habitus** and the specific cultural fields and contexts in which subjects find themselves.

The concept of the habitus can be understood as history naturalised. The values and dispositions gained from our cultural history are incorporated into, and constitutive of, who we are and how we see the world. As people pass through various cultural fields and institutions, and come under their influence, they are disposed to regard those values, discourses, ideals and ways of doing things as natural and, to some extent, universal. That is why there is often a considerable amount of misunderstanding and conflict when practitioners from different kinds of fields (business and the arts, for instance) come together. While we are being disposed towards certain paths or ideas we are generally not conscious, however, that we are being 'spoken' by that field. Of course, because people come into contact with, and move through, so many different kinds of fields (such as education, the family, church and sport), there is always something of a negotiation or compromise required by practitioners.

Every cultural field has its own authorised languages (what Michel Foucault calls 'discourses'), as well as specific values, ways of doing things, expectations, hierarchies, dress codes and meanings. In order for a person to fit in and progress (for instance, be employed and promoted in a business or bureaucracy), they must more or less unconsciously adjust themself to that field. This requires (actually demands) knowledge of a field's rules (written and unwritten), genres, discourses, capital, values and imperatives. Cultural fields have their own conditions of entry, predicated on an acceptance of the worldview(s) of the field. For Bourdieu 'the field is the subject'.

Imagined communities, culture and the collective habitus

The habitus can usually tolerate change and social upheavals, and subjects moving from one field to another, because there is a continuity of meaning that characterises and permeates the overall culture in which those fields are embedded. This communal culture is promoted and perpetuated by such organisations as government bureaucracies, the media and the education system. This is one of the developments that followed from the logics, imperatives and practices of the reason of state. It was facilitated, initially, by the widespread dissemination of printed texts, combined with massive advances in the number of people who possessed reading and writing skills. If we accept Benedict Anderson's (2006) suggestion that nation-states are really 'imagined communities'—that is, populations who come to believe and act as if they constitute a single, natural and more or less homogeneous entity—then we can say that all the different nations, even the most supposedly natural, powerful, traditional or longstanding ones, such as Britain, France, China and India, have been politically and culturally 'imagined into existence'. In fact, the existence of any sociopolitical entity depends on the maintenance of this sense of a shared culture that is based on shared purpose, traditions, values, language and way of life. One of the ways in which modern nation-states have attempted to communicate their identity, as well as maintain social and political control over their populations (the two activities are very closely related), is by identifying and disseminating (through schools, pamphlets, media broadcasts and websites) examples of 'national culture'. At the same time, most governments also put considerable energy and money into building places and technologies of discipline and surveillance for their own populations. Police forces, secret services, prisons and the whole bureaucratic mechanism are there to ensure that the people remain committed to, and believing in, the idea of their nation, and that they behave accordingly.

For most of the twentieth century, nation-states have attempted to regulate, control or influence the production of meanings within their boundaries, and this is still the case today. States have attempted to maintain this control because they have recognised the extent to which the production of meanings is able to 'express, or set the groundwork for, the mobilisation of group identities' (Appadurai 1997:13). Culture is one of the ways in which states facilitate their aims and objectives, and perpetuate their existence. The media, print and electronic, have played a critical role in the construction of national identity by interpellating (or, calling into being) small groups of people who may be separated by religion, geography, dress, customs, values, language, political affiliations or history. Newspapers, radio broadcasts, film and television (and more recently digital technology) have all played a part in the constant reiteration of national pride and traditions.

Culture (in the form of language, history, dress, meanings, genres, rituals, art and sport) operates both as a means of indicating sameness, membership, recognition, continuity and inclusion (the 'between us' of communal identity), on the one hand; and difference, rejection, disavowal, unconnectedness and exclusion ('I am not that') on the other. Moreover, it does this throughout and across nations and societies. Communities are always being 'called up' at the level of gender, race, ethnicity, age, sexual preference, geography, profession or sport. Moreover, every subject is going to be hailed or addressed, often simultaneously, by a variety of institutions, texts and discourses, some of them quite antithetical to one another. Think of the difficult game Barack Obama had to play when he gave his 'victory' or 'acceptance' speech (in January 2009) after winning the American presidential election in 2008. He had to present himself (to the people, Democrats, other politicians, different gender categories and openly racist groups from the American South and Midwest) first and foremost as an American: that is, as a category of subjectivity that defines itself, at least discursively, as being unified in its diversity. What this meant is that Obama could not appear to be speaking to, associating himself with, singling out or representing one particular group. There was a clear recognition, not just on the part of that community, that Obama's election was significant because he was the first African-American president. It followed, for some groups (again, think of the southern United States), that as an African-American he would govern for, and privilege, 'his community'. Now of course this has never been articulated (in the media or during past presidential campaigns) when Anglo-Celtic or other white men have been elected. This is because, for a long part of American history, the white male has been the default 'universal' American subject. It only raises its head as an issue when the president comes from outside that group.

How did Obama play this out? First, by insisting that the significance of the occasion, the real meaning of his election, was in the opportunity it presented to reunite America. In other words, he was saying that under George W. Bush the government had favoured some groups and discriminated against or ignored others, and that he was going to change that. Second, he chose to refer to just about every traditionally 'disadvantaged' group (women, the disabled and the poor) except African-Americans. The only reference to the struggle of African-Americans against racism and other forms of violence came, interestingly enough, via implicit citings of Martin Luther King's speeches and Sam Cooke's civil rights anthem 'A Change is Gonna Come'. If America could be said to be characterised by a collective habitus (animated and activated only at rare and specific times and sites), then the discourse that best articulated that habitus was one of 'opportunity for all'. By refusing to make any specific reference to his own skin colour or to privilege the struggle of African-American's, Obama's speech both performed and endorsed that habitus.

Modern and postmodern subjectivities

To what extent is this picture of the modern nation-state as the catalyst for, and guarantor of, the collective habitus still relevant? Has there been any profound change in the processes of subject formation with the change from the modern, relatively stable world of newspapers and television to the postmodern, globalised and digitally mediated present? We made a reference early in this chapter to two closely connected factors that have played a significant role in the production of contemporary subjectivity: **liberalism and capitalism**, and by extension the technological developments that have transformed the capitalist media. In an essay on the relation between postmodern culture and developments in communication technology, Mark Poster (1995) claims that the electronic media have facilitated a 'profound transformation of cultural identity' (87),

Go online

Liberalism and capitalism

one that is more or less analogous with the break between the Middle Ages and incipient modernity:

> technically advanced societies are at a point in their history similar to the emergence of an urban, merchant culture in the midst of feudal society ... At that point practices of the exchange of commodities required individuals to act and speak in new ways ... Interacting with total strangers, sometimes at great distances, the merchants required written documents guaranteeing spoken promises ... A new identity was constructed ... among the merchants ... in which a coherent, stable sense of individuality was grounded in independent, cognitive abilities. In this way the cultural basis for the modern world was begun, one that eventually would rely upon print media to encourage and disseminate these urban forms of identity ... In the 20th century ... radio, film, television, the computer and now their integration as 'multimedia' reconfigures words, sounds and images so as to cultivate new configurations of individuality. If modern society may be said to foster an individual who is rational, autonomous, centred and stable (the 'reasonable man' of the law, the educated citizen of representative democracy, the calculating 'economic man' of capitalism, the grade-defined student of public education), then perhaps a postmodern society is emerging which nurtures forms of identity different from, even opposite to those of modernity (1995:80).

Poster suggests that contemporary subjectivity is caught between two more or less discontinuous regimes. There is a modern form, which is contemporaneous with the sphere and influence of the capitalist print media and its texts (such as books, newspapers and pamphlets). It was facilitated by advances in communication infrastructures and technologies, such as roads, railways, canals and steamships. It was produced under the auspices of significant social, cultural, political and economic fields and institutions. It included sites such as the family, church, sport, schools, universities, the sciences, museums and galleries, youth groups, newspapers, the law courts, factories, parliament and government agencies and bureaucracies.

This regime has not been without its own tensions, to some extent divided between logics associated with the reason of state and the emergence of a capitalist-inflected liberalism. The former approaches the subject in terms of the wider question of the relation between state imperatives and population management; the latter is at best indifferent, and at worst inimical, with regard to the role of the state, and instead champions Poster's 'calculating economic man of capitalism'. The development of liberalism went hand in hand with an emphasis on the notion of individuality and self-responsibility, and the spread of free-market capitalism. The pervasiveness of free-market capitalism in the nineteenth and early twentieth centuries meant a move away, not only from government control and regulation of important economic matters, but from the notion of government responsibility to and for society or communities. In classical Marxist terms, the most important content of the state—people and land—were taken out of the context of being part of a society or community, and became commodities in the marketplace.

The logical extension of liberalism and the free market economy was a move from state- and bureaucratic-based decision-making (which could be determined by non-economic considerations) to a form of decision-making arising out of a much more complex network of financial institutions that were not necessarily based in one state. Today states, to a certain extent, have lost their political and economic autonomy, and are influenced in their decision-making by international institutions and multi- and transnational corporations.

The media, for instance, is no longer as susceptible to government needs as it was in the first half of the twentieth century. In *The Power of Identity* (1997b), Manuel Castells tracks the changes from the early 1980s—when virtually every television network was state controlled and radio and print media carefully regulated—to the 1990s and on to the present century. It was in the twenty-first century that— as an effect of the emergence of new technologies and of media mergers—most governments lost the ability to control the transmission of media, and became increasingly influenced by, and even dependent upon, the **fourth estate**. Now, instead of having power over the media, governments have had to fall back on lesser forms of influence. Arjun Appadurai (1997) suggests that it is becoming increasingly difficult for any state to produce a sense of social and national community because of the wide reach of the electronic media, and the increasing fragmentation of identity (189). Castells identifies twentieth-century technology as having brought about 'one of those rare intervals in history ... the transformation of our material culture' (1997a:29). The 'usual suspects' on the list include computers, electronic mail, the Internet, digital, cable and fibre optic technologies, mobile telephones, satellite technology, television, film, and telephone or video conferencing. Each can be located within the general categories of digitalisation, networking and information processing.

Digitalisation is probably the most important technological advance in the area of communications. It is central to networking potentialities because it is characterised by growing convergence, and thus brings together a variety of media (telephone, television and computers) and types of texts (pictures, sounds and words). Digitalisation offers greater flexibility, because communication technologies are no longer text specific, and can 'talk' to each other. Castells writes:

> the information technology paradigm is based on flexibility. Not only processes are reversible, but organizations and institutions can be modified, and even fundamentally altered, by rearranging their components ... a decisive feature in a society characterized by constant change and organizational fluidity (1997a:62).

This also speeds up and facilitates information processing, because the changes in speed and mass associated with developments in communication technology allow greater amounts of information to be stored and circulated, and moved across mediums at real-time speed.

This decline of state regulation of the media and, as a consequence, of the stability of national identity, is associated with the inability of governments to control or limit the pervasive reach of transnational media corporations such as

Fourth estate The institutional status of the press. The first three estates are executive, legislative and judicial powers. The expression raises the status of the press to that of a pillar of democracy.

Digitalisation The process whereby information is produced as a universal binary code, and is thus able to circulate more freely and at greater speed across communication technologies, and not just within them.

News Corporation, AOL-Time-Warner, Bertelsmann and Viacom. Flows of images, information and ideas from across the globe offer citizens a smorgasbord of forms of identification; and of course provide reportage that might be very much at odds with the local government's interpretation of national or global events. The Marxist theorists Michael Hardt and Antonio Negri (2001) pick up on this notion, pointing out that one of the distinguishing characteristics of the contemporary globalised world is the **imbrication** of capitalism, the media and biopower. They argue that the first task of the grid of **globalisation** is not just to produce consensus among subjects, but more dramatically to ensure that all thought, every notion of morality and ethics, and the dispositions and values of subjects, are produced within the framework of global capitalism. This has led to a situation where the media and communication industries now occupy a dominant place with regard to the social, precisely because their role is to transform the social into something else: a kind of simulation of the capitalist system of production. In other words, more or less everything that is considered inalienable within society—sporting teams, artistic production, human body parts, death or children—is to be reformulated and rethought as alienable: as being subject to the market. The imperative, then, is to produce subjects disposed to see and understand the world almost exclusively through capitalist eyes and categories.

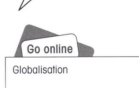

Imbrication An overlapping pattern.

Globalisation The contraction of time and space brought about by new communication technologies, and the free circulation of texts across conventional borders; the cultural, social, economic and political movements, and new technologies, that displace people and texts from local to global settings.

Hardt and Negri (2001) suggest that while capital has always been disposed towards the global, it is only in the post-Second World War period, and most particularly since the 1970s and 80s, that capital has effectively replaced the nation-state as the organising apparatus and principle of the management of populations. And as the nation-state has progressively been integrated into the networks and system of global capitalism, the function of biopolitical management and control, formerly undertaken by public institutions, has given way to apparatuses and ideologies of capital and the commercial media. In one sense this can be presented in terms of a straightforward shift from what was largely a public communication system in the first part of the twentieth century, to what is the overwhelmingly commercial system today. But Hardt and Negri (2001) push this argument to another level. They suggest that the civic sphere within which the production and negotiation of meanings (and consequently, subjectivities) takes place is now almost entirely a global civic sphere constituted by the communications equivalent of Castells' 'network society'.

Go online

Globalisation

Appadurai has raised the question as to the effect that the forces and processes of globalisation have on the **habitus**. Appadurai suggests that the more or less unregulated flow of cultural texts—in concert with the continuous 'flowing of peoples' that characterises the contemporary world—works to 'move the glacial forces of the habitus into the quickened beat of improvisations for large groups of people' (1997:6). He picks up on the work of the French theorist Michel de Certeau (1988) to argue that people are continuously confronted with images, narratives, information, voices and perspectives, from all corners of the globe, that do not equate with the received ideas of their habitus. Rather than having stable subjectivities, people have to make do with whatever is at hand. So, for instance, regardless of their own national or ethnic identity, they might borrow identities

Go online

Habitus

from Hong Kong kung fu films, American sitcoms or Indian melodramas. This means that they are necessarily distanced not just from 'official' cultural texts and their meanings, but from any institution or text that claims to have a monopoly on meaning, simply because, in a globalised world, what is understood as normal is always subject to (very rapid) challenge and change.

By way of example, we will consider what seems to be one of the most natural of modern categories of subjectivity—the child and children—and see how, first, it is tied up with, and emerges from, the spread of discourses, logics, imperatives and disciplinary techniques associated with the reason of state; and second, how this subject category has been transformed, over the last few decades, by new media technologies and the pervasiveness of capitalist logics and imperatives.

The child as subject: From normalisation to commoditisation

Every cultural field, institution and form of discourse is required to respect, or at least pay lip service to, the inalienable status of the child. What this means, among other things, is that children are supposedly not reducible to, or a part of, the capitalist economy and its logics. At the same time children are increasingly being treated, and function, as commodities and consumers. Advertising campaigns for consumer products like films, clothing and food are often specifically directed at pre-teen groups, who are seen as being able to access considerable levels of disposable income. This disjunction usually informs media representations and public sphere discussions of what could be described as the increased sexualisation, in contemporary Western culture, of child subjectivity.

We pointed out in our previous chapter that in the first volume of *The History of Sexuality* (2008) Michel Foucault identified the ways in which the bodies of the various categories of 'the people', including children, became scrutinised for signs and symptoms that would show their health and normality—or otherwise. From birth, the subject's body is evaluated, measured, tested and categorised with the purpose of reading and determining the 'truth' of the body. That truth is obtained by comparing the body and its markers to the various grids of knowledge brought to bear by different institutions. While the child was generally understood as being a stable category ('everybody knows what a child is'), in reality it was transformed and revised as new forms of knowledge were developed. Moreover, children are being targeted in advertising texts that sell desirable lifestyles, activities and fashions—often strongly sexualised. This means that the category of the child is no longer separated from regimes and notions of sexual desire and desirability. This production of desiring and desirable subjects occurs more or less simultaneously and continuously, and once started cannot be readily reined in. Popular culture has become saturated with a new set of categories and subjectivities (predicated on the newly and overtly sexualised child, for instance) that clash with more traditional and inalienable (and usually official) categories of, and discourses about, child subjectivity.

If adults experience or manifest any form of sexual excitation arising from watching or contemplating or being with a child (via an advertising photograph, a film, a fashion shot, or a computer game as much as conventional pornography), this is usually considered a form of deviance. At the same time, adults are often disposed (in mainstream computer games, fashion photographs and films, as well as overtly pornographic DVDs) to respond with desire to the sexualised child. To fail to become aroused by a scantily clad child model, or by a few lines of a drawing suggesting large breasts or curvaceous legs is, for some subjects, to fail the test of normal masculinity.

Why are these developments considered to be a problem? More specifically, why are they often represented in the media as symptoms of a much wider crisis of childhood? Partly it can be understood as an issue of subjectivity-as-genre; what children are doing is, to use Judith Butler's term (1993), 'performing' generic characteristics associated with adulthood. Why are certain generic characteristics inappropriate to be performed by children? Because children are (supposedly) incapable of looking after themselves, making judgments about their practices, or knowing what is 'good for them' (particularly when it comes to sexuality). Adults can sexualise themselves in a variety of ways (adult men and women may seek to make themselves attractive to another person), but it is presumed that either they know, or should know, what they are doing, and are prepared to take the consequences. In the contemporary world, desire is an ever-present and largely unquestioned component of adult subjectivity: what advertising texts tell us, implicitly, is that if we are not attuned to, and animated by, our desires there is something wrong with us (we are not normal). This is (still) not deemed to be the case with children.

There are two sets of questions that arise from this issue. The first pertains to how children are represented as, and disposed to be, desiring, sexual subjects when discourses of and about their normal subjectivity do not allow for any notion of sexual desire. The second is concerned with the sociocultural processes and imperatives that theoretically remove children from the marketplace, and how these sit alongside the countermove (from capitalist enterprises, texts and discourses) to commoditise everything, especially those areas and things that have been deemed inalienable. So how are these seeming paradoxes negotiated and played out in the contemporary media?

Before we locate these issues within specific examples and sites of media representations and discourses, it is worth bearing in mind the dominant role the commercial media has come to play in all aspects of subject formation. We have made the point that regimes of normalisation and capitalism determine or predispose our everyday visuality, including not just how we see the world and people around us, but also how we view and understand ourselves. The field that is most active in facilitating and naturalising these two regimes is the media. It is impossible to make sense of how and why people think, behave and come to see the world without making reference to the media and their ever-widening sociocultural roles. The media are a repository for what Judith Butler (1993) calls 'authorised performances of subjectivity'. The media provide a kind of 'store window' of desires and performances, and a selection of subjectivities from which viewers can theoretically 'pick and choose'. The reality, of course, is somewhat more complex. As Judith Butler points out, the forms of subjectivity that are made available in the media, and the provision of the role models and exemplars that do a great deal of the work of commoditising those performances, are always bound up with various kinds of sociocultural authorisation: Is this normal? Is this fashionable? Is this desirable?

Go online

The Miley Cyrus 'scandal'

How does the commercial media deal with the question of the newly sexualised, desiring child? Let us look at the situation involving **Miley Cyrus**, the daughter of American country singer Billy Ray Cyrus. In 2007, when she was under 16 years of age, she took part in a series of media events (a *Vanity Fair* shoot by Annie Leibowitz, also involving her father; and music clips for songs such as '7 Things' and 'Start All Over') where she was represented as sexually desiring and desirable. Moreover, these texts simultaneously emphasised her status as a child and a sexual commodity, without any sense of contradiction or ambiguity. This all drew a considerable amount of media attention—in newspapers, talkback radio, television news reports, Internet blogs and YouTube clips—about whether or not her behaviour in the media was appropriate. More specifically, it called into question her status as a role model for young girls.

The *Vanity Fair* photographs were read as sexual (and sexualising) for a variety of reasons: Cyrus was naked from the waist up (but with her breasts covered) in one shot, and in others the way her body was arranged (shots of her breasts from the side, held tightly in a black top; lying back staring knowingly at the camera) suggested sexual availability and knowledge. This sexual and sexualised reading was generally privileged over other explanations (Leibowitz is a photographer whose work is associated with, and part of the field of, art and aesthetics; draping the daughter's body over the father connoted familial affection) because of various intertexts, specifically photographs on the Internet showing her pulling down a top to reveal her bra, and another of her naked in a shower (behind frosted glass). The simultaneous combination of the insistence and denial of overt sexuality gave rise to a parody, also on YouTube, featuring a fake scenario of Annie Leibowitz urging Billy Ray to put his hand on his daughter's breast, while in the foreground a Disney executive explains that he is at the shoot to ensure that Miley Cyrus's 'family image' is not being damaged. What made all this particularly scandalous was precisely this insistence that the subject of desire and desirability was a child. In the *Vanity Fair* shots she is presented as a little girl—kissing and cuddling daddy. In the clip for 'Start All Over' she is initially presented as cuddling under the sheets of a doll-like bed.

Go online

Pavement magazine

The Miley Cyrus example is becoming increasingly commonplace, even as it generates moral denunciation, ridicule and scandal. A similarly blatant example can be found in the Spring 2006 issue of the glossy fashion magazine *Pavement*, which was published in New Zealand (it stopped publishing in 2007). The cover of this 'special teen issue' shows a prepubescent girl in a short, off-the-shoulder dress with one half-formed breast partly visible. Regardless of the girl's age, she is made to look like she is 13 or so. The idea is clearly to refer to the idea of, and desire associated with, paedophilia. Most of the images in the issue are presented so as to emphasise the innocence of the models. They are fresh-faced (presumably deliberately made up that way), and their bodily arrangements (hugging themselves, finger on mouth, eyes downcast) make them look like children even when they are 18 or 19 years old. In the issue, sexuality is mostly implied or alluded to, but there are photographs of models either directly engaged in sexual activity (a boy has his hand down a girl's jeans leg in a Lee advertisement), or approximating soft-porn positions (legs opened wide to the camera, breasts and legs bared).

These types of representations of sexual and sexualised, and desiring and desirable, child and teenage models are matched by media warnings about the immorality and undesirable consequences of such practices. Consider the following article in the *Sydney Morning Herald* newspaper, 10 October 2006:

> The sexualisation of children is changing the experience of childhood, yet there has been little public discussion of its implications … Children, particularly girls, are under increasing pressure from advertisers and marketers to adopt a sexy persona from very young ages. Those who apply the pressure claim they are simply responding to little girls' interest in looking pretty … This sexualising pressure places children at risk in a number of ways … The focus on sexual couplings found in girls' magazines, pitched at readers aged five to 13, may have dangerous implications for children who are approached by predatory adults. These magazines encourage girls to have crushes on men older than themselves, with heavy coverage of adult female celebrities and their boyfriends, as well as articles on and posters of adult male actors and singers … To sexualise children in the way that advertisers do—by dressing, posing, and making up child models in the same ways that sexy adults would be presented—also implicitly suggests to adults that children are interested in and ready for sex. This is profoundly irresponsible, particularly given that it is known that pedophiles use not only child pornography but also more innocent photos of children (*SMH* 2006).

This article does a number of things, but most obviously it switches attention away from the commercial media's commoditisation of the child. The subject category of the child itself remains sacrosanct and unambiguous: children are vulnerable and innocent, and they are being taken into territory (sexuality, relationships, desires) that is against their interests and threatens to do them great harm. The media and advertisers are characterised as encouraging unhealthy practices and tendencies. What is much more significant, however, is they are accused of facilitating the work of paedophiles. The discourses here are both of physical danger and moral crisis: children are 'at risk', and there are 'dangerous implications' from 'predatory adults' ready to take advantage of girls disposed to have 'crushes' on older men. Moreover, even 'innocent photos of children' can be 'used' by paedophiles.

One of the great, unresolved tensions of the way the media turn children into sexual commodities is that such a project necessarily seeks out, mines and encourages desires that are forbidden and not socially acceptable. If we return to the examples of Miley Cyrus and the *Pavement* 'teen issue', all that the two enterprises have to commoditise is a particular kind of sexuality that can be differentiated from other sites more or less offering sex for sale. As Jean Baudrillard (2003) points out, the logic of capitalism is the logic of fashion, and the logic of fashion is predicated on difference and differentiation. The function of this system of differentiation:

> goes far beyond the satisfaction of needs ... the system never operates in terms of real ... differences between persons. What grounds it as a system is precisely the fact that it eliminates the specific content, the ... specificity of each human being, and substitutes the differential form, which can be industrialized and commercialized as a distinguishing sign. It eliminates all original qualities and retains only the schema generative of distinctions ... Differences ... become ... the matter of exchange ... This is a fundamental point, through which consumption is defined ... as a system of communication and exchange, as a code of signs continually being sent, received and reinvented—as language (2003:93).

Two things are happening within this system of differentiation. First and more generally, the human subject is turned into a commodity: the representations of the young, fresh-faced, pale-skinned and skinny girls (and boys) staring rather uncertainly at the camera in the *Pavement* issue, and the teenagers who are the basis for those representations, are being treated as things-for-profit. As Appadurai puts it, they have been **commoditised** or been moved into the commodity situation, which he defines as the situation in which 'exchangeability ... for some other thing is its socially relevant feature' (1988:13). Second, they have been specifically commoditised in terms of the difference of their sexuality, or perhaps it is the kind of desire that they bring to the table: they are innocent (but available for corruption) and vulnerable. Moreover, there is also the *frisson* (the charge, the buzz) of their illegality: they may be of legal age (the magazine provides the age of each model), but they look (or are set up to look) illegal. In other words, this and other media, fashion and advertising sites are not facilitating paedophilia, as the *SMH* article claims—they are peddling it. Now to do this is clearly monstrous (in terms of the moral discourse of the normal and the healthy), which is why the *SMH* article has to veer away from the practices themselves (articles and images that sexualise children) and find some other, more easily identifiable monsters (paedophiles), if only to provide an explanation for the widespread discussion of, interest and circulation of child sexuality.

Commoditisation The process of producing something predominantly in terms of its exchangeability.

Conclusion

What these and other related examples point to is a crisis, not of inalienable childhood, but of traditional categories and discourses that have effectively produced, regulated and authorised the subjectivities of children. Now, as Foucault (2003) has pointed out, this crisis is always with us: such categories and discourses are never stable or uncontested, and one of the consequences of disciplinary and regulatory discourse is in a sense to produce 'others' who are not healthy, productive, reliable or good citizens. The interesting point, is the way rapid changes to communication and information technology, and the expansion of relatively unfettered, free-market capitalism (the two developments are closely related) have, in a very short time, cast off or made redundant categories and discourses of regulation and normalisation that have traditionally exercised a powerful influence over the kinds of subjectivity available to large sections of the population. In our next chapter we will look in more detail at how the media as a cultural field negotiates and represents these kinds of issues in terms of its specific logics and imperatives.

Additional reading

Introductory

Danaher, G., Schirato, T. and Webb, J. (2000). *Understanding Foucault.* Sydney: Allen & Unwin.
  An accessible and well-exemplified introduction to Foucault's work.

Webb, J., Schirato, T. and Danaher, G. (2002). *Understanding Bourdieu.* London: Sage.
  A useful introduction to Bourdieu's work, with a chapter on the media.

Advanced

Bourdieu, P. (2000). *Pascalian Meditations.* Cambridge: Polity Press.
  Bourdieu's best and most worked-through account of how the habitus works through the body.

Foucault, M. (2008). *The History of Sexuality.* Vol. 1: *An Introduction.* London: Penguin.
  Foucault's influential book of the relation between sexuality, disciplinarity and normalisation.

THE FIELD OF THE MEDIA

Introduction

One of the most common conceptions about the media is that they could and should act in a disinterested way. Disinterested here does not mean uninterested; instead it means that the media should act in impartial and unbiased ways. The expectations are that the media enact connections between individuals through telecommunication, networks and technological devices (from the telephone to the Internet); bring creative work and entertainment to audiences (through music, books, television, Internet, films and games); and extend or even constitute public debate (through the news media). All of this is meant to be done through (relatively) independent channels, networks and voices. For instance, we do not expect our telephone companies to prioritise one phone call over another according to who the caller is; or our Internet service providers to apply different data transfer speeds (email, file transfers or downloads) depending on the type of users. This is what a disinterested media means: we want media companies and institutions to apply rules and procedures that ensure the free and fair transfer and dissemination of information and data. This should strike anyone who pays attention to the media as wishful thinking. But let us stay with this idea a bit more, because we need to realise that to analyse the media we should look at both what they do and what they should do.

The media and society

■ Two contradictory positions

Two contradictory positions

The expectation and hope that media can act in a disinterested way reflect the fact that citizens in modern democratic societies expect and want to believe that the media, and especially the news media, will act, intervene in and contribute to civil society, and act as an instrument of economic and social progress. The media are therefore expected to represent and analyse the operations of power and politics; contribute to public, regulatory and legislative debates governing media laws and rights; and yet remain independent from direct interference from political and economic interests. If, in the process, the media benefit economically from this position, then the profits and the resulting financial stability ensure further development and independence.

In this model of the disinterested media, one of their main tasks is to facilitate the unimpeded circulation of information. This implies that the media hold a special place in civil society, as they are both expected to act on behalf of, and with, the public's larger good, while at the same time being driven by business and economic imperatives. This position is reflected in the different constituent parts of media industries and professions. For instance, textbooks for news media students will position this distinct role and responsibility as the key to the professional mission and integrity of the job. Similarly, media watchdogs, in the form of independent groups and associations, specifically monitor, on behalf of the public, the commercialisation and control of airwaves that are publicly owned, and defend the principle of network neutrality (see chapter 8). This is a principle that would guarantee that those companies who control the Internet do not treat Internet communication any differently than any other. In these examples, what counts is the maintenance of standards, rules and safeguards to ensure the protection of the media's role and independence.

Conversely, one of the most common critiques of the media is that they cannot extricate themselves from political, economic and institutional pressures, and the assumption that disinterest is possible is dismissed. Evidence of this is present both in alternative media circles, such as citizen journalists, and independent producers who stand in opposition to the so-called corporate media. This position relies extensively on tracing the links between media ownership and corporate control: in other words, find the money and you will find the interests underlying the media. In addition, if one can connect the money with political interests, then the myth of disinterested media gives way to that of the manipulative and coercive media. There is, of course, plenty of evidence to support such a critical position: one of the most commonly used examples is that of the elaborate thread of financial and political connections exemplified in **Rupert Murdoch**'s News Corporation and, even more striking, the career of Italian politician and media mogul **Silvio Berlusconi**. Berlusconi, in addition to having been prime minister of Italy at four different times (most recently in 2008), also controls the three most popular private television channels as well as a number of wide-circulation newspapers. His control

Go online

Rupert Murdoch

Go online

Silvio Berlusconi

Go online

Media, power and economics

of an extensive media empire, and his remarkable hold on power despite charges of corruption and nepotism, attest to the fact that media and political controls are mutually reinforcing.

The analysis of the relation between **media, power and economics** has been developed by Edward S. Herman and Noam Chomsky in *Manufacturing Consent: The Political Economy of the Mass Media* (1994), which was originally published in 1988 and became the subject of a documentary directed by Mark Achbar and Peter Wintonick (1992). The study looks at how the entanglement of economics and class interests produces news media that tend to present dominant perspectives, filter the news and set the agenda in a manner that is congruent with these interests. It is not that someone in a news room is told what to say (even though this can clearly happen; see Greenwald's documentary *Outfoxed: Rupert Murdoch's War on Journalism*, 2004), but rather that the specific corporate and financial structure of a news media company will produce a set of attitudes and dispositions that will lead to an editorial policy. This produces a journalistic practice that reinforces the dominant interests of the company and its allies in other parts of the culture. In other words, the interests of the company and those it serves are naturalised in editorial practices.

The point of this chapter is not to advocate or defend either position. They both provide incisive and important questions and answers, and we need to understand them, since they shape so much of intellectual and public discussions of the media. Rather, this chapter will take on the points raised above and contextualise them within the context of the media as a cultural field. This chapter focuses on how the media work, and how the internal logic of the field produces the rules governing the practical and actual functioning of the media.

Bourdieu's notion of a cultural field

Cultural field A social system—with institutions, agents, subjects, discourses and practices—that structures and reproduces power relations within and without. The field's practices are organised and validated through the habitus.

The idea of a **cultural field**, as used in this chapter (and discussed in chapters 2 and 3), emerges from the sociological writings of Pierre Bourdieu. He was a sociologist and public intellectual who specialised in the analysis of power relations, practices and rules in the context of cultural fields and specific institutions, such as schools, universities, the art world, television and social groups. He saw cultural fields as functioning in relatively autonomous ways. For Bourdieu 'a field is a separate social universe having its own laws of functioning independent of those of politics and the economy' (1993:162). Imagine for a moment walking into a room where a group of experts are discussing the relative merits of different wines from a variety of vineyards, and making assessments based on a comparison of colour, robe, hue, aromatics, florals, fruit, tannins, structure, texture and length. Clearly, to make a useful contribution to a discussion of these wines you should be a member of the field, and have the ability, not only to use a specific technical and perceptual vocabulary, but also to do so in the right way and at the right time. Of course, wine connoisseurs will tell you that it is perfectly fine to use whatever terms you want, but your status in the field of wine connoisseurship (or outside the field) will be assessed instantly by how you perform. This performance would require an understanding of the rules of the field that are not formally articulated or specified. Outsiders will not recognise these unwritten rules, and will break them (and in the process 'give themselves away'). For instance, the entire discussion might avoid any reference to the prices of the different wines, the economics of the wine trade and the agricultural policies and regulations imposed upon the winemakers, even though the field of wine connoisseurship and the field of commerce are strongly connected. That is how fields work. To those inside, the language, rules and practices are perfectly sensible and useful. To those outside, they are a mystery. Now apply this to any kind of media contexts: a television set with all its highly specialised functions, a gaming development company, a newspaper newsroom or the board of directors' room of a major media company. Something is at work in all of these contexts, but only those within the fields know how things work.

For Bourdieu, it was essential to understand how a field organises, structures and justifies itself, and how its agents internalise its logics. His approach was to develop an understanding of fields that offered a more grounded approach, which contrasted with other theories of subjectivity, such as those proposed by Louis Althusser (see chapter 2). For Bourdieu, a field is an active, dynamic structure where a lot of things are happening, and with a logic and structure that allows and causes things to happen in everyday practices. He did not want to close down what could happen within a field, but rather was interested in looking at how its agents could use its powers and tools to produce different kinds of outcomes. Bourdieu was specifically interested in understanding and analysing how the rules of a specific field come to be formulated around 'a system of common reference' (1993:177)—values, roles, discourses, imperatives and hierarchies—and how their logics reproduce the field's culture, ethos, rules and power differentials.

This means that, for Bourdieu, fields have to do two things. First, they must constantly project their importance, values and significance in relation to other fields and to society at large. They must find ways to self-validate, and to make inside and outside agents speak in the terms set up by the field. Second, they have to make their members act, participate and 'fit in' without having to think about what they are doing, or why they are doing it. The rules of the field have become second nature to participants.

Bourdieu often referred to sport, because we are all more or less familiar with the logic of sport as viewers and participants, and because of its strong relation with the field of the media. Like other fields, sport is about the practice of individuals within well-defined constraints. Sport is also about play. For Bourdieu this is both a serious matter and a characteristic of all fields. Players in a football (soccer) game are constrained by rules and regulations that have been set up long before they take the field. The referee is the immediate representative of some of these rules, or at least the formal ones. However, he or she is not the sole enforcer of these rules. The players all share an ethos associated with competition, teamwork, strategic thinking, trust and organisation. They all have specialised roles to play, and have to combine the objectives and strategies of the team as a whole with their own individual skills and techniques, and with the actual conditions of any given game and in any given situation in the game. In order to be successful, the players need to have internalised all of these concepts, while constantly inventing, creating and acting within the clear constrains of the rules and the objectives in the game (not all soccer teams play to win; many play not to lose). All the time they are working under the directives and authority of the manager and the senior players. Individuality expresses itself within that logic, and as an ability to select and enact the best options of a game situation.

The best players are those who shine in harmony with the flow of the game. They demonstrate a literacy regarding the rules and play of the game, and translate these rules into actions. They act without thinking, but their actions are the expression of an ability to internalise the game, and externalise this understanding in the immediacy of the moment. One of the most common ways in which the language of players and experts will characterise a player's literacy in the game will be to translate that in terms of the character, courage, bravery and genius of a player. The result is that players acquire status among their peers, the experts and the public. This status constitutes an example of what Bourdieu calls **cultural capital**, which can be defined as anything (such as qualifications, objects, forms of literacy or connections) that has value, and can be exchanged, within a cultural field (1993). Players can use this status as cultural capital for financial gains and celebrity, but also to gain power within their organisations. At the level of professional players, the field of soccer interacts with other fields, such as the field of the media, business and entertainment. This example reveals some key characteristics of a field that can be applied to all fields, including the field of the media. In order to constitute itself, a field needs institutions, discourses, imperatives, values, rules, administrative organisation, technologies, habitus and cultural capital. We will discuss these in the rest of this chapter.

Bourdieu did not specifically address the issue of a general field of the media, but he certainly saw it as a component of the cultural field. In a book on television (a series of lectures he gave when he took on the role of a public intellectual), he discusses what he calls the **journalistic field**, specifically applied to television journalism (1998a). He states that the journalistic field constitutes a microcosm with its own rules, which needs to be understood and analysed according to its internal logics. We need to consider the media, with their industries, institutions, technologies, professions, discourses and practices, as a distinct field. We saw in chapter 1 that the field of the media is the result of historical and technological development. What characterises the media is the transmission and experience of information in a variety of forms—from data to visual, audio and narrative texts—and with the support of technologies and networks of distribution and transmission. The media constitute a field, as they produce a coordinated and organised system combining all these elements with a relative degree of autonomy, but also in relation to other fields, especially power and economics. One of the major constituents of the field of media is the organisation of activities into industries ruled by industrial, legal and economic logics.

Cultural capital A term associated with the work of Pierre Bourdieu, referring to anything deemed to be of value and exchangeable within a cultural field.

Journalistic field The rules, roles, institutions and practices relating to journalism in all its forms.

Media industries

Media industries exist in a variety of forms and sizes, and for different purposes. As the term 'industries' suggests, what characterises them is the systematic and technological organisation of their activities, and their reliance on existing industrial models. They depend on the division of labour, the specialised assignment of tasks and duties, the rationalisation of production and distribution systems, and an elaborate system of legal and ownership organisations. These are what Bourdieu described as the objectivities of the field. These are the structures and organisation that constitute the sphere of relative autonomy of the field, where certain forms of power and cultural capital can have a direct influence on the running of the media entity as corporate and commercial structures. This is the context in which New Zealand-located filmmaker Peter Jackson, for instance, has the leverage to initiate projects, find the funding and mobilise an extensive network of people with creative and technological skills, while negotiating the intricate demands of New Zealand corporate and tax systems and labour laws, as well as the vicissitudes of Hollywood finances. What allows him to negotiate all these extremely complex areas is the influence he has acquired and maintained, and his ability to translate this for his and the studio's self-interests. The contemporary Hollywood studio system, of which Jackson is a part, provides a useful example of the internal logic of media industries.

Janet Wasko, in a book entitled *How Hollywood Works* (2003), details the workings of the studio system and its different structural components. This analysis of the film industry offers a classic model of media industries, not just cinema. Wasko details the structures of the industry by following a linear organisation from the conception of a film to its consumption. She demonstrates that the rationalisation of the movie industry's organisation follows a classic industrial model based on the division of labour. She identifies four stages and four areas that constitute the structural organisation of the field:

1 production
2 distribution
3 exhibition and retail
4 promotion and protection of the industry.

For the sake of clarity, these four stages are presented in a linear, and temporal fashion, but the structures of media production are such that all these stages overlap, and might even be concurrent.

■ Stage 1: Production

Gaining the green light

For a film studio this is the first stage. It is where projects originate, are identified and negotiated. This happens well before cameras start rolling. This can be done from within the studio through the acquisition of rights to a book, a play or a television show. In that case, a producer will hire screenwriters to develop a script. When the project is deemed good enough and potentially profitable, the director,

Go online

Making documentaries and DVDs

actors and other creative and technical staff will be hired. If the project is conceived outside of a studio, it might be pitched to different studios and sold to the best bidder, or at least to the studio that will give it the green light. This is done through the work of agents or independent producers. In either case, the project only goes ahead when contractual agreements are completed. This will involve lawyers, agents, managers, financiers and distributors, and a whole series of agreements about payments, associated rights and percentage of the film revenues. Even at that stage, the project is both the focus of much creative development and already a commodity in the field. The point is that this only has value in the field itself. Elsewhere, for instance at a cocktail party, any discussion about what 'would make a great film' has no value per se, and the status of that idea is entirely different from that of an idea picked up by a studio or a producer.

This stage is invisible to the public, and any information about this is either done in the form of parody, such as Robert Altman's *The Player* (1992), or described in a retrospective fashion, in the extra material on DVDs where filmmakers might talk about this process. An interesting example of a television series on the film industry is the HBO show *Entourage* (Ellin 2004–2008). This series is based on showing the fictional development of the career of a film star and his relationships with his manager, agent and friends. Even though the show simplifies the workings of Hollywood, it does demonstrate the tensions between achieving success, celebrity and financial gains, and the commercial imperatives of the industry. It shows the rules of the game, and how they manifest themselves in the negotiation of salaries, control and creativity. The narrative tension of the story is based on contrasting the artistic interests of the would-be star with his strategic negotiation of the business environment. He wants to make projects he deems creatively worthy with small budget productions, but he also stars in a blockbuster film *Aquaman* (directed by James Cameron, who plays himself in the show), which extends to action figures and an attraction park ride. The television show also brings to light the work of talent agencies. These exert great control over the industry—since actors are no longer contracted to studios—and have acquired a lot more creative and financial leverage and increasing salaries.

Pre-production

The second phase of the production process is pre-production. The film has been given its green light and now the production requirements of the film are addressed: locations are scouted; production designs for the overall look of the film, the costumes, sets and special effects are initiated; crew are hired; and rehearsal for actors might take place at this stage. A hierarchy of roles and responsibilities is clearly in place between executive producers (those who head the studio or have the financial leverage); the producer(s), who is in charge of the execution of the film and all its aspects; and the director, who has the creative responsibility, if not control, of the project, and works most closely with other key creative personnel (director of photography, production designer, sound designer, music composer and, especially, actors). One of the most obvious differences between most films and narrative television series (Chase *The Sopranos*; Simon *The Wire*;

Gilligan *Breaking Bad*) is that the producer(s) is more clearly the author of the show in a television series. In pre-production, all aspects of production are prepared, as well as a shooting script and a schedule that will itemise all that has to be shot, and the order in which they have to be shot.

Principal photography

In the third process, the shooting (principal photography) takes place on location and/or in studios. The culture of the film set is probably the most documented, and in many ways the most subject to mythologising. This is the stage that is the most visible, and often represented in fictional films, in behind-the-scene documentaries and especially in the promotional 'making-of' genre. Season 4 of *Entourage* starts with an episode that mimics a behind-the-scenes documentary on the set of an independent project that is marred with difficulties. Because viewers know they are watching a fictional account, and they know the characters well, they can see the ways in which the different interviewees perform for the sake of the documentary, and provide confessions and narratives that tend to be self-serving.

Sets function in extremely complex ways. They involve tens if not hundreds of crew and actors, and are structured around clearly divided production departments, in the context of labour and union rules, and with the creative imperatives remaining, normally, the unifying principle. Sets are the scene of tensions, conflicts and collaboration, and are both constituted in the moment of each production and as residual and long-standing (studio and union) rules and tradition.

The director does not run the set; the first assistant director does. He or she keeps proceedings to schedule, coordinates the work of all departments, keeps records of daily progress and frees the director from the logistics of the set. The first assistant director can also be the extended eye and hand of the producer while being the director's best ally.

Post-production

The next stage, which most likely is concurrent with the main phase of production, is post-production. The use of the prefix 'post' refers to the fact that this stage corresponds to a sequence in the development of the project, but it might not necessarily correspond to a temporal sequence. In many ways the use of the term is a convention, especially for films that rely extensively on special effects. Post-production will often start a long time before actors become involved and principal photography starts. Post-production also involves editing, sound and music and other forms of treatment of the image, which take place between the moment when principal photography is completed, and when a print is struck and sent to movie theatres.

■ Stage 2: Distribution

Although the creative aspects of filmmaking are clearly associated with production and its different phases, distribution is the key to the film being made and/or reaching an audience. Many projects are made and funded only after a distributor has come on board. The distributor might make demands on the script, casting or other aspects, with the aim of making the project a strong business proposition. When presented to distributors well before production, the film has already become a commodity, and the studio has to convince the distributors that the film and all its related forms of income will make a profit for all. This leads Wasko to state that, 'The major distributors dominate the film business' (2003:59). This is not the popular image of the movie industry, which places emphasis on the directors, stars and stories, rather than on the corporate and marketing realities of distribution.

Distributors are essentially wholesalers who serve as intermediaries between production companies and exhibition outlets, including movie theatres, video and DVD rentals and retail, pay television, free-to-air television and airline companies. They make decisions about release dates, promotion and advertising, and control the flow of money between exhibitors and studios. The distributors try to multiply all the ways in which a film can generate profits around the world, and across all technological platforms. The distributors' power over the film industry is illustrated by the fact that when DVD technology was commercialised, they enforced a series of technical limitations in the form of the creation of six different geographical zones. A DVD sold in the US, for instance, cannot be played on a DVD player bought in another part of the world. This means that a film can be released for sale on DVD before its theatrical runs in other parts of the world has expired, and it also means that the geographical division of distribution can be enforced to protect the elaborate network of distributors, exhibitors and retailers and their economic interests. Prices are set in each of the zones depending on what retailers expect consumers are willing to pay.

■ Stage 3: Exhibition and retail

Distributors sell the rights to exhibit films in a variety of ways, in different places and through different technologies. The main exhibition and retail contexts are movie theatres, cable and satellite television (where a consumer subscribes to an entire film channel), pay television or video-on-demand (when a subscriber will purchase the rights to screen an individual film) and DVD rentals and sales. The distribution of films over the Internet is an increasing outlet for the industry. Films can be rented or bought from commercial sites such as Amazon, iTunes, BigPond Movies, Netflix, Movielink and Blockbuster.

This leads the film industry to seek alliances and partnerships with a variety of players to find mutually beneficial agreements. An example of this is Movielink, which was established in 2001 as a joint effort between several studios, which then became a subsidiary of Blockbuster in 2006, and finally was absorbed by the latter in 2008. The Movielink service (now Blockbuster) combines the libraries of studios such as Warner Bros, Metro-Goldwyn-Mayer, New Line, Lionsgate, Universal, Twentieth-Century Fox, Paramount, and Sony Pictures Entertainment. It allowed these competitors to collaborate to offer a wide range of films. This is a good example of how the field both ensures its financial gains, but also constantly protects and promotes its interests.

■ Stage 4: Promotion and protection of the industry

Go online

Promotion and protection of
the industry

The fourth stage Wasko (2003:188–220) identifies is the promotion and protection
of the industry. In this stage the industry tries to achieve four different but
complementary objectives. First, it tries to extend its markets, business and profits.
It achieves this through the extensive marketing and advertising of films. This
involves activities such as market research, test screenings, paid advertising in
newspapers, billboards, websites and trailers. It also involves non-paid exposure
in media outlets, such as press conferences, star appearances on talks shows and
interviews with individual film reporters, where local television presenters can get
a one-on-one interview with a star or director for as little as a few minutes.

Second, it tries to promote the industry by developing close relationships with
the commercial and industry presses. Entertainment news has become a major
part of news coverage on television, on the Internet and in newspapers. Programs
such as *Entertainment Weekly* and the television channel E! Entertainment Television
(available on cable and satellite television in many countries around the world) play
out the close relationship between celebrities and studios, their interests in exposure,
the promotion of new films and the advantages to the channel in terms of ratings.

Film reviewers may not be so easily wooed by the glamour of celebrity, but the
studios have learned how to work with critics by organising special screenings,
and facilitating access to stars, directors and studio executives. Reviewers themselves have learned how to play the game. Most film reviewers' responses to, and
evaluation of, films are cast in the terms set by the industry itself. Film reviewers
often see themselves as enforcers of the rules of entertainment, storytelling and
filmmaking techniques. In other words, most film reviewers will judge a film in the
terms that Hollywood has itself codified, enforced and publicly discussed over a
long period of time. In any case, the studios have also learned how to work around
critics. In some cases, they will release films without allowing preview screening for
the press and reviewers. The Hollywood film industry has its own trade press (that
includes *Variety* and the *Hollywood Reporter*), where information about industry
deals, technologies, markets, box office returns, the economy and government
policy is published. Even though it is subject to the Hollywood publicity machine,
the trade press is widely read and influential.

Third, the industry reinforces its cultural capital through the organisation of
awards and festivals. The most famous of these is the Academy Awards, a made-
for-television program transformed into media spectacle and entertainment. The
Academy Awards acts as a demonstration of quality and achievement sanctioned
by the important-sounding Academy of Motion Picture Arts and Sciences. It also
works as a great advertising boost for films, actors, directors and other creative and
technical personnel. The build-up to the Awards, the coverage and the impact of
the results, promote the industry's image and significance. Similarly, film festivals
(such as Sundance, Toronto, Venice, Berlin and Cannes) provide cultural validation
for the artistic merits of the film industry. Most of these festivals also function
as a market for film distribution. At the Cannes Film Festival, for instance, films
(including many independent films) are not simply awarded prizes, but find

distributors. Therefore, awards and festivals function both as official and cultural validation of the industry for public consumption, but they also reinforce and promote the business and power games of the industry.

Fourth, the Hollywood industry is deeply invested in managing its relations with public institutions and government. One of the great fears of the Hollywood studios is the direct intervention of government and public institutions in their affairs. Historically, the film industry has always tried to keep politicians and regulators at bay by enforcing self-imposed standards. This is the reason why the powerful Motion Picture Association of America (MPAA) was formed in 1922. Since then, censorship and the rating systems in the US are enforced by the industry itself. The documentary *This Film Is Not Rated Yet* (Dick 2006) discusses the rating boards and the major studios' control of the process, and the artistic and financial limitations it imposes. Industry control, according to the filmmakers, does not imply understanding the creative process, but rather a careful positioning of the industry so that the interests of major studios are protected and the attention of government is kept away. According to Wasko, 'the MPAA is especially active in fighting various threats to the industry, everything from government intervention and trade policies to copyright infringement and First Amendment issue' (2003:212). The First Amendment in the American Constitution protects freedom of speech.

Discussions about the evils of Hollywood (most recently through the political and cultural influences of neo-conservative politics and its constant criticism of popular culture) have had much purchase in the media. The call for further censorship and restrictions is a constant presence in political debates. However, the MPAA has managed to avoid political control by cultivating connections with politicians of all parties, and making campaign contributions to politicians and parties, mainly to the Democratic Party (Wasko 2003:213). Hollywood executives and celebrities are willing to lend their names to social and cultural issues, while politicians gain exposure and tackle issues that are important to the film industry. Copyright infringement and piracy and runaway productions (Hollywood productions that use foreign locations and services, such as Jackson's *The Lord of the Rings* trilogy, 2001–2003) are some of the most pressing issues of the industry, and they involve the political and diplomatic means of government. The MPAA has been relatively successful in making the American government intervene on behalf of the industry in other countries, including threatening trade penalties for allowing piracy through Internet distribution. This includes the Swedish police raiding the office of a BitTorrent (a peer-to-peer computer application that allows the exchange of files) website accused of copyright infringement.

Media industries workers

Go online

Media industries workers

Throughout this discussion of the process of production in the Hollywood systems we have focused on different (at times concurrent) stages. We have also introduced the different categories of creatives, executives and crews. It is useful to identify those more precisely, as they are key agents in the field and have very different roles and responsibilities. In a book titled *The Cultural Industries* (2002:52–3), David Hesmondhalgh describes the processes of media production and all the different roles. He specifically identifies key areas and jobs (these have been modified slightly here):

1 'Primary creative personnel': Hesmondhalgh also calls them 'symbol creators'. They are the musicians, writers, screenwriters, designers and other creative people whose ideas initiate and drive the production process. They are also the people in media industries who are most likely to self-exploit by working very hard for little financial return, and for whom the self-image and cultural capital associated with the role is a form of reward.
2 'Technical crafts workers': The crews and technicians who are hired for their specific set of skills (53). This could be a lighting or audio technician, for instance. Usually their input is limited to materialising the creative and technical directions provided by the primary creative personnel.
3 'Creative managers': Including commissioning editors for television channels, producers, editors of books, and magazines (53). These are people who initiate or commission projects, find the funding, have the institutional and industry contacts and leverage, and provide the required support to creatives.
4 'Owners and executives' (executive producers, CEOs): Provide the institutional and business context, and make the larger strategic decisions for the company (53).
5 'Cultural intermediaries': Include reviewers and critics, and those who provide commentary on cultural activities and shape public taste in the media often by reinforcing what are already accepted norms and tastes. For instance, as discussed above, reviewers and critics respond to media products (such as films, shows and books) most often in the terms set up by the industry. Reviewers do not challenge the industry. Rather, their opinion and views reflect the expectation that the media industry should fulfill its assigned role. For Pierre Bourdieu, cultural intermediaries validate, consecrate and reproduce the views and tastes shared by the dominant social groups.

Each of these categories holds specific roles in the industry, and their power and responsibilities are not necessarily congruent with the others. The logic of the field is what allows such an array of interests and functions to coexist.

This extensive discussion of media industries, specifically the Hollywood studio system, has demonstrated how the field is constituted by different groups of people and roles. What binds the industry together is the logic and discourses of the field and legal, corporate and institutional structures of media industries.

Media ownership and concentration

The many activities of Silvio Berlusconi, Italian prime minister and media owner, can be used as an illustration of the ways in which ownership, concentration of power and economic means may be conflated in the media. The rules and practices of media control have become one of the most debated and scrutinised areas of media studies, if only because both media scholars and citizens have become increasingly aware of the ways in which ownership structures of media companies have a direct effect on the outputs, practices and roles of media. Here we will specifically focus on private ownership of media companies, and especially on the media conglomerates: economic, legal and corporate structures that control vast ranges of media activities. Media ownership is also an area where the relation between the field of the media and other fields, such as economics and politics, interface most directly.

In the case of Silvio Berlusconi, the fact that he has held the office of Prime Minister of Italy, and has had direct and indirect control of major media outlets, has meant that he has sought, and been able to influence, public debate. He has merged his political and commercial interests (including passing legislation and deregulating the media in ways that were self-serving), and transformed the figure of the politician into that of an omnipresent media character. His popularity with the Italian electorate seems to be based on his blurring the distinction between statesman and celebrity. Paul Ginsborg, in *Silvio Berlusconi: Television, Power and Patrimony*, argues that 'the process by which modern consumerism, commercial television and political power are linked is an entirely new one' (2004:8).

Berlusconi's situation is one example. There are others, including those involving the President of Russia, Vladimir Putin, and French President **Nicolas Sarkozy**, both of whom exert significant influence over their national media industries and scenes. They have made it a priority to cultivate personal relations with media outlets, and feed the media the kind of celebrity stories that they readily carry. These include stories about Putin's physical prowess and hyper-masculinity, and Sarkozy's soap opera-like love life.

This increased, mutually beneficial relationship between media and politics can also be seen in the transformations of politicians into media commentators, and vice versa. With former politicians becoming expert commentators (such as President George W. Bush's key strategist and adviser Karl Rove, and former presidential candidate Mike Huckabee), the role of commentator is becoming increasingly that of contributor to a manufactured partisan spectacle, where substance and quality of analysis give way to the repetition of ideological positions in order to score points.

Go online

Nicolas Sarkozy

■ Media conglomerates

Go online

Media conglomerates

With the increasing globalisation of corporate ownership in the mid-twentieth century, there have been moves toward the integration of media companies into ever-increasing media conglomerates. Conglomerates are made up of companies that either belong to the same parent company, or are linked by a series of financial dependencies or part ownerships. This move towards greater concentration and control of media interests by fewer but ever-expanding corporations sped up even further from the beginning of the 1980s. The rise of neo-liberal economic principles (see chapter 2) has been translated into the deregulation of rules governing media ownership and the concentration of media holdings in most Western countries. Moreover, the rise of the logic of market capitalism in many other parts of the world, with the emphasis on maximising profits through building media connections across many areas (such as film, radio, television, newspapers, Internet, music and publishing) has been a governing principle. Media conglomerates have been buying or merging with companies, or have put in place complex arrangements where they could have part ownership in other businesses. In the 1980s, mergers between hardware and consumer electronics companies were of particular concern. There were fears that companies such as Sony would tie in their purchase of CBS Records and Columbia Pictures with their consumer electronics products. This never really materialised, but something more worrying has happened.

Media conglomerates have built an intricate series of connections between media companies, which use these links to build up media products with a variety of commercial outputs, and expand and saturate the market with many media products, which actually originate from just a few media conglomerates. The apparent abundance of media products often conceals this fact. The Time Warner Company, for instance, has interests in many media sectors. It controls television stations including HBO and CNN; production and distribution companies including Warner Bros., New Line Cinema, Fine Line Features and Castle Rock Entertainment; numerous magazines, including *Time* and *Sports Illustrated*; online services including AOL; publishing companies; theme parks and a professional baseball team (the Atlanta Braves). It also has partial ownership of Amazon. The commercial and business logic of such a conglomerate is to maximise the connections between its various sectors. This gives rise to the **media franchise**, in the sense that a single text can have many outputs and can be reproduced over an extended period of time. A recent example of this is Peter Jackson's *The Lord of the Rings* trilogy (2001–2003). Tracing all the forms and outlets of the franchise can be a surprising activity. In this instance there are:

> **Media franchise** The commercial exploitation of a media product as a brand, which involves licensing of all aspects of the media text (characters, costumes, imagery in a film, for instance) and the development of further products such a sequels, novels and computer games.

- three theatrically released features
- DVDs of each of the theatrical releases
- DVDs with extended versions of the films
- CDs with soundtracks
- games for PC, Playstation 2, Xbox and Game Boy
- books of illustrations, pictures and commentary
- a website
- merchandise (such as figures, objects, weapons, costumes, jewellery, t-shirts and posters).

Since New Line Cinema is part of the Time Warner media conglomerate, all these products were distributed or sold by subsidiaries. Therefore all profits went back to the parent company. This caused Peter Jackson to sue New Line Cinema, which he accused of having undersold the merchandising and copyrights of the films, therefore cutting Jackson out of much more lucrative revenues. Jackson contended that if the merchandising rights had been open to competitive bidding, he would have benefited much more, as the merchandising rights would have been sold to the highest bidder. According to an article in the *New York Times*:

> The suit charges that the company used pre-emptive bidding (meaning a process closed to external parties) rather than open bidding for subsidiary rights to such things as *Lord of the Rings* books, DVDs and merchandise. Therefore, New Line received far less than market value for these rights, the suit says.

> Most of those rights went to other companies in the New Line family or under the Time Warner corporate umbrella, like Warner Brothers International, Warner Records and Warner Books. So while the deals would not hurt Time Warner's bottom line, they would lower the overall gross revenues related to the film, which is the figure Mr Jackson's percentage is based on ... Mr Jackson's lawsuit and similar suits filed in the last few years, called vertical integration lawsuits, argue that the idea of the media conglomerate is at odds with the interests of the creative minds behind the content (Johnson 2005).

The suit was settled (unsurprisingly) out of court in December 2007. Clearly, none of the parties had an interest in keeping proceedings in court and in the public eye. New Line would not want to establish a precedent and reveal the financial arrangements it made. By settling out of court, New Line avoided a potentially unfavourable court decision becoming a precedent, to be used by other complainants against it, or against other media companies. Jackson probably also felt that a long public fight with a major Hollywood studio would not have benefited his status as a New Zealand-based filmmaker making films with studio money, especially in a context where there is already substantial resentment against runaway productions; that is, films funded with studio money spent on foreign locations with foreign crews.

■ Vertical integration and modern corporate ownership

Vertical integration
An industrial structure where all of the stages of an industry are controlled by a single entity; for example, in film, the control of production, distribution and exhibition.

As the *New York Times* article suggests, these practices imply a de facto **vertical integration** of the industry, or at least an effort by media conglomerates to achieve it. Vertical integration used to be the practice before an American Supreme Court decision in 1948, which required all the Hollywood studios to dismantle their ownership of production, distribution and exhibition. The Supreme Court saw vertical integration as breaking anti-trust laws and preventing competition. The constitution of media conglomerates has not directly reconstituted vertically integrated structures, but the terms of media ownership are such that public regulators and government have been reluctant to unravel the complexities of their arrangements.

There are many issues and challenges related to the corporate ownership of media industries and the ever-expanding scope of their influence. They can be summarised in six key points:

1 *The concentration of media companies in the hands of individuals* who seek and use their power for political and economic advancement for themselves and their allies. Such cases include Silvio Berlusconi, and in the English-speaking world, Rupert Murdoch and News Corporation.
2 *The concentration of ownership of local media outlets.* Increasingly, local and regional media outlets (radio, television and newspapers) are owned by a single parent company. This raises the problem of the lack of divergent voices in a locality.
3 *The lack of critical media scrutiny.* How can a media outlet owned by a media conglomerate criticise another company or its practices when it belongs to the same conglomerate?

4 *The erasure of boundaries between media genres for the benefit of multiplying profit.* This can often take the form of the news arm of a media outlet covering as news one of its other forms of activities. For instance, networks about to launch a new program or series might interview one of the stars of the new show in a news or current affairs segment. This can result in the branding of the media company taking precedence over its functions.

5 *The protection of shared interests of dominant groups.* The more powerful a media conglomerate becomes, the more intent it will be on defending its interests, and aligning itself with powerful political and legal institutions. Powerful conglomerates are able to exert much influence on government through lobbying, political donations and direct influence. When Tony Blair, former prime minister of Britain (1997–2007), resigned, one of his first public speeches was an indictment of the media's reliance on entertainment- and personality-driven coverage. The irony is that Blair benefited, at least initially, from the strong support of Rupert Murdoch's British outlets, was an accomplished media performer (making a memorable speech after Princess Diana's death) and used one of the most strategic, effective and infamous spin doctors (Alastair Campbell) during his tenure as prime minister.

6 *The potential disappearance of political and cultural dissent.* A widely acknowledged example of this, and something the American media have recognised, was the lack of scrutiny of the Bush administration's invasion of Iraq. From the terrorist attacks of September 11, 2001 in New York and Washington to the invasion of Iraq in 2003, the American media failed to question the link the Bush administration was making between those attacks and Iraq. Fox News television was an unapologetic mouthpiece of the neo-conservative movement in the USA, and was beating the drum of war. But the other major news outlets also readily accepted the erroneous facts and information presented by the government. Since then most of these media outlets have performed an exercise in self-scrutiny, and conceded that they failed to question power for fear of becoming targets of political and public pressures.

Media conglomerates are powerful structures that exert increasing influence on public debate. The more financial stakes a media conglomerate has, the more likely it is to seek to influence government, regulations and laws. In this context, the maintenance of alternative media voices has become an important priority. Similarly, public and media institutions play an important role in maintaining the specificity of the field of the media.

Go online

Media institutions

Media institution An official body involved in the promotion, defence, reproduction, governance and regulation of the industry. Media institutions define the sphere of influence of media industries, and defend their interests in relation to other fields. They enforce the self-imposed rules of media industries, and translate government laws and regulations into actions and rules. They also intervene to resolve conflicts and pass judgment on potential failures to follow rules and guidelines that are self-imposed or government-imposed.

Media institutions

If media industries are in the business of producing, distributing and selling media commodities, **media institutions** are involved in the promotion, defence, reproduction, governance and **regulation of the industry**. Media institutions define the sphere of influence of media industries, and defend their interests in relation to other fields. They enforce the self-imposed rules of media industries, and translate

Go online

Self-regulation and journalism

government laws and regulations into actions and rules. They also intervene to resolve conflicts and pass judgment on potential failures to follow rules and guidelines that are self-imposed or government-imposed. As Bourdieu signalled in his analysis of cultural fields, institutions play a key role in allowing the reproduction and maintenance of the field's relative autonomy, but in order to achieve that, it needs to establish its significance, power and acquire cultural capital.

In the previous section we discussed how the Motion Picture Association of America (MPAA) has been protecting the interests of the Hollywood film industry since 1922 by establishing strong control over the industry, without having to rely on laws and regulations. For instance, the rating system controlled by the MPAA in the United States does not require all films to be rated. Getting a film rated is a purely voluntary process in the USA. However, as *This Film Is Not Rated Yet* (Dick 2006) demonstrates, the absence of a rating means that a film will struggle to find any distributor or exhibitor to bring it to the public. In other words, even though there is no binding regulation that requires all films to be rated by the MPAA, working outside of the self-imposed industry rules and processes means that there are few avenues for independent films. Participation in the rating system is voluntary; however, choosing to bypass the process is akin to commercial suicide. The forms of power MPAA exercises are field specific, and compliance with the rules of the industry does not require legal enforcement in all cases. This is important to acknowledge, as we tend to assume that restrictions, control and exclusion are the outcomes of government control. Conversely, assuming that all forms of institutional power limit the actors in the field fails to acknowledge the fact that one of the functions of media institutions is to ensure some degree of autonomy for the media. The examples below will help explain this.

Media institutions are either public or private bodies. In most countries, media institutions are a combination of bodies that have been established by government, industries or professional bodies. This does not mean, however, that their activities will be scrutinised by these bodies. Media institutions not only need to work in an independent way, but they need to be seen as working independently. They have industry and social functions, but they also have a public profile. We can characterise the sphere of influence and legitimacy of media institutions around the following key characteristics and functions:

1 *Media institutions embody and defend some field-specific values.* These can be rather abstract, and captured in documents such as codes of practice, codes of ethics, statements of intent or general principles. They are not laws or rules, but objectives. These values are usually the outcomes of the history of the field (for instance, journalism and its contribution to public debate developed over many centuries), and are a means for the field to assert its independence, its discursive justification and its ethos, and they constitute a form of cultural capital. These values are not enforceable as such, but are guiding and are underlying motivations. To a large extent, the members of the field must internalise these principles and values.

2 *In order to translate values into action and intervene both within and outside the field, media institutions rely on rules and procedures.* These are the mechanisms through

which the institution can act and have influence. For instance, the public will be able to complain about media programs or advertising through specific channels. In New Zealand, viewers and listeners can make a formal complaint through the Broadcasting Standards Authority (BSA), a public body that is accountable to the government. The process is clearly defined, and the decisions made by the panel of experts, industry and community representatives are made public. The advertising industry in New Zealand, on the other hand, is subjected to a self-regulatory and industry-controlled body, the Advertising Standards Authority. It functions very much like the BSA, with similar procedures (complaints, reviews, decisions and public communications), but has no accountability to the government. It is funded by the advertising and media industries.

3 *Media institutions have elaborate systems of governance, responsibilities, and systems of accountabilities.* Usually people sitting on the governing boards and decision and review panels of media institutions are a combination of individuals from some of the following categories: respected professionals with a high standing in the field; representatives of media companies and corporations; representative of unions or staff; and representatives of the community at large and/or government. The balance and the extent of the representation on these boards are different in each institution. However, the combination of members with high professional and social standing is usually a priority. One of the ways in which these institutions can achieve industry and public credibility is through the transparency of their consultation and decision-making processes. The performance of transparency is more important than the transparency itself, and is a matter of great debate. In the USA, the Federal Communications Commission (FCC) is made up of five members who are appointed by the President and confirmed by the Senate. The FCC regulates communications— television, radio, wire, satellite and cable—and makes extremely important decisions about media issues, such as the management of public airwaves, rules about media ownership and telecommunications policies. The members are usually appointed along party lines (the chair and majority of the commission usually sits with the party in power). The FCC holds extensive public hearings when conducting policy reviews or introducing new regulations. However, much criticism has been directed at the FCC for ignoring the public input, and ruling in favor of media concentration and media corporate interests. This raises the issue of accountability: it can be in the form of annual reports submitted to official and government bodies but also made public, to the board of directors of the institution and/or to industry bodies.

The example of New Zealand On Air provides a useful case study regarding the role of public institutions. In a context where it is more expensive to produce New Zealand programs than it is to purchase foreign ones, the government has found it necessary to establish a public body to provide funding for television and radio broadcast. It also provides public funding for music made by New Zealand artists and production companies. The funds are awarded on a competitive basis, and are available for production companies in association with both public and private radio and television channels.

In its statement of intent, NZ On Air articulates its values and guiding principles, which include:

> Broadcasting plays a powerful role in shaping a nation's culture and identity. Seeing ourselves on screen and hearing ourselves on air helps us to connect as a society, and to know who we are as a nation in the South Pacific.

NZ On Air is expected to participate in the development and articulation of cultural and national identity. These are rather abstract objectives, when the decisions NZ On Air makes are about giving public funding for television and radio programs. However, this means that NZ On Air has to reconcile the notion of nation-building with the broadcaster's commercial imperatives. Even though NZ On Air sets up some general direction for the development of certain genres (documentary and comedy have been the object of specific attention most recently), it strives to avoid intervening in commercial decisions for the broadcasters. As stated before, it seeks to achieve transparency in its decision-making process: it makes public the outcome of its decision panels and it provides a yearly report to government, which is publicly available. Negotiating the pressures from government, industry and the public are key components to the working of public media institutions.

The New Zealand Press Council is a typical example of an industry, self-regulatory body. There are similar bodies in other countries, such as the Australian Press Council and the British Press Complaints Commission. The Council consists of a Chair (in 2009, a retired High Court judge), as well as representatives of the public, newspaper and magazine publishers, and unions. Its rules and principles are stated on its website and include:

> To consider complaints against newspapers and other publications …
>
> To promote freedom of speech and freedom of the press in New Zealand; to maintain the New Zealand press in accordance with the highest professional standards (New Zealand Press Council).

Most of the complaints are not upheld, but the justifications for the decisions, and the reiteration of the principles underlying the freedom of speech, professional standards and public interest, are a key function of the Council. In other words, the Council articulates the practices and beliefs of the field of journalism. One of its tasks is therefore to formulate the ethos of the field (its beliefs, its validated principles and practices and its disposition to act in certain ways) for its members and for the public at large. When the complaints are upheld, the sanctions are less significant in terms of their material and financial implications than they are for the status of the publication in the field. Usually a newspaper or magazine against which a complaint has been upheld has to publish a retraction.

Breaching the principles and policies with which publications have chosen to comply has a negative impact on the credibility of the infringing publication. In a recent decision in 2007 in relation to an article by Deborah Coddington in *North and South* magazine entitled 'Asian Angst: Is It Time to Send Some Back?' (2006), the Council found that 'the magazine breached its principles on accuracy and discrimination' (New Zealand Press Council 2007). While reiterating the principles that publications could express strongly-held positions, the panel stated that *North and South* had resorted to a 'gratuitous emphasis on dehumanising racial stereotypes and fear-mongering', especially because it presented crime and population statistics in ways that were misleading (New Zealand Press Council 2007). The decision reflects the fact that it is not so much the expression of opinions that were an issue here, but the accuracy of the information and the misleading conclusions. In other words, the decision reasserted the necessity of relying on good journalistic practices. The legitimacy and ethos of the field are reinforced, while social responsibility and accountability are ensured. At the same time, government intervention is avoided. Media institutions, such as the Press Council, play a key role in reasserting and defending the interests and the ethos of the field.

Habitus, practices, discourses and doxa

Go online

Habitus, practices, discourses and doxa

In this chapter we have discussed structural, institutional and ownership aspects of the media industries. These are what we introduced (following Bourdieu) as the objectivities of the field. They encompass everything from creativity, production, regulation and control. The final component of the field of the media that we will discuss here is the **habitus** of the field. According to Bourdieu, the habitus is the result of the structures of the field and the practices, forms of behaviour, beliefs and actions that are made possible within these structures. The members of the field internalise these practices, and they become unconscious points of reference, justification and action. The habitus disposes them to perceive, feel, think and act in ways that can be recognised and validated by other members of the field. It can also become the basis for the formulation of an ethos that compels members of the field to act in a certain way, but can also be a means of affirming the autonomy of the field. Journalism has strongly established practices and values that are almost universally captured in codes of ethics in most countries of the world. This leads journalists to act and think in the terms that have been validated and defended by the profession. It also means that in the face of encroachment on the independence of journalists, practices that are not encompassed in the ethos of the field, or have not been internalised, threaten the autonomy of the field.

> **Habitus** A concept based on the work of Pierre Bourdieu. Habitus is history naturalised. The values and dispositions gained from our cultural history are part of who we are, how we see the world and how we do things.

Earlier we discussed how the logic of media conglomerates and corporate intervention in the running of media industries is a source of constant conflicts and tensions. An interesting fictional example of the tension between the habitus of the field of journalism and the economic and corporate imperatives can be found in the fifth and final season of the HBO television show *The Wire* (Simon 2008). In that series a substantial part of the action is set in a newsroom that bears the name of a real newspaper, *The Baltimore Sun*. The narrative contrasts the ethos of one of the editors of the papers and most of the journalists with that of an ambitious and devious journalist, who ingratiates himself with the executive editor and the corporate structure of the newspaper. What the program demonstrates is the extent to which the journalists' ethos and habitus dictate their ways of operating with and relating to their sources, the subjects of their stories, colleagues and corporate structures. The show also documents the shift in the newspaper's culture and habitus in the face of cutbacks caused by the decline of the print media. In this instance, the writers of the show (one of them a former *Baltimore Sun* reporter, David Simon, who is also the key producer of the show) pass a very pessimistic judgment on the future of newspapers and the autonomy of journalists.

How the habitus in the field of the media functions is of course dependent on the different media industries, and is only accessible to those who function in that capacity. However, habitus alone determines how and what the field produces. In a book entitled *Production Culture: Industrial Reflexivity and Critical Practice in Film and Television*, John Thornton Caldwell explores what he calls the 'cultural practices and belief systems of film/video production workers' in Hollywood (2008:1). In other words, he studies and documents the habitus of these media workers and their relation with the field. Caldwell's study extends what is a growing body of work on the study of media industries from the perspective of those involved in all its various aspects. He analyses—through interviews, textual analysis and ethnographic observations—the practices, beliefs and discourses of members of the industry at all levels of responsibility; and their involvement in the process of self-theorising of practices, activities and industrial relations. In a context in which job insecurity, economic volatility, the expectation of self-exploitation and the necessity of strategically managing one's career advancement are the rule, Caldwell looks at the ways in which managerial, creative and technical staff in Hollywood perform and explain their roles in the field, and produce competing discourses about the industry. Some of them are for public consumption (gossip), while others are purely for internal purpose (the production of collective identities especially for technical crew). Caldwell concludes that the deeply-seated practice of self-reflexivity is the key to understanding production processes in Hollywood. Hollywood is not simply in the business of producing entertainment but also in the process of producing a habitus, a culture, that ensures its sustainability, relative autonomy and creativity.

One of the most obvious ways in which the habitus manifests itself is through the circulation of beliefs articulated as **doxa**. It reinforces the field's beliefs and practices, and must be deployed by the field's participants at the right time. Advocating and repeating doxa is a form of speaking from a position of authority invested by the institutional status of the field. It also reinforces one's sense of belonging to, and acceptance within, the field.

Doxa A common and an unquestioned statement that stands as self-evident truth.

■ Universal story-telling as doxa

A very specific example of doxa in the field of the media is the discussion of storytelling and filmmaking, and its reliance on what the field sees as the universal appeal of stories. The point of deploying the doxa that good stories are those that have universal appeal is not to determine whether there is a fundamental and universal form of storytelling (the attempts to justify the universal appeals of stories from an anthropological perspective are always rather dubious), or whether successful films are those who succeed in this way, but rather how the term gets deployed in the field, and how using the term reinforces the speaker in the structure of the profession.

On the website of Robert McKee—author of *Story: Substance, Structure, Style and the Principles of Screenwriting* (1997), and creator of Story Seminar, which has been delivered around the world (both McKee and his seminar are portrayed in *Adaptation* (2002), written by Charlie Kaufmann and directed by Spike Jonze)—we can read the following description of the seminar:

> Over three intense days, McKee's Story Seminar effectively demonstrates the relationship between story design and character. Quality story structure demands creativity; it cannot be reduced to simple formulas that impose a rigid number of mandatory story elements. Robert McKee's course teaches you the principles involved in the art and craft of screenwriting and story design, and proves the essence of a good story is unchanging and universal. Whether on the big screen, on television, in novels, on stage and in ALL creative work, everything works in the shadow of classic story design (McKee 1997).

The seminar promises to instruct participants on the deeply seated structures of universal storytelling and to offer this as a key to successful screenwriting. Similarly, the most common form of critical and reviewers' evaluation of a film is its reliance on the same universal characteristics. A Google search combining the terms 'film' and 'universal appeal' provides about 370,000 answers demonstrating that the idea has considerable currency. The claim about the story's universal appeal is a way of saying that the film will not scare away viewers with an obscure and culturally incomprehensible story, and that the viewers are likely to recognise the film's characters, situations and emotions from other films.

In the end it does not matter whether stories can have universal appeal. What matters more is the context in which the phrase is deployed, by whom, for what purpose, and backed by what kind of cultural capital and status in the field. Clearly one of the functions of such a phrase is to give credibility to the speaker and the story mentioned, and to provide an explanation that appears insightful, but actually does not require much explanation.

By way of example, consider *Whale Rider* (Caro 2002), a film set in a small Māori community in New Zealand that achieved international success and wide critical acclaim. On the surface, this success seems remarkable because of the fact that the film is about a culturally specific set of characters, and that it speaks of cultural conflicts in a community most viewers would never have experienced (even in New Zealand). Yet the appeal of the film was related to the fact that it touched people around the world. The director of the film, Niki Caro, expresses this in the following way:

> It's very interesting to me with this film to have taken it all around the world now and to see something that is so culturally specific to this tiny, intense, strong indigenous culture has this amazing ability to reach out universally to audiences (Thompson 2003).

And of course most reviewers of the film commented on the universal appeal of the story and characters. It would be more accurate to say that the appeal of the film came from the narrative and characterisation techniques that have been widely implemented by filmmakers around the world, through the influence of people such as Robert McKee. It relies on a classical and widely used three-act structure (the story is divided in three movements, with strategically placed plot elements), and uses characterisation devices that are common to contemporary film. This might explain why the content of the film seems universal: the film is carefully structured, and the pace of the narrative development allows the viewer to experience the plot in a way that is familiar and makes sense.

The point here is not to be dismissive of the currency of the idea of universal appeal, but rather, to understand what functions it has in the field, and the ways in which it provides an agreed-upon discourse to describe something that will make sense to all, including viewers. This is how habitus works: it allows things to happen, to function and for things to be validated and to produce effects.

Conclusion

We have, in this chapter, discussed the media as constituting a field in the sense that Pierre Bourdieu (1993) has proposed. This has allowed us to understand how media industries are structured, how agents in the field adopt or are assigned specific roles, and how they participate in the reproduction and maintenance of the values and discourses that justify and provide the field with credibility. What is missing from this discussion is the audience. In the next chapter, we discuss how media texts and experiences produce and act upon, but also are negotiated by, different types of audiences.

Additional reading

Introductory

Hesmondhalgh, D. (2002). *The Cultural Industries*. Thousand Oaks, CA: Sage.
Provides a thorough yet approachable discussion of the legal and corporate
structures of the cultural industries, including media industries.

Wasko, J. (2003). *How Hollywood Works*. Thousand Oaks, CA: Sage.
A detailed analysis of the structures, policies and practices of the Hollywood film
industry.

Advanced

Bourdieu, P. (1998a). *On Television and Journalism*. London: Pluto Press.
A reasonably accessible book outlining the economic and political pressures
imposed on the field of television journalism, and the impact they have on
professional practices and the independence of the field.

Caldwell, J. (2008). *Production Culture: Industrial Reflexivity and Critical Practice in Film
and Television*. London: Duke University Press.
Provides an extensive sociological and ethnographic study of the contemporary
Hollywood industry, including all levels of production.

MEDIA AUDIENCES

Introduction

In many important respects, research into audiences forms a cornerstone of media studies. This chapter explores its centrality to the field and looks at different aspects of audience studies. We will begin with a brief examination of the history of the audience, from early studies of group psychology, the pioneering work on radio listeners during the Second World War, criticisms of mass-produced popular culture, to challenges offered by scholars in the 1970s. The idea of the audience, as a phenomenon, as well as an object of study (and, notably, concern), has changed during that time. We will also explore a number of case studies that have appeared over the last 30 years, many of which analyse how individuals and audiences make sense of contemporary media texts in multiple ways, and across wide-ranging contexts. We will close with a consideration of the status of the contemporary audience, in the context of challenges to models of mass media, global circuits of production, distribution and consumption, as well as new viewing and listening contexts and interfaces, including mobile phones and portable music devices. In these respects, we will consider how economic, institutional, technological and social changes have combined to produce different audience types and experiences.

History of the audience

Go online

History of the audience

As long as there has been human culture, there have been audiences. The Latin root word of audience, *audientia* ('to hear'), gives us a sense of how we might imagine the very basic function that early communication served, with an emphasis placed on its oral nature and the close proximity the voice required. In a broader sense, those early cave paintings, rituals and ceremonies discussed in chapter 1 also imply and necessitate a viewing and listening audience. They serve as a binding mechanism, which bring people together in common purpose. In the first instance, however, they assume someone is looking and/or listening. These early media texts not only suggest a reader, viewer, subject and listener, but also a broader community, as well as a sense of belonging built around an event, and thus a shared collective experience.

The idea of the audience as something worthy of in-depth study emerges during the first part of the twentieth century. Here it begins to take more shape, particularly among sociologists, psychologists and, of course, those interested in the media. However, as an object of study and analysis, and most pointedly, anxiety, the notion of the audience can be traced back to a concern with crowd psychology in the nineteenth century. Early studies in sociology and psychology, such as those undertaken by the French scholar Gustave Le Bon, sought to understand the mechanics of group activity (what he referred to as a 'social organism') expressing a 'will', which was something distinct from individual behaviour (Le Bon 1903). Le Bon's theories also found an English home in the work of Wilfred Trotter, who gave us the term 'the herd instinct', by which he meant the way in which group instinct typically triumphed over the good sense of the individual. 'The masses' in all of these senses became something that appeared to have a will of its own, and needed to be viewed with concern (Trotter 1924).

Both Le Bon's and Trotter's ideas and concerns about the collective mind of the masses informed the work of Edward Bernays. The nephew of Sigmund Freud (the founder of psychoanalysis), Bernays combined his uncle's concepts about the unconscious with Le Bon's and Trotter's ideas about crowd psychology, as a way of trying to understand how large groups of people can and, he argues, should be manipulated. Much of Bernays' thinking came into focus because of the rise of propaganda during the First World War. Propaganda, most often in the form of advertising, was used to gain financial and emotional support from citizens of those countries involved in the war. Relying on the notion of an 'imagined community', propaganda for the war was a prime example of how a citizen is 'hailed' as a subject of, and to, the nation.

Bernays noted the apparent success of propaganda in garnering support for political and economic interests. He was particularly interested in manipulating people, as he feared the irrational side of human behaviour. As a way of developing his ideas about propaganda being a tool of mass manipulation and putting them into practice, he devised what would later be called **public relations**. His ideas had

Public relations The practices that mediate between an organisation or institution and the wider public; especially, methods of gaining goodwill for companies, government organisations or individuals without paying for advertising.

a profound impact on the advertising industry from the 1920s on, as it began to use a range of measurement tools to better determine and shape its markets. Target marketing as we know it today owes much to his ideas. Bernays was later employed by a number of companies to devise marketing strategies, and was also an important part in organising the media spectacles that made up the political campaign of US President Calvin Coolidge. Bernays' book *Propaganda* (1929) attempts to make a legitimate case for deliberately influencing public opinion. He saw propaganda as an important part of what makes democracy work, viewing it as a way of channelling irrational desire into proper outlets of consumption and orderly social behaviour.

The Frankfurt School

Go online

The Frankfurt School

Following on from Bernays, the notion of propaganda and the role of the media in manipulating people on a large scale were taken up by a number of other critical thinkers in the 1920s and 1930s. Most notable of these were those involved with what is referred to as the Frankfurt School. This was a not a proper school, but rather a group of intellectuals associated with the University of Frankfurt am Main in Germany, whose most active phase extended from the late 1920s through to the early 1960s. Significant members of this group included Max Horkheimer, Theodor W. Adorno, Walter Benjamin and Herbert Marcuse. An extended lineage can include Jürgen Habermas, who continues to grapple with many of their ideas (see chapter 6). As German intellectuals, they were active prior to the rise of Nazism (many of them were Jewish), and many later fled to America when the Nazis assumed power. In both the European and American contexts, they tried to understand the relationship between mass culture and ideology, and considered popular culture—such as music, film and propaganda—as tools to be used by those in power to reproduce the unequal social relations that are the hallmark of capitalism. For this reason, they looked to the work of Karl Marx, among others. Not unlike Bernays, they too were drawn to Freud's notion of the unconscious, but were more interested in understanding its relationship to capitalism in a critical, ideological fashion.

Culture industry In Adorno and Horkheimer, the way in which cultural products (such as films and music) are produced in mass form, much like an assembly line produces cars. For them what was significant was that cultural products produced on such a scale began to resemble one another, in that they were 'standardised', but also in that they generate the same kind of responses.

Pseudo-individuality A term coined by Theodor Adorno to explain the false sense that a mass media text offers its reader, viewer or listener of being addressed in a singular form; that is, being addressed as 'you'.

As part of this larger concern, Max Horkheimer and Theodor Adorno (1972) took a keen interest in mass-produced popular culture, and were concerned with what they called the **culture industry**. By this term they meant the way in which cultural products (such as films and music) are produced in mass form, much as an assembly line produces cars. For them, what was significant was that cultural goods under capitalism are produced in such a way that they become commodities. As things are now orientated towards the market, they become goods for sale and exchange, able to be bought and sold. They are produced on such a scale that they began to resemble one another, in that they are 'standardised', but they resemble each other also in that they generate the same kind of responses. The audience is presented with mass-produced texts that create in each individual viewer or listener the illusion of independent and free thinking. It may address 'you', in the form of the 'between-us', but this is a form of false consciousness, or what Adorno referred to as **pseudo-individuality**. Horkheimer and Adorno believed that mass-produced cultural commodities encouraged a passive experience of culture, an effect that saw the reader or viewer regress to a child-like state. Popular culture for them works its ideological magic by massaging the ego of the viewer or listener, giving him or her a sense of pleasure and gratification in such a way that any critical engagement with the world is made to disappear. In their estimation, popular culture does not allow any space to consider your own or anyone else's socioeconomic situation. Rather, it acts as a form of escapism: it provides the illusion of being able to escape from the dreariness of the workday world through the fantasy worlds offered by film, popular music and other mass media texts. Horkheimer and Adorno considered this to be dangerous, because this was the way in which certain interested social classes could maintain the status quo, and thus their particular economic, social and political power.

Media effects argument

Go online

Media effects argument

While they did not coin the term, Horkheimer's and Adorno's ideas about the ideological effects of the mass media in many respects anticipate what would come to be called the **media effects argument**. This is also sometimes referred to as the **hypodermic model** (Lasswell 1938), which suggests that people take in media texts without any kind of filter or critical reflection, just as a doctor gives a patient drugs with a hypodermic syringe. This argument, as developed over the course of the latter half of the twentieth century, has been the subject of much heated debate. However, it remains one of the most common ways of describing how the media supposedly work on audience members. With its focus primarily on young people, the media effects argument translates very effectively into concern about their, as well as the audience's, welfare. This is particularly the case with representations of violence on television, in films and, most recently, in video games such as *Grand Theft Auto*. The main focus is typically on young people, and how they are processing all the images they take from television, films, the Internet and video games. Simply put, a violent act on screen is understood to have a negative impact on young viewers. The media effects argument suggests that it may even lead them to commit violent acts.

> **Media effects argument**
> Model suggesting that audience members ingest the media uncritically, often resulting in the simple equation, for example, that violence on screen begets violence off screen.
>
> **Hypodermic model** Refers to a conception of media effects, suggesting that people take in media texts without any kind of filter or critical reflection, just as a doctor gives a patient drugs with a hypodermic syringe.

The roots of the media effects argument can be found in the work of Frederic Wertham. His book, *Seduction of the Innocent* (1955), (and his testimony to a number of government panels in the 1950s) had a profound impact on how various authorities, as well as the general public, came to understand the media and its supposed negative effects on young people. Wertham's book examined the nature of comic book culture in the US in the 1950s, looking mainly at horror and superhero genres (such as Superman and Batman). He outlined what he saw as a number of violent and sexually suggestive aspects of comics, many of which supposedly appeared as hidden messages. As a result of his testimony before a number of committees and advisory boards in the US, and after pressure from the Senate, the comics industry voluntarily adopted a code of standards that it still uses today. Wertham's study is arguably the moment when the media effects argument takes root in the public's imagination. From this point on, the media serve as scapegoats for a variety of social ills, from encouraging violence, to sexual deviance, corruption of young people and communism.

Critics of this model suggest that the experience of media is much more complex and informed by a number of diverse factors, and that audiences are more sophisticated than the researchers often give them credit for. David Gauntlett (2004), for example, has claimed there are a number of problems and assumptions that undermine the media effects argument. He suggests that many studies approach social problems 'backwards', by which he means that there is little consideration of other social factors (such as race, ethnicity, gender, class and family histories) that might be better indicators of the source of violent behaviour. Wertham's studies were done on juvenile delinquents, so suggesting that the cause of their violent actions was to be found in the media is highly debatable.

The argument also treats children as inadequate; a great deal of the research into media effects fails to give children much credit when it comes to understanding media texts. Gauntlett suggests that many of the studies are marked by an explicitly conservative ideology and filled with moralising, which in certain cases can often lead to suggestions of censorship. As he also notes, the way in which people are studied is often artificial. By putting people in contexts that are unfamiliar—such as focus groups or a controlled space—and away from the contexts within which they normally consume media, the responses to representations of violence are skewed.

For Gauntlett, the media effects argument is selective in its criticisms of representations of violence in the media. Many of these studies fail to consider violence outside of its fictional context (for example, not looking at the effect of seeing 'real' violence on the nightly news, versus seeing fictionalised violence in films or television). They also rarely look at the role of violence in constructing a narrative and character. Depictions of violence may in fact be a criticism of violence in society, and our fascination with it. An instance of violence on screen should also be considered to be part of the larger narrative; taking a representation of violence out of its context amplifies its impact without acknowledging its role in a larger act of storytelling.

Many of the media effects studies adopt a stance that has little time for the masses or popular culture. Wertham, for example, criticised comic books, which he found crudely drawn and full of childish content. Much like the Frankfurt School, many of these studies were not interested in working through the broader appeal of popular culture. The role comics played in boosting soldiers' morale during the Second World War, for example, has rarely been discussed at length.

Many defenders of the media effects argument are passionate about their belief in the power of the media to influence young people negatively. Their beliefs, however, are rarely more than just that, as Gauntlett suggests. There is little in their argument that can be backed up with rigorous scholarship and research.

Moral panic A media response to events which may be construed as evidence of social problems. Their presentation in the media makes them appear to be spectacular events that the community or nation should be alarmed about.

Moral panics

Go online

Moral panics

The media effects tradition exists today in many different forms. One of the more persistent variations of it is found in the notion of the **moral panic**. The term 'moral panic' was used first along with the idea of the 'folk devil'. Stanley Cohen (2002), who was studying the way in which representations of young people circulated in the media, coined these two terms. He examined the way two groups, the Mods and Rockers, fought over the course of a few weekends in the early 1960s at Brighton Beach, UK. As a result of their violent encounter, there was some damage to the resort and a number of arrests. Cohen analyses how the media were inclined to frame this story in specific ways, the effect of which was to identify a 'folk devil', in this case both the Mods and Rockers, and create what he called a 'moral panic'. A moral panic was a collective response to an event that might be seen to question or undermine the privileged principles and values upheld by society. For Cohen, the mass media play a role in amplifying these events in such a way that they become larger than the event itself, or what we have elsewhere called a spectacle (see chapter 7).

The moral panic can be said to follow a sequence:

1   A conflict of some sort occurs and is singled out by the media (as front page news, often with a graphic image accompanying the text).
2   The event is deemed a threat by the media, and is framed as having the potential to undermine a culture's values.
3   The perpetrators are singled out (and often demonised).
4   Various experts (such as doctors, psychologists, police and lawyers) are called upon to both confirm societal values and offer solutions to the threat. It is typically read it as a 'symptom' of a larger problem.
5   Public outcry forces the government or other authorities to step in, introducing a bill or enacting a law in an attempt to alleviate the threat and return order to society.

Current versions of moral panics often circulate around new technologies and new forms of media. These include social networking sites such as MySpace, Facebook and Bebo. Much like the media effects argument, the concern is mainly about safeguarding young people. In New Zealand, there have been a number of moral panics regarding text bullying on mobile phones, boy racing, drug use and underage drinking. While these may be construed as evidence of social problems, their presentation in the media makes them appear to be spectacular events that the community or nation should be alarmed about. Moral panics say a great deal about how the media work to manufacture stories, often with an ideological bias. They also reveal the ways in which a culture deals with its social problems.

Go online

Uses and gratifications

Uses and gratifications

Uses and gratifications model A model that attempts to explain the different kinds of interactions people have with media texts, as a way of explaining how certain individual and social needs may be met through an engagement with media texts.

In the early 1970s, a different model for understanding how people relate to the media was put forward. It differs in many important ways from the media effects–hypodermic model, placing more emphasis on how people actually use the media. Jay G. Blumler and Elihu Katz (1974) developed what is referred to as the **uses and gratifications model**. According to their study, rather than simply ingesting media uncritically, people use the media to meet a number of different needs.

People are not simply passive consumers of media texts in this model. According to their study, uses include:

1   *Escape:* Some people use the media to get beyond their everyday lives.
2   *Social interaction:* Media texts allow families and friends to discuss and share their experience; people come together around a particular program, and use that as a way to bond with others.
3   *Identification:* Characters and stories are appealing because they resemble aspects of the viewers' lives and experiences, allowing them to feel a sense of connection.
4   *Information and education:* News, documentaries and other genres serve to give viewers details about people, places and things that they might otherwise know little about.
5   *Entertainment:* Quite simply, there is something pleasurable about the media that appeals to audience members; its stories may be exciting, diverting and amusing.

The uses and gratifications model offers a more complex view of how audiences interact with the media. Its strength as a new model for understanding media consumption is that it affords opportunities to think about audience interaction in a range of different ways.

Reception theory

Reception theory A theoretical model used to explore the way in which meaning in a text is generated through a reader's or viewer's experience of that text.

Go online

Reception theory

Reception theory is another way of getting beyond the blind spots of the media effects argument. However, it differs in important ways from the uses and gratification model. It asks what people see in the media and how they interpret media texts. It was arguably developed in relation to literary texts, but has proved useful in the study of media texts in general. The most notable version of reception studies is found in the work of the British scholar Stuart Hall, who introduced the encoding–decoding model. At the same time Blumler and Katz were developing their uses and gratifications media model in the early 1970s, Hall (2005) offered this important reevaluation of the media effects tradition. This was an effort to better understand the processes of media communication, which he suggested were made up of circuits of meaning. Hall suggests that modern communication apparatuses, such as radio and television (and later the Internet), do not construct their messages on a standard linear message–sender–receiver format. Instead, contemporary media rely upon a much more complex feedback loop that requires an understanding, from both producers and consumers, of storytelling, narrative and genre, as well as the contexts of production and consumption. Using the example of the news story, Hall develops his model of encoding and decoding, which offers an important framework for understanding the production and consumption of media texts.

Each side of this equation mirrors the other. On the encoding side (the production side), a raw event, something that happens out there in the world, is put together into story form, according to a range of criteria and mechanisms. This is echoed on the decoding side of his equation (the consumption side). We can exemplify with reference to the production of a news program:

1 *Technical infrastructure:* Such as cameras, studios and editing suites.
2 *Relations of production:* Economics of broadcasting (commercial broadcasting versus public broadcasting) and questions of ownership.
3 *Frameworks of knowledge:* Such as editing, camera angles, musical accompaniment and length.

These are mirrored on the decoding side of the model:

1 *Technical infrastructure:* Access to television or equivalent (via cable, Internet or satellite).
2 *Relations of production:* Questions of general access, tied to social and economic relationships (such as class, gender and ethnicity).
3 *Frameworks of knowledge:* Background information, story recognition, level of education and understanding of genre (such as investigative report, human interest stories, celebrity gossip or sports segments).

What links these two sides, Hall suggests, is a shared understanding of what makes up a story. There is an expectation on the part of the producers that viewers will understand elements of a raw event assembled into a recognisable story format. However, as he also notes, there is no guarantee that both sides understand the story in the same way. Stories are made up of complex sign systems, both visual and aural. The things we see and hear, the images combined with the soundtrack in a news story, are subject to what we have earlier referred to as the arbitrary nature of the sign. There is nothing natural about the correspondence between the organised sounds and images in a news story and what they come to mean. It is convention that links the meaning we take from events and how they come to be represented to us in particular forms (such as genres or narratives). The relationship between what we see and hear through our television—in other words, the meaning we take from these sights and sounds—is based on a set of shared cultural codes. However, we may not all sit in the same position with regard to these codes and conventions. There are, for example, a range of ways in which we might read a given news story, disposed as we are by our own experiences, expectations and literacies.

For Hall, meaning is not simply contained in the text itself. Instead, it is worked out by reference to a set of cultural codes, or what we are calling literacies. Thus, our class, gender, race, ethnicity, sexual orientation and age influence how a text will be read. Our experience of the world, for example, may not fit with what we see represented on screen. The result can be competing interpretations of a given story, which can be seen as an example of what is called **hegemony**. This term, taken from the Italian Marxist Antonio Gramsci, is another key idea in media studies (see Gramsci 1971). It describes the way in which a dominant group tries to gain the consent of a subordinate group (or groups). It may do this through political power, from the top down (coercion), but it may also do it more effectively through cultural means, from the bottom up (consent). The dominant group's values may be

Hegemony A term used to talk about political predominance, usually of one state over another. The use of the term in media studies has developed from the work of Antonio Gramsci, who showed that the ruling classes need the acceptance of their subordinates. To gain hegemony through an agreement of opinion is a struggle: a constant negotiation and renegotiation, organisation and reorganisation, of structuring experience and consciousness.

asserted through what is called a privileged reading of a text, for example. Telling the story in a particular way does this. Using editing, camera angles, narration, music, orientation and other techniques gives news stories a specific look and slant. The story may purport to tell all sides of the event, appearing to take an objective stance, but a careful analysis can reveal that it is biased towards a particular worldview. Hegemony, in this instance, presents a preferred worldview as the commonsense one, affirming the status quo as eternal and unquestionable.

For Gramsci (and Hall), however, what makes hegemony unique is that it is part of a dynamic struggle over meaning and cultural value. Because culture is never static, it means that those in power must always reaffirm and reassert their privileged control over it, as it can never be total or complete. There are gaps, in other words, that permit people to misread, intentionally or not, cultural texts. This allows them to resist, and even challenge, the privileged reading of a text. Hegemony, then, is about the struggle over meaning, and for media studies this is an important reconsideration of how power can be understood as much more widely spread and much less centralised.

Hall builds on Gramsci's ideas about social and cultural power by thinking about how media texts, in this case news stories, can be read from different social positions. Using the news, he classes these possible readings into three positions:

1 dominant–hegemonic
2 negotiated
3 oppositional.

An example of how these positions might work can be taken from a fictional nightly news story. Imagine the story involves a politician putting forward a Bill that advocates a tax break for corporations. Those who share this point of view, in other words, who are part of the dominant–hegemonic group, would see this as reflecting their worldview in a positive way. They would read this story relatively 'straight', as it confirms their ideological stance with regard to the economy. A middle-class viewer might take a negotiated position, as someone whose taxes may go up, but who recognises that, in order to help the economy grow (which may or may not benefit them in the end), businesses should be given a tax break. An oppositional reading, on the other hand, would see this as yet another concession to those in power. Someone in this position recognises a contradiction between the worldview privileged on the screen, and his or her own experience of the world.

One simple way to consider how we might begin to analyse a story, then, is to consider not only what is represented, but rather what is not represented. Could the story have been told differently? What does the choice of music tell us about the constructed tone of the story? What about the editing? How much context do we really get in a news story, and how much ends up being cut out? While Hall places an emphasis on news stories, this model of reading can be equally applied to other narrative texts as well. It is useful to media studies, because it suggests that there is a range of possible readings of a given text, and that we each bring something to bear upon our understanding of the media. We can read a text straight, or we can read 'against the grain' of a text. From our background and current experiences, our encounter with any media text can confirm or deny our worldview.

Hall's work, along with that of a number of other scholars, constitutes a shift in how audiences have come to be understood. There is stronger emphasis placed on what is called the **active audience**. The meaning is not simply in the text, but relies upon a whole set of other, related, social factors. Other researchers have done extensive work using Hall's model, three of which are discussed in more detail below.

> **Active audience** Rather than being simply passive receivers of media texts, members of the audience engage with the media in a wide variety of ways.

■ David Morley

David Morley is an important figure in a subfield of media studies known as television studies. Morley's work, specifically on the British television current affairs show *Nationwide*, is an important part of audience studies (see Morley 1980). In this study, conducted between 1975 and 1979, Morley drew parallels between the codes of the program and how they might correlate to the social and cultural status of audience members. This builds on Hall's model of encoding and decoding. Morley's preferred method of obtaining data was to gather together specific groups (such as university arts students, women college students and men college students), to which he put a series of questions. He was trying to create a cultural map of how people read texts on the basis of categories such as class, race, gender, age, sexual orientation and ethnicity.

■ Ien Ang

Ien Ang's books—*Watching Dallas: Soap Opera and the Melodramatic Imagination* (1985), *Desperately Seeking the Audience* (1991) and *Living Room Wars: Rethinking Media Audiences for a Postmodern World* (1996)—have done a great deal to elevate television studies to a central place in media studies. Much of this work is based on similar interview methods adopted by Morley. Ang's initial study of the American television show *Dallas* was concerned with the issue of viewer pleasure. As she states, 'What matters is the possibility of identifying with [the object of pleasure] in some way or other, to integrate it into everyday life. In other words, popular pleasure is first and foremost a pleasure of recognition. But what do *Dallas*-lovers recognize in *Dallas*?' (1985:20). Ang relies on the uses and gratifications model to make her argument, noting the role that entertainment plays in viewers' pleasure. The notion of recognition is an important part of how that pleasure is experienced and articulated, particularly as it relates to a soap opera's realism. Ang found that many of those involved in her study judged the characters according to how 'genuine' they appeared. She also discovered that many disagreed with the ideology of the show, yet still found it pleasurable. A Marxist, for example, could recognise in the crass excess of *Dallas* a critique of capitalism.

■ John Fiske

John Fiske is another scholar whose ideas have informed work on media audiences, primarily in television studies (see Fiske 1987). Much like Hall and Morley, he argues that people make their own meanings on the basis of their experience of the world, informed as it is by gender, sexuality, class, ethnicity, age and other social categories. Fiske focuses much of his research on the ways in which popular culture might be seen to contain, as well as enable, consumers. His work looks at hegemony in many different contexts of popular consumption, from television to fashion.

Fiske places a great deal of emphasis on what he understands to be small acts of resistance on the part of audiences. He sees in them the slow erosion of the structures of domination and subordination. However, his work has been criticised for a number of reasons. The emphasis on consumption seems more inclined to celebrate capitalism for allowing resistance, rather than offering alternative modes of challenging power structures. The stress on pleasures of the text has also been seen by some critics on the left as just another way of reasserting the media effects argument, with its ability to produce apathetic, apolitical consumers utterly absorbed in popular culture.

Active audience, subcultures and fans

Go online

Active audience, subcultures and fans

Countertext A text produced in relation to an original text, as a way of celebrating, expanding or undermining the source text.

Bricolage The French word for 'the use of only materials or tools at hand to achieve a purpose' a term first used by anthropologist Claude Lévi-Strauss to describe the way in which everyday objects have their meaning transformed by a new kind of use.

The criticisms of Fiske are important to note, particularly for thinking about the ways in which popular culture might be seen to encourage a lack of engagement with, or an unwillingness to affect, real political change. The notion that the audience is active in its reading of media texts still has a great deal of currency. There are a number of ways of looking at the relationship between audiences and texts, such as the ways in which readers interpret them, the creation of communities of readers, and the idea that readers and consumers can, and often do, produce their own texts and **countertexts** in response to an original source. Readers, authors, consumers and producers get muddled together in many of these cases. In this final section we will consider the significance of these shifting roles.

■ Subcultures

In Dick Hebdige's study of British punk subcultures in the 1970s, *Subculture: The Meaning of Style* (1979), he suggests that punks acted as noise in the system of traditional representation, particularly in relation to the media. As a way of making this noise, they learned to take what had been discarded by the dominant culture— a process Hebdige calls 'excorporation'—and transform it into something with new meaning. Punks appropriated and reassembled objects and media texts in a process Hebdige calls **bricolage**—a term he borrowed from anthropologist Claude Lévi-Strauss. In many respects punks epitomised the notion of hegemony, with their own struggle over the value and meaning of culture. Hebdige suggests that by using images and objects in ways that were contrary to their accepted meaning (safety pins as jewellery, bin-liners as clothing, swastikas as a fashion statement), punks sought to intervene in the dull spectacle of mid-1970s British popular culture by turning it on its head. This appropriation was combined with music-making that did not seem to rely on any kind of training. This was the case with the punk band the Sex Pistols, who found themselves on top of the pop charts with songs such as 'Anarchy in the UK' and 'God Save the Queen'. The do-it-yourself (DIY) approach to making culture outside the mainstream encouraged many young people to find the means to create their own forms of culture.

Hebdige, however, notes that many of these acts of appropriation were very quickly absorbed back into mainstream media. Hebdige called this part of the process 'incorporation'. He suggests that this took two forms, which he equated with the processes of ideology and commodification. Ideological incorporation refers to the way in which the threat that punk posed was neutralised by the media. Initially, punk was treated as a form of moral panic. Not long after its first appearance, however, perceptions about punk began to change. In certain mainstream magazines at the time, young punk women who had children were presented as just like other mothers, through generic storytelling and photo essays, with the only difference being their hairstyles and clothing. They were incorporated back into a discourse about the family. In this way, they came to be represented by the media, which once scorned them, in such a way that any threat or danger they posed, any sense of moral panic that once existed, was made to disappear. The **commodification** side of the incorporation process refers to the ways in which the music and fashion that emerged through punk were taken up by mainstream culture. Shortly after the appearance of the first Mohawk haircuts, for instance, they began to appear on high-fashion catwalks, and boxer shorts with images of the Sex Pistols' 'Anarchy in the UK' went on sale in clothing stores throughout England.

Subcultures did not begin or end with punk (Mods and Rockers are two earlier examples). Throughout the twentieth century, outsiders have grouped together as a way of creating a space separate from mainstream society. They still exist today, and exhibit many of the characteristics Hebdige describes. There have been, however, numerous reconsiderations of this kind of subcultural theory. Sarah Thornton (1995), for example, has offered a set of criticisms that focuses mainly on the role that media play in subcultural practice. Borrowing from Pierre Bourdieu, Thornton outlines the ways in which subcultures might be rethought. In Thornton's view, we can see in various subcultures, what we can call a field of subcultural production. Many musical subcultures work through their own sets of institutions and related cultural intermediaries (such as college or independent radio, alternative magazines, Internet websites or blogs), different kinds of economies (such as borrowing and lending, and equitable fair trade), and have created dense local and global networks of distribution for promotion, touring and distributing music and music-related media. They also operate according to their own logic, rules and regulations. Thornton suggests that in this context there is a great deal of emphasis placed on cultural, or what she calls subcultural, capital as the preferred currency. This means having the right kind of subcultural literacies, an ability to use skills, expertise and even reputation as a way of shoring up a position in the field, whether as a musician, radio DJ or a journalist. Success in this field, for instance, is not tied to financial gain; in fact, that could well be taken for failure in the form of 'selling out'. The gauge of success is instead about critical

Commodification The transformation of an object, text or experience into a commodity; something which can be integrated into the logic of consumer culture and can be purchased outside of its original context.

acclaim, respect from your musical peers, an appeal to a certain kind of authenticity or a modicum of 'cool'. The getting and spending of subcultural capital is all about having the kind of knowledge and skills that allow you to deploy and use it in the right way, knowing when to reveal and conceal it in measured amounts, all as a way of guaranteeing and maintaining your position in the field.

For Thornton, there is an important consideration to be made in this kind of field, and it is one that previous models of subcultures failed to consider in any great detail. The media play an important role in the distribution and display of subcultural capital, and they also play a role in binding subcultures together. Hebdige's model of subcultures overwhelmingly sees the media as an afterthought, as outside the process of subcultural formation. The idea is that the media, primarily in their mainstream form, corrupt and contaminate the subculture, somehow throwing doubt on its authenticity. Thornton suggests instead that we need to understand that media are crucial to how groups like this form. In fact, seeing the media as unified, consistent and monolithic is misleading. It would be better to consider the media according to the way their various audiences are framed. To this end, Thornton proposes we think about media as taking three forms: mass, niche and micro. By **mass media**, she is referring to magazines and media with a wide target audience, and a broad appeal in terms of content. **Niche media** target more specialised audiences, and are devoted to more specific lifestyle aspects of a given group. The last category, **micro media**, which includes **fanzines**, is not limited to audiences or markets. Many fanzines, for instance, place more emphasis on an idea of community over that of the market (though they may well just be creating a different kind of market).

Mass media Media with a wide target audience, and a broad appeal in terms of content.

Niche media Media text targeting specific markets, based on demographic criteria such as age, sexuality and ethnicity.

Micro media Media, such as fanzines, targeted at specialised, highly focused interest groups.

Fanzine A small, often hand-printed, magazine dedicated to a specialised topic or cultural phenomenon.

■ Fan cultures

Thornton's points about micro media, such as fanzines, can be extended to consider other ways of understanding how audiences are active. Fans, and fan communities, are another way to think about how people consume popular culture, not simply as individuals, but as a social activity. Fans, short for 'fanatics', are keen on a particular aspect of popular culture. They may become absorbed by it, and collect obscure details about a television show, a musician or film director. They may amass large collections of music, or have shrines filled with memorabilia dedicated to the chosen object of their fandom. Typical representations of fans in popular culture show them as dysfunctional, obsessive loners or stalkers, often referred to as 'geeks' or 'nerds'. Examples of this can be seen in films such as *Nurse Betty* (2000) and *Galaxy Quest* (1999), though a slightly more human portrait can be found in the documentary *Trekkies* (2002). These caricatures of the fan, however, represent only one dimension of their passion and commitment to a singular object.

There are ways in which fans are more than simply consumers of popular culture, and they may use a variety of media in which to communicate their love of a particular television show, magazine, celebrity or band. Like Thornton's three-tiered model of the media, fan culture can be understood as taking different forms. There are mainstream magazines that cater to fans of soap operas; for example, magazines that target a single series, many of which are published nationally and internationally. But contemporary fan cultures also show affinities with punk and its do-it-yourself ethos. There are many more underground or alternative micro-media forms, such as fanzines. More recently, fans have been able to develop online communities, setting up bulletin boards online or creating blogs devoted to their particular form of fandom.

Henry Jenkins has written a great deal about the subject of fans, and in his book *Textual Poachers: Television Fans and Participatory Culture* (1992) he discusses in details what he refers to as **textual poaching**. By this he means the manner in which readers and consumers of popular culture have found ways to use the original text as source material for their own form of creative expression. Some notable examples of textual poaching can be found in the fan culture associated with the original *Star Trek* television series (originally aired in 1966–1969, it has been in syndication since the 1970s, and has also generated a host of television spinoffs and films). A number of fans, many of them women, found ways to make sense of the somewhat inconsistent aspects of the storyline from the original television show. They produced stories that began to fill in the gaps the show failed to account for. In certain cases, many female fans produced new kinds of storylines that involved a fictionalised love affair between Captain Kirk and Spock, in what are commonly known as Kirk–Spock stories (this new genre of storytelling was referred to as 'fan' or 'slash' fiction, the latter a reference to the slash between the two names). A selection of television shows, films and novels have generated their own **fan fiction**, including *Buffy the Vampire Slayer*, and, more recently, the Harry Potter films and novels. Jenkins and others have studied the way in which fans not only make sense of these stories in relation to the original source text, but also begin to use the material to create, and, more importantly share, their stories with other fans. Many of these stories were originally circulated in fanzines. More recently, online communities have provided opportunities to share, critique and collaborate on new stories.

> **Textual poaching** Taking source material from an original text and resituating it in a new text. A form of quotation.
>
> **Fan fiction** A subgenre of writing, where the readers of an established genre expand upon its possibilities, usually by writing new fiction about the characters within that genre.

Media Studies 2.0

Go online

Media Studies 2.0

Textual poaching is still an active part of how some people consume media today. This is reflected in online sites such as MySpace, Flickr and YouTube. Blurring the line between audience and producer, the appearance of user-generated content sites has provided new forums for creativity, sharing texts and fostering a sense of community. In many cases, the audiences are producers, which gives the idea of the active audience a different kind of meaning. In this final section, we will look at the visual and audio appropriation of popular culture, the culture of the remix, and culture jamming. We will highlight a number of issues, not least of which is the changing nature of the audience.

There have been numerous historical examples of fans and audiences becoming more involved in producing a range of media texts; much of this has been made possible through the emergence of new technologies. Good examples can be found in popular music. Since the late 1960s, for example, when disc jockeys in dance bars first started mixing records, the idea of a single unified musical text was already being challenged. Throughout the 1970s, disco DJs in the US and Europe learned to single out the beats or instrumental portions on a record, looping and elongating a track by using two turntables and a mixer. They could create lengthy mixes where songs never seemed to start or end; instead, songs would just blend into a seamless soundtrack. In Jamaica in the 1960s and early 1970s, another culture of remixing began in earnest as producers took snippets of their favourite imported songs from the US and stretched out the bass lines, deepening them to create what was soon known as dub. In the late 1970s, early hip hop culture in New York was taking lessons from both dub and disco to create a new kind of subculture based on the beat and, later, the **sample**. Using the technology of the sampler, a device that allows you to cut out various elements of a song and then loop them endlessly, people could now quote portions of their favourite songs and create their own musical texts based on the work of others. While still a staple production tool in the making of pop music generally, sampling technology would soon give birth to other new musical genres, such as house, techno, jungle, drum and bass and grime.

Sample A small fraction of music, copied from another source, incorporated into a new piece of music.

Mashup A musical collage made up of a vocal track from one song mixed with the instrumental portion of another.

More recently, the musical **mashup** has signalled another merger of musical texts and technology. Using an instrumental version of a song, and merging this with another vocal cut, usually in digital mp3 format, anyone could use basic musical editing tools on his or her computer to generate new tracks. Initially, these circulated mainly online, through file sharing, or on websites and Internet bulletin boards, a phenomenon that reaching its highpoint with the release of Dangermouse's *Grey Album* (2004), which featured a combination of The Beatles' *White Album*, mixed with Jay-Z's *The Black Album*. Because the *Grey Album* was initially designed to be an art project, Dangermouse had not sought permission to use The Beatles' material, and the album was immediately withdrawn from circulation after the copyright owners, EMI, objected to the unauthorised use of their songs (McLeod 2005).

As the case around the *Grey Album* indicates, both sampling and mashups raise issues about the complex relationship between copyright, intellectual property and creativity. Recently, the Australian band the Avalanches had to wait more than a year to release its album *Since I Left You* (2001), because the more than 900 samples used had to be cleared by the record labels and artists (including the first sample Madonna ever allowed of her music). There are many arguments made on all sides of this debate, from artists defending their right to borrow a guitar riff or a beat to make a new track, to the labels that appear to be working in defence of their artists (but are not averse to licensing their songs off to be used in commercials or movie soundtracks). Some see this is a political, aesthetic and philosophical issue that is concerned about allowing artists the right to borrow and quote freely as a longstanding part of the creative process.

Remix The transformation of a musical or video text using various editing techniques.

The culture of the **remix**, and the complex legal issues that go with it, is not restricted solely to musical texts. Online video sites, such as YouTube, Daily Motion and Vimeo, allow, and encourage, a whole range of content to circulate. People can create their own short films, upload video diaries, editorialise, put up their favourite music videos, make their own videos for their favourite songs or even remix videos or film clips as they see fit. In the latter case, the ability to recognise generic codes has provided a number of remixers with the ability to convert movie trailers for horror films such as *The Shining*, for example, into upbeat family-friendly tales, re-titled *Shining*. Translating a movie trailer such as *Requiem for a Dream* (2006), a dark drama about drug abuse, into an uplifting, sprightly story of a boy getting the girl, requires a knowledge of how music, editing and voice-over narration all contribute to what defines any genre. Turning a drama into a comedy means having the literacies—the right kind of cultural capital—required to make the switch, but also a working knowledge of, and access to, the technology at hand (editing software, for example). While some of these reworked texts might be seen as tributes to the films themselves, they are rarely seen as innocent remixes. Many get pulled down by studios and copyright holders (although there are still dozens available online), as do the hundreds of musical clips put up without record label permission. The fact that many of these videos are removed suggests that remix culture, and a great deal of YouTube content in general, points to a certain anxiety about authorship. In many cases, the clips posted on these sites have no clear author or director, save for a username that may well be a pseudonym (used to avoid any consequences due to copyright infringement).

All of these instances of remix culture are a symptom of a larger shift in how people relate to the media. The blurring of the line between producer and consumer, fan, audience member and the market points to a complex cultural and social phenomenon. Alison Hearn (2008) has recently suggested that sites such as YouTube, and the photo-sharing website Flickr, encourage people to be creative in a DIY fashion, they are in fact creating yet another market space, where people learn to self-promote, and more pointedly brand themselves as commodities. Both users and viewers are transformed into numbers to be sold back to the advertisers who finance these sites. This is not unlike the function of the audience in most cases of the media. Whether it is a television audience, radio audience or Web surfer, the audience exists as a kind of currency that is exchanged among advertisers and the media host. What makes YouTube, and other websites that rely upon user-generated content, different is that it could be said to conflate markets, audiences and communities in ways that are often difficult to disentangle.

A recent example of this confusion can be found in the success of the clip 'Where the Heck is Matt?'. In this **viral video**, you can see the character Matt in various locations around the world, dancing a gawky made-up jig. Initially you see him performing alone, to be joined as the clip unfolds by whatever crowds he can gather. The soundtrack is a swelling piece of world music, with lyrics written by the nineteenth-century Bengali poet Rabindranath Tagore, and sung in Bengali. At the end of the clip, the sponsors of the video, Stride Gum, flash their logo. Reading the comments on the clip, the vast majority are positive, stressing how uplifting and inspirational it is. No mention is made that Stride underwrote his travels, and there is no objection to the appearance of the **logo** at the end of the clip. The addition of the logo, however, undeniably makes this an advertisement, but for what exactly? The YouTube interface blurs the lines between corporate- and self-advertising,

Viral video A video clip that spreads with such great speed that it is seen in many different contexts by many different people, and is thereby widely recognised.

Logo A trademark or symbol that identifies a company or organisation.

between the commercial brand and the branded self. User-generated content is what defines the YouTube brand, and viewers, who may also be producers, have now become part of the complex overlapping of market, audience and community.

Other examples of the active audience have a more overtly political agenda. One of these is **culture jamming**, which refers to the practice of publicly interfering with the messages of advertising. This has become a common sight in city spaces. For many years, media activists have been trying to draw attention to the ways in which public space has been gradually commercialised and privatised, mainly through advertising. Using techniques drawn from the culture of graffiti—which is not unlike early punks—they refashion public advertisements such as billboards by defacing them, altering images and text alike. They turn the media text against itself, using the language of advertising to undermine the otherwise privileged reading. Often the result draws attention to the contradictions of consumer culture. Many of these techniques can also be found in the magazine *Adbusters*, where readers are encouraged to submit their own forms of media intervention.

New technologies, such as mobile phones, provide another vehicle through which people are encouraged to intervene in the spectacle of modern culture, sometimes by becoming yet another kind of spectacle. The culture of **flash mobs** was a phenomenon that took advantage of the immediacy of email and mobile phone technologies to organise micro-events in cities around the globe. These could be small pranks in public squares, or focused groups who could gather in restaurants, bars or department stores. They would be sent instructions via text message or email telling them where to go and then told to say a particular phrase or do a specific activity. While generally more playful than culture jamming, these events and the use of technology points towards ways in which networks, social and technological, can lead to shifts in the way in which people use the media, beyond being passive, inert audiences.

As these last instances of media interventions demonstrate, we are well past the idea of a monolithic group of people passively consuming whatever is fed to them. The point can be illustrated also by another portable technology that has transformed the notion of the audience: the iPod. This portable mp3 player provides listeners with the ability to create their own playlists and to generate a soundtrack for activities such as walking, commuting, exercising or studying. The iPod can be used as a way of managing our emotional lives, in much the same way we use music generally, to set a tone or mood. It is a tool we can program with our favourite songs or movies, as a way of creating our own acoustic or visual space that we carry around with us, and we can create soundtracks that might be suited to any task at hand. This is, for example, the way in which the iPod has been consistently marketed, with images of rapt listeners ecstatic in their own acoustic space. This privatised, individualised and portable use of music does not suggest that the audience has entirely disappeared. However, it is another indication that with the appearance of new technologies and media the shape an audience can take has been transformed, atomised and redistributed through this new technology, and bound up in a complex array of networks, social and otherwise (for more on this, see chapter 8).

Culture jamming The use of media against themselves to point out their ideological intent; for example, the use of techniques such as graffiti on advertising texts to call attention to a particular bias and/or solicitation to buy a particular product.

Flash mob The temporary gathering of people, called together for a collective prank, usually alerted through email or text messages.

Conclusion

The iPod, as a cultural icon of the empowered listener, is a provocative example on which to close this discussion of the audience. There are, as we have outlined in this chapter, a variety of ways in which we engage with media texts, as individuals and as part of a broader social community or network. There is space, as we have seen, for the audience to be active, to use the media as a tool, either for themselves or against the media itself. However, this is not to suggest that power and ideology have disappeared. We are still caught up in larger and more expansive networks of economic, political and social control, as the YouTube example illustrates. The manner in which media are produced and consumed has changed in a way that suggests that power is not simply coming from the top down, as Horkheimer and Adorno (1972) otherwise suggest. Power can be distributed in different kinds of ways, through different channels, and analysing it requires an acute awareness of the complexity of the contemporary audience, as many of the models outlined here demonstrate. Increasingly, media texts are produced for narrower and more specific audience types, with regard to lifestyle, age, gender, sexuality, race and ethnicity. In the last few decades, we have moved away from broadcasting as the preferred model to narrowcasting, with programming increasingly tailored to different tastes. The audience as entity and concept is constantly changing, subject to ever finer gradations of marketing techniques as well as sociological study. The individual and collective experience of the media in this shift is caught up in technological changes and economic imperatives as well as the emergence of new media in ways that the following chapters will consider in more detail.

Additional reading

Introductory

Gauntlett, D. (ed.) (2000). *Web Studies: Rewiring Media Studies for the Digital Age*.
London: Arnold.
A useful consideration of the Internet and related culture.

Jermyn, D. and Brooker, W. (eds) (2003). *The Audience Studies Reader*. London: Routledge.
This collection provides an overview of key writings on audiences.

Advanced

Adorno, T. (1990). *The Culture Industry: Selected Essays on Mass Culture*. New York:
Routledge.
The best known critical theory account of culture.

Bourdieu, P. (1989). *Distinction*. London: Routledge.
A highly influential book on the relation between culture and audiences.

CHAPTER 6

MEDIA AND THE PUBLIC SPHERE

Introduction

The contemporary hyper-mediatised world is dominated by rapidly changing new media technologies, and characterised by the proliferation and fragmentation of publics, spheres and information. At the same time, the concept of the (mediated) public sphere as a democratic social space in which public opinion is formed is one of the central discourses or myths through which the field of the media recognises and represents itself. Media and public institutions have evolved in parallel since the beginnings of representative democracy in the seventeenth century, in a constant play of mutual interaction (McNair 2006). Brian McNair (2006) has defined the **public sphere** as the whole set of media outlets by means of which particular groups of individuals are provided, or provide themselves, with the information they need to participate in the political processes that affect their lives. When we are talking of the public sphere, we are using a shortcut for what really are many public spheres. The public sphere is always segmented into subspheres, organised by demography, political viewpoint, lifestyle and ethnicity. The media outlets and communication practices within the public sphere come out of these subspheres, and will cater to them and their niche markets (McNair 2006).

What is the status of the public sphere in today's changing media landscape? In this chapter we will exemplify the concept of the public sphere and evaluate its roles, forms and functions in contemporary society.

Public sphere Where, and how, we interact with society. It is a network of spaces and activities. The media are part of the public sphere, and provide the forms of transmission and distribution we need to participate in the political processes that affect our lives.

Public spheres

Go online

Public spheres

On 4 November 2008 the Democratic Senator Barack Obama was elected the first African-American president of the United States. The media worldwide quickly offered images, stories and interpretations of this historic event. What for a long time had been seen as politically impossible had become real. 'Change has come' and 'victory for the people' were two of the resounding calls, inspired by Obama's victory speech in Washington. The international news coverage of the 2008 US presidential election on the day, before results started to come in, was dominated by images of long lines of people waiting to vote. The media reported an 'unprecedented turnout' for this 'historic' election. More than 130 million Americans voted: more than for any election since 1960. After his historic win, Barack Obama started his acceptance speech—his first speech as the American president elect—with this image of the huge numbers of people voting:

> If there is anyone out there who still doubts that America is a place where all things are possible; who still wonders if the dream of our founders is alive in our time; who still questions the power of our democracy, tonight is your answer.
>
> It's the answer told by lines that stretched around schools and churches in numbers this nation has never seen; by people who waited three hours and four hours, many for the very first time in their lives, because they believed that this time must be different; that their voices could be that difference (*BBC News*, 5 November 2008).

He continued to say that this victory belonged not to him but to the American people, and that his and the Democrats' campaign began not as a political power game in Washington but from the people, from ordinary citizens:

> It was built by working men and women who dug into what little savings they had to give $5 and $10 and $20 to the cause.
>
> It grew strength from the young people who rejected the myth of their generation's apathy; who left their homes and their families for jobs that offered little pay and less sleep; it grew strength from the not-so-young people who braved the bitter cold and scorching heat to knock on the doors of perfect strangers; from the millions of Americans who volunteered, and organised, and proved that more than two centuries later, a government of the people, by the people and for the people has not perished from the Earth.
>
> This is your victory (*BBC News*, 5 November 2008).

What Obama refers to here—the power of democracy, people leaving their homes to vote, or to support a political campaign in order to create social change—is what we call the public sphere.

The terms private and public sphere refer to the two main realms of our social life. The public sphere is where, and how, we interact with society. It is also where society and the state come together. It is most simply and best described as a network of spaces and activities (Morris & McCalman 1999) where we live our political lives. In order to participate in political processes, we need to have spaces to form opinions or to act, and we need the information to know how (or why) to act. For all of these activities we need communication: information, ideas and opinions need to be transmitted, interpreted and exchanged in order to be turned into knowledge and action. The media provide these forms of transmission and distribution that connect us in our various living environments. As we will explain in more detail later in this chapter, the media, particularly new media technologies (such as the Internet), largely constitute both the spaces and activities that make up the contemporary public sphere.

Let us look at some examples of such spaces and activities. The spaces we heard about in Obama's speech are the public spaces around the churches or the schools where people lined up waiting to vote, or the streets election campaigners walked and the doors they knocked at to collect money. But the 2008 US presidential election also happened in virtual spaces. YouTube is an example of how new media technologies can influence and even transform political processes. Both candidates, Senators Barack Obama and John McCain, used YouTube for posting videos, advertisements and speeches. Its supporters used these postings not only to put out the candidates' political messages, but also to encourage participation. One of the best examples of this was the 'Yes We Can' music video released in support of Barack Obama on YouTube in February 2008 ('Yes We Can' was performed by many celebrities, and was led by Black Eyed Peas member will.i.am). The lyrics are quotations from Obama's speech (also titled 'Yes We Can') in New Hampshire. The video won awards, including the first ever Emmy Award for Best New Approaches in Daytime Entertainment (Reuters 2008); and at the time of the election, had more than 12 million views on YouTube. It also became the unofficial and highly popular slogan for Obama's campaign.

A further level of the possible connections between politics and media is the fact that Obama played the clip prior to a rally of about 20 000 people on the campus of the University of Wisconsin–Madison on 12 February 2008. The Republican John McCain, whose campaign was cash-strapped compared to Obama's, decided to use more YouTube space and spend less money on purchasing TV spots. Obama broke all records for fundraising during his campaign by using the Internet to collect huge numbers of small donations. After winning the election, the Obama campaign created a website, Change.gov, to provide guidance and information during the 'transition to power' process. The site lists the issues that Obama will have to address urgently, and solicits suggestions from US citizens about these issues. The presidential addresses (traditionally broadcast on radio) are also archived on the site. Obama broke with the tradition of the presidential address by also posting his on YouTube.

YouTube was not just used by the candidates during the 2008 US presidential election campaign, but also by members of the public to communicate their political views. The most viewed election-related video on YouTube (with almost 13 million views) is by an Iraq war veteran in response to Obama calling the Iraqi War a mistake. The video ends with the line 'John McCain for President', after the Iraqi veteran has explained in portrait shot why the Iraq war is not a mistake and why he supports McCain. Just before the last line, the veteran had walked out of the picture and away from the camera, to the music of 'I'm Proud to be American'—revealing that he has lost a leg and wears a prosthesis ('Dear Mr. Obama').

This brief snapshot of the 2008 US presidential election demonstrates the varied and complex relationship between media and politics, and how the media have become central to what are considered to be fundamental assumptions of democracy: freedom of opinion, expression and information. The example of the 2008 US presidential election also shows the centrality of communication to political life (Terranova 2004:132):

> Healthy democracies need a healthy public sphere, where citizens (and elites) can exchange ideas, acquire knowledge and information, confront public problems, exercise political accountability, discuss policy options, challenge the powerful without fear of reprisal, and defend principles (Chambers & Costain 2000:xi).

Habermas's concept of the public sphere, and beyond

Academic debates about the public sphere have been strongly influenced by the German scholar Jürgen Habermas. In a book first published in 1962 (Habermas 1989), he describes the emergence of a sense of the public, understood as a public body of citizens who, through public opinion (the exchange of views and discussion about social life), begin to participate in political life. Habermas provides a historical narrative of the changing forms of public life and of the political culture of early modern Europe, and suggests that there has been a degradation of public life in our societies today.

Habermas's concept of the public sphere is complex, and he has continued to re-describe and refine it in subsequent publications. Four main points recur. The public sphere is, first, a sphere of our social life in which public opinion can be formed and expressed and in which citizens can behave as a public body. Second, it is a network for communicating information and points of view. Third, it is a sphere in which public information is available, which in turn enables the democratic control of state activities. Fourth, it mediates between society and state.

Habermas's notion of the public sphere has been criticised for several reasons (see Thompson 1990). It is seen as idealising and romanticising what has traditionally been a privileged and restricted sphere (dominated by such groups as men and the upper classes). Another set of problems lies in Habermas's over-pessimistic assessment of the rise of the mass media, particularly their role in destroying the previous face-to-face conversations of citizens debating in, for example, coffee houses.

For all its faults, why has Habermas's concept continued to be influential? As we have already argued, the public sphere is a concept that can be useful in understanding the relationships between the media, the state, the people and the economy. Habermas's model remains the starting point for discussions of the relationship between media industries and political processes. This model is also potentially useful, because it defines a standard for a democratic media infrastructure. In his words:

> Only when the exercise of political control is effectively subordinated to the democratic demand that information be accessible to the public, does the political public sphere win an institutionalised influence over the government through the instrument of law-making bodies (Habermas 2006:102).

In this model, the public sphere works as a counter to state authority. The media and media technologies are crucial in enabling this task of criticising the state and its ruling structure. Here is a good summary of the criticism that Habermas did not pay sufficient attention to this aspect, and why it is necessary to look at the impact that media technologies might have on social and political life:

> Habermas suggests that, while the traditional fora that nurtured the public sphere have long since declined or disappeared, the idea of the public sphere could be reactivated on a different institutional basis. The problem with this suggestion is that the development of technical media has dramatically altered the nature of mass communication and the conditions under which it takes place, so much so that the original idea of the public sphere could not simply be reactivated on a new footing. The media of print have increasingly given way to electronically mediated forms of mass communication, and especially television; and these new media have transformed the very conditions of interaction, communication and information diffusion in modern societies. The original idea of the public sphere, bound to the medium of print and to conduct face-to-face interaction in a shared physical locale, cannot be directly applied to the conditions created by the development of new technical media. If we are to make sense of these conditions and of the opportunities afforded by them, we must pay closer attention than Habermas does to the nature of technical media and their impact on social and political life (Thompson 1990:119–20).

This 'nature of technical media and their impact on social and political life' is what will occupy us for the rest of this chapter.

But before we move on, let us summarise the main points. The public sphere is not an institution, but both a communicative network (Eriksen 2004) and a set of sociocultural practices. There is not one single authoritative public sphere: rather, the public sphere consists of many spheres. In order to fulfil its potential function, the public sphere is dependent on media. The following sections explain in more detail the notion of the public sphere as a sociocultural practice.

Media and democracy: Citizenship

> Everyone has the right to freedom of opinion and expression; this right includes freedom to hold opinions without interference and to seek, receive and impart information and ideas through any media and regardless of frontiers (Universal Declaration of Human Rights 2009).

Freedom of speech and freedom of information are two of the central assumptions of modern political thought. The relationship between transparency of communication and democracy is foundational. Modern conceptions of democracy start from demands for free speech and political representation (Terranova 2004:131). Without a public space, in which to express and communicate ideas and form shared opinions and access information, there is no democracy.

As you can see in the quote from the *Universal Declaration of Human Rights*, the role of the media has been part of this conceptualisation. In this section we look at the kind of public spaces and activities created by media and communication technologies that enable people to participate in political life. We pointed out that what lies behind this is the idea of social action. This idea of social action extends back to the idea of **citizenship**. A citizen, in very broad terms, is a member of a political community (usually the sovereign nation state) who both enjoys the rights, and assumes the duties, of membership. This membership in a political community can provide a source of identity (to be a Kiwi in Aotearoa New Zealand, to be an Aussie, and so forth). Citizenship is also a legal category and status, defined by civil, political and social rights. Citizenship defines citizens as political agents who have the right to participate actively in a society's political life and institutions.

In both its individual and social sense, citizenship is linked to what Benedict Anderson has called imagined communities and the rise of the nation state. A nation is an **imagined political community**. It is 'imagined' because its members do not know most of the other members, and yet feel they are united and are part of a community (Anderson 2006:6–7). After explaining why the development of nation states needed imagined communities, Anderson discusses the media through which these imagined political communities were imaginable and imagined. Print capitalism, the novel and the newspaper, for example, made it possible for people to think about themselves, and to relate themselves to others. Media are thus interlinked to the idea and possibility of citizenship. The development of print media, literacy and a reading audience made possible the development of national communities and of civil society. The growth of printing, for example, was a technological change that enabled a public space and debate (see Bennett et al. 2005:29–32; see also chapter 1). Citizenship is a concept that describes the possibility of reaching beyond oneself, of creating new relationships not just with the world or one's state in general, but also between individuals and groups. In this respect culture, and especially popular culture, is essential to the concept of citizenship (Nash 2008:168).

The media as fourth estate

The evolution of the nation state, political theory and democratisation has gone hand in hand with the development of modern mass media. The idea of the media as the **fourth estate** belongs in this historical context. The notion of the media as the fourth estate means that the actions of the state are represented, debated and evaluated in the public sphere, a set of processes carried out or facilitated by

Go online

The *Universal Declaration of Human Rights*

Citizenship The duties and rights associated with being a member of a community and country. Organises and structures relations between members of the shared community, and their individual relation with government and society.

Imagined community In Anderson, this refers to the sense of shared histories, values and narratives that allow for and produce a sense of common interest. The basis for this sense of community is an imaginary relation with others one has never met.

Go online

The media as fourth estate

Fourth estate The institutional status of the press. The first three estates are executive, legislative and judicial powers. The expression raises the status of the press to that of a pillar of democracy.

the media, mostly by the subfield of journalism. In this view, it is the job of the press to scrutinise the operations of power (Lister et al. 2003:177). Ideally, when there is state and other abuses of power, journalism is meant to move 'from the work of mere reportage, interpretation and commentary to exposure, criticism and advocacy, thereby becoming political actors in their own right' (McNair 2006:57).

The current political and social context of the question of the relationship between media and democracy is what many have described as disillusionment with politics and the media. Pierre Bourdieu, for example, criticises the closure of the political world unto itself and its forgetting of social reality, and discusses the role of the media in this process (see Bourdieu 2008). What Bourdieu and others describe as the disenchantment with politics and with the media means that politics is seen as not fulfilling its democratic function any more. It also means that the field of the media is seen as not meeting its role as the fourth estate. Think, for example, about the declining membership of major political parties since the 1960s, the declining participation in electoral politics (hence the excitement over voters turning out in 'epic numbers' for the 2008 US presidential election) and a general popular alienation from formal political institutions and processes (see Castells 1997; Flew 2008). Similarly, the media, and particularly the mass media, have been criticised for replacing spaces and discourses of critical reason and political engagement with entertainment and spectacle. In Habermas's (1989) original formulation of the public sphere, for example, the mass media have played a key role in dissolving a healthy public sphere. Or, in the tradition of the Frankfurt School (which influenced Habermas), the mass media are part of the processes of mass culture that support political elites.

The Internet and other new communications technologies were initially greeted with great enthusiasm, because of the potential they offered to revitalise the public sphere. The Internet, as the new communications medium, was heralded as constituting a new public sphere. This capability is seen to lie in the very characteristics of the new and emerging information and communication technologies: digitality, interactivity, hypertextuality, dispersal and virtuality (see Lister et al. 2003:13–37). In their introduction to new media, Martin Lister and colleagues summarise the various issues that emerge with the question of the Internet as a new public sphere:

> Despite the existence of more nuanced accounts of the mass media which offer a more complex view of their social significance, it has now become clear that some of the main proponents of the twenty-first century's new communications media are actually celebrating their potential to restore society to a state where the damage perceived to be wrought by mass media will be undone. In some versions there is an active looking back to a pre-mass culture golden age of authentic exchange and community. We can especially note the following:
>
> ■ The recovery of community and a sphere of public debate. In this formulation the Internet is seen as providing a vibrant counter public sphere. In addition, shared online spaces allegedly provide a sense of 'cyber community' against the alienations of contemporary life.

- The removal of information and communication from central authority, control and censorship.
- The 'fourth estate' function of mass media is seen here to be revived as alternative sources of news and information circulate freely through online publishing.
- The creative exploration of new forms of identity and relationship within virtual communities.
- Online communication is here seen as productive not of 'passive' supine subjects but of an active process of identity construction and exchange (2003:70).

Can the Internet fix what is wrong with the conventional mass media? Can it constitute new forms of communication and new spaces for democracy: new electronic places for political discussion, political communication and, ultimately, political action? Can it provide the means to fulfil the traditional function of the media as the fourth estate? These questions are at the core of the relation between media and democracy. In today's political and media landscape, this relation of media and democracy revolves around the question of how technologies are transforming political citizenship, and how we can behave politically in the structures we live in.

How we behave politically is currently a hot topic in popular media culture. The notion of citizenship, for example, is widely discussed and debated within main-stream media and popular culture. Al Gore's highly influential film about climate change, *An Inconvenient Truth* (Guggenheim 2006)—which makes campaigning and doing something about climate change a personal, political and, above all, moral issue—is a good example of this concern. Tanja Lewis (2008:227–30) puts this concern into the wider context of a growing discussion in mainstream media of the impact of capitalist modernity. In the face of a world increasingly threatened by both environmental destruction and the biggest international financial crisis since the Great Depression of the 1930s, the question of citizenship, and with it the means for potential civic engagement, have a special urgency.

This situation is played out across the media, and not just in news or current affairs. Many reality TV shows deal with questions of civic responsibility. In New Zealand in 2007 a series called *Wa$ted* was screened on TV3. The series featured a different New Zealand household for each program, and showed ways to cut daily energy use and general waste. The show won the 2007 Energy Efficiency and Conservation Authority (EECA) Energywise Supreme Award: it was chosen for this award—which is for innovation and achievement in the energy efficiency sector—instead of actual energy efficiency projects. The EECA's justification for this was that *Wa$ted* helped to move the issue of energy efficiency into the mainstream and bring it to the attention of millions of viewers. The show is a typical example of the current trend in the ways in which popular media treat the question of our political behaviour. They reframe political discourse and move it 'away from a sole focus on traditional modes of activism and on formal politics to a growing interest in personalised lifestyle-related issues and a choice-based ethics' (Lewis 2008:238). This move of activism and formal politics closer to lifestyle and consumerism will have many implications on political and social life.

In our previous sections we have explained the relationship between the media, the public sphere and democracy. In the following section we will expand on this political dimension of the public sphere, and look in more detail at the idea of social or political action and how the media construct, and reconstruct, this idea, as well as their role in enabling it. The sections following will look at political and social agency, the idea of civil engagement and the role of communication and media technologies.

Public debate, public opinion and the question of consent

We have established that the public sphere is one of the crucial spaces of democracy. It is a space where democracy is imagined into existence through the idea of a public and the idea of democratic ideals. But we have also seen that it is one of the spaces where democracy is practised (alongside participation in electoral politics, for example). The call for citizen participation, as we have seen it in Obama's campaign, is closely linked with these ideas and ideals; and citizen participation is the crux of realising these ideals. If a public sphere is to exist and function, it needs to have influence. This means that:

> in a democracy political elites should reflect and be responsive to what publics articulate ... expressions of popular will and public opinion disseminated through media should, to the extent that they can be gauged, be capable of having real impact on political institutions, of making a difference to people's lives (McNair 2006:139).

This claim for the public sphere to have political relevance is a tall order. However, it shows how the concept of the public sphere matters, and how it has the potential to be an extremely powerful tool. Citizen participation can take different forms in a society. Voting every few years—electing politicians to represent our interests—is one such form. However, this is a rather 'limited interaction between the governors and the governed' (Lewis & Wahl-Jorgensen 2005:98). There are many other possible forms of political engagement, such as volunteering and participating in petitions or protests.

The form of participating that has been at the foundation of democratic governments is the idea that the will of the people is the source of political legitimacy. And the will of the people is expressed through public opinion and debate. As we have described in the previous sections of this chapter, public opinion and debate, and the means through which they happen, make up the public sphere. In this sense, what constitutes the public sphere is the formation, expression, exchange and discussion of public opinion: the communication and negotiation of politics. Therefore, in this section we will look at the processes of public opinion and debate as they are facilitated and structured by the media. What is public opinion, and what is its function?

■ The potential of public opinion and public debate

Public opinion is theoretically what the people want and think, and democratic governments gain legitimacy in reflecting the will of the people. Public opinion can take on several functions. Policy-makers use it to determine whether proposed or introduced policies find approval, for example. Public opinion is also used in the electoral arena of politics to determine voting intentions. Opinion polls have become a crucial part of what Pierre Bourdieu calls the 'political game' (2008:62). Because of the increasing influence of opinion polls (the many forms of opinion surveys conducted today) on politics, public opinion and the capability to influence the polls becomes increasingly important for politicians, and within political communication more generally. Public opinion, therefore, lies at the heart of politics, and is the key to understanding one of the main problems of political action: the interaction between individual opinion and collective opinion as represented and enacted by delegated governments (for more detail on this, see Bourdieu 2008:61–3). The way we understand public opinion and public debate (the process by which public opinion is formed) is therefore about how we define political action and how we think it can be facilitated.

> **Public opinion (and public debate)** What the people in a state want or think; the 'will of the people'. Public opinion, in the form of opinion polls, can have a political role in that policy-makers use it to decide whether proposed policies will find approval, and politicians to determine voting intentions. Public debate is the process by which public opinion is formed.

As expressed in Article 19 of the *Universal Declaration of Human Rights*, current conceptions about democracy start from the demands for free speech and political representation. Remember that these rights include accessing information, having one's positions represented in the public sphere, and being represented in the debates about issues vital to one's society. Freedom of information and freedom of communication are necessary ingredients for developing informed opinions, expressing them and then basing one's actions on them. Within this context, public transparency (and hence accountability) of institutions of governance (national and international) is paramount. Without this transparency and accountability, it would be difficult to uphold democratic ideas. The relationship between communication and democracy, and the role of public opinion and debate in it, is at the heart of the analysis of the international media landscape.

Because of this relationship between communication and democracy, public opinion has significant political potential. John Pilger, an investigative journalist and documentary filmmaker, argues that in the wake of the so-called 'war on terror'— and its subsequent threats to civil rights by increasingly limiting international anti-terrorism laws—a movement is growing of citizens who are getting involved in opposing the US-dominated 'military plutocracy' and a one-world power system. In this view, public opinion can be a new superpower, if we realise the power of not accepting the status quo (Pilger 2004:xxix; Terranova 2004:131).

Theoretically, public opinion—through freedom of information and freedom of communication—can exercise scrutiny over power elites. The potential of public opinion is also expressed in the fact that an inclusive public debate is one of the hallmarks of a functioning democratic society. Other such checkpoints are political equality, popular control of government, civil rights and human rights (*Democratic Audit of Australia* 2008). However, in this potential also lie the challenges of public debate and opinion. Public opinion and access to information can be limited and manipulated. As much as the freedom to information and communication can be a strong tool of empowerment and inclusion, excluding or marginalising people from the rights to 'representation in the spheres of both politics and communication' (Terranova 2004:131) can disempower people and citizens very effectively. Let us look at this issue in more detail.

■ The challenges to public opinion and public debate

John Pilger is extremely critical of the media and particularly the news media. In his award-winning documentary about the Iraq war, *Breaking the Silence* (2003), he argues that the American media played a vital role in the invasion of Iraq. He accuses them of echoing and amplifying state propaganda, instead of challenging and contextualising it.

The view Pilger expresses is at odds with the idea of the media as independent and committed to discovering and reporting the truth, rather than merely reflecting the world as powerful groups want it to be perceived (Herman & Chomsky 1994:xi). Pilger addresses the importance of propaganda in explaining how the media actually work. His work stands within a well-established tradition of media analysis. Already in the 1920s, Walter Lippmann (1997) described public opinion in terms of the **manufacture of consent**. He claimed that propaganda had become a regular organ of popular government. The role of the mass media in this process has been analysed by Edward S. Herman and Noam Chomsky in their book *Manufacturing Consent: The Political Economy of the Mass Media* (1994). In this book Herman and Chomsky argue that the powerful are able to 'manage public opinion by regular propaganda campaigns' (xi). They have developed a propaganda model of the mass media that provides an institutional critique showing the actors that define the media within the global market system, such as governments, leaders of the corporate community, media owners and executives, and other individuals and groups with vested interests (see Herman and Chomsky 1994:1–36).

Manufacture of consent
The management of public opinion by propaganda and other strategies to reach an agreement of opinion.

Pilger's insistent calling to account of the media for their failure to fulfil their democratic postulate of accurate reporting shows why the question of the relationship between media and democracy matters. The argument about the media's implication in the injustices wrought in the name of the so-called 'war on terror' has been made in other numerous cases, too. Herman and Chomsky, for example, have argued the same for the Vietnam War:

> It would have been impossible (for the US government) to wage a brutal war against South Vietnam and the rest of Indochina, leaving a legacy of misery and destruction that may never be overcome, if the media had not rallied to the cause, portraying murderous aggression as a defense of freedom, and only opening the doors to tactical disagreement when the costs to the interests they represent became too high (xv).

The author of a recent book on the politics of the information age begins on a crucial question: 'Is it still possible to talk of the media as a "public sphere" in an age of mass propaganda, media oligopoly and information warfare?' (Terranova 2004:4) The media are not simply a new public sphere that ensures the general principle and right to freedom of information and communication. There are a number of challenges to the media as a public sphere. To start with, the media are not an independent and abstract entity consisting of enabling media technologies. Rather, they are part of wider political and economic fields and contexts. This influences the processes of media production and consumption. Most importantly, the media are firmly embedded in the global business of media industries. Currently there is an extremely high concentration in the ownership of global media corporations. This does not foster a diversity of viewpoints and coverage of facts, and makes 'information management' easier. Pilger and others make the point that these global media corporations want to produce obedient customers rather than free-thinking citizens (Pilger 2004:xxvii). A good example of how media ownership influences the potential of public debate and opinion is the media landscape in Italy. During Silvio Berlusconi's time as prime minister, many have questioned whether Italy functions as a democracy, given his controlling interest in commercial broadcasting and his government's political influence over public broadcasting (Semetko 2004:351).

Another set of challenges to public opinion is posed by the many new laws that have been introduced in the wake of the terrorist attacks of September 11. Then there are also the challenges to the democratic function of the public sphere and public debate posed by the technological character of the media. The context of post September 11 has brought about the imposition of many forms of surveillance technologies on the Internet. Access to information and communication can also be limited by technological inequalities. The digital divide still exists (Golding 1999). Moreover, both access and technological infrastructure can be politically controlled. In Cuba, for example, Internet access in 2008 was still restricted to only a few workplaces, schools and universities. The government says that because of the US trade embargo it cannot connect to the undersea fibre-optic cables. In Cuba, online connections currently are via satellite, a service that is expensive and has limited bandwidth.

No wonder then that many have pointed to an important tension at the heart of the public sphere. On the one hand, the *raison d'être* for the public sphere is democracy; on the other hand the discourse of the public sphere is dominated by the observation that it needs democratisation. What has gone wrong? The challenges to the public sphere as a space of democracy will occupy us for the rest of this chapter. These challenges stem from the fact that the media do not simply create a new public sphere. The public sphere is fragmented and contentious: a crowded, noisy, chaotic, competitive and rancorous communication space (McNair 2006; Papacharissi 2002; Tsaliki 2000). It is important to realise that the public sphere is not a tidy model; rather, it is 'temporary and multiform, not fixed and regulated' (Hermes & Dahlgren 2006:261). Therefore the practice of public opinion and the conditions for the production of consent need to be understood.

The practice of public opinion and the production of consent

Pilger and others who discuss the role of the media in creating a 'public sphere of political debate' (Raymond 1996) pose the question as to whether the media—and particularly the news—can play a part in the evolution of democratic politics worldwide (McNair 2006:135). Understanding the conditions of the production of consent can help us understand the factual and potential role of the media in society. What, for example, are the capacities of the media for realising social change? How do the media partake in a manipulative politics that excludes or represses voices differing from the dominant powers? The practice of public opinion centres on the question of consent.

Consent (or **consensus**) in a general sense describes the processes of reaching a common feeling, an agreement of opinion. However, the word has a wide range of meanings. Since an agreement of opinion is an essential aspect of democratic politics, the word can easily be used for political ends in the political game. Raymond Williams, in *Keywords* (1983), points out that the word is difficult to use, because of its politics and because of its range of meanings. It ranges from the positive sense of seeking agreement through an inert or even unconscious assent, to the '"manipulative" kind of politics seeking to build a "silent majority" as the power-base from which dissenting movements or ideas can be excluded or repressed' (77–8). The master example for how the politics of consent operate in the political game is the current power of public opinion polls. As with Bourdieu, for Williams, 'public opinion politics' can explain why the processes of consent are politically so important.

Another crucial concept in media studies to explain the processes of politics and the workings of the media within it is **hegemony**. Again, Raymond Williams's *Keywords* offers a concise explanation of the concept (1983:144–6). Generally, the term is used to talk about political predominance, usually of one state over another, and hence is also used when describing 'superpower' politics. The use of the idea of hegemony in media studies has developed from the work of Antonio Gramsci (1971). His work extended the meaning of hegemony as political predominance of relations between states to relations between social classes. Gramsci describes how the ruling classes depend (for their power) on the acceptance of their interests by those they subordinate, as the natural order of things. Power, therefore, is not just influenced by political or economic power, but also by cultural power: by influencing experience and consciousness and the expression of both. In that sense, the idea of hegemony becomes important in societies 'in which social practice is seen to depend on consent to certain dominant ideas' (Williams 1983:145). To gain hegemony through an agreement of opinion is a struggle: a constant negotiation and renegotiation, organisation and reorganisation, of structuring experience and consciousness.

Power by acceptance is about finding a commonsense position. One example where this struggle is currently evident is the debate over the intrinsic value of nature and the environment. Is it a commodity and resource, or is it worth protecting in its own right? An example of these kinds of hegemonic struggles within a media text is Pilger's *Breaking the Silence* (2003). One of Pilger's strategies in the documentary is to make a semantic play on words that highlights the politics of naming. This is represented in opposing word pairs: *decent* regimes or *hostile* regimes, war *on* terror or war *of* terror, and so forth. In the interviews

Consent (or consensus)
The processes of reaching an agreement of opinion. The term is important within media studies because consent can also mean an unconscious assent, which in turn can easily be used for the manipulative purposes of building a silent majority from which different opinions can be excluded.

Hegemony A term used to talk about political predominance, usually of one state over another. The use of the term in media studies has developed from the work of Antonio Gramsci, who showed that the ruling classes need the acceptance of their subordinates.
To gain hegemony through an agreement of opinion is a struggle: a constant negotiation and renegotiation, organisation and reorganisation, of structuring experience and consciousness.

Pilger conducts, there is a constant struggle over, and negotiation of, these words. For example, in the military camp the public relations officer keeps speaking of 'holding facilities', while Pilger calls them 'detention centres'. At the end of his documentary, Pilger proposes a redefinition of 'public opinion'. It can be a superpower alongside the superpower of the United States, he says, if we do not remain silent and do not simply accept the acts committed by our governments in our names (such as the invasion of Iraq).

As Chomsky, Pilger and many others argue, the negative side of this emphasis on public opinion and consent is the potentially manipulative power of the 'manufacture of consent'. In the wake of the war on terror, the media have been increasingly criticised for being part of this kind of manipulative politics. Where are the spaces for expressing ways of seeing, and acting in, the world that are different to the dominant US worldview? Hegemonic power struggles happen in political and economic institutions, but also in cultural spaces, such as the public sphere. As we have explained in this chapter, the public sphere is a concept that relies on the idea of public opinion, particularly the conceptualisations of the public sphere based on Habermas's work. Importantly, Habermas's ideal notion of the public sphere, with its emphasis on rational agreement, has been criticised in this context. In *The Postmodern Condition* (1984), Lyotard raises the issue that anarchy, individuality and disagreement, rather than rational accord, lead to democratic emancipation. The question of what role the media can play in creating democratic politics gains new significance in this context. Are the media, as Pilger and many others accuse them, merely a mirror to the dominant powers, or can they create spaces for dissent and counter-narratives? We base our following discussion of mainstream and alternative media on this question.

■ Mainstream and alternative media

Media studies analyses the structural contexts of the media industries. One strand of this analysis is that the gap between the media (particularly journalism) and information control (particularly in wartime) diminishes or disappears. The media are part of economic and political structures, and are influenced by agents with powerful vested interests. Currently, for example, much of the editorial content of the news media stems from public relations companies. This is the context of the emergence of alternative and unofficial media.

Within the field of the media, there has always been alternative sites and practices. In the eighteenth century, for example, pamphlets and periodicals functioned as alternative media. They were highly political, satirical and oppositional to the ruling powers. They were made possible by the advent of a new technology, the printing press, then a new means of communication. But they were also made possible by political, cultural and economic developments: the relaxation of government censorship and licensing regimes; political unrest; and urbanisation, which created new audiences for public debate.

Pilger claims that in the wake of September 11 and the US invasion of Iraq, public opinion is stirring in opposition, 'perhaps as never before' (2004:xxix).

Go online

Mainstream and alternative media

He describes the growing network of alternative media and its potential impact on political life:

> It is this network that has helped raise the consciousness of millions; never in my lifetime have people all over the world demonstrated greater awareness of the political forces ranged against them and the possibilities for countering them. 'The most spectacular display of public morality the world has ever seen,' was how the writer Arundhati Roy described the outpouring of anti-war anger across the world in February 2003. That was just the beginning and the cause for optimism. For the world has two superpowers now: the power of the military plutocracy in Washington and the power of public opinion (2004:xxix).

In this view, the media themselves become an issue and site for popular and political action. If the media do not function as the fourth estate—and what is more, if the media become part of state control and other vested interests through information control (Miller 2004)—then a fifth estate has to be created as a civic force to provide a counterweight to the new media rulers (governments and corporations) by monitoring, analysing and denouncing them (Pilger 2004:xxviii–ix).

■ The Internet and the public sphere

The key question raised by emerging alternative media—and the continued growth of new uses of media technologies for information and social interaction—is whether media technologies and the global communication system enable and improve the processes of public debate and political action (McNair 2006:140). When the Internet emerged as a new media form and technology (or rather, a conglomeration of technologies), there was initially a great deal of cyber-optimism and a utopian rhetoric surrounding new media technologies (Papacharissi 2002:9). This initial cyber-optimism is now dated. The Internet and other new media technologies have not produced a better, more democratic world. The debates over the possibilities of the Internet and other media technologies, however, remain important (Kahn & Kellner 2005: 76). This is not least because of the tension at the heart of these new media technologies: on the one hand they enable new, progressive political uses (which reconstruct and remediate models of citizenship and political activism); on the other hand they are both a tool and product of global techno-capitalism.

In this context, important reservations have been expressed in critiques of the Internet as a public sphere. Methodological and theoretical objections rest mostly on two crucial issues. The first is about public communication and our understanding of our place within it. The second issue is about the political and practical contexts of this view. By definition, a public sphere should be characterised by universal access. But in reality access to the Internet and its cyberspace remains a scarce resource, determined by economic and social power. Lister and colleagues explain that:

> Universal access is in this case built out of the technology by the logic of upgrade culture—that is to say there will always be better software and faster computer architecture creating uneven access conditions. The economics of the entire computer production industry is based upon an accelerating principle of

'faster and smaller'. This induces in many users a kind of technological anxiety produced by the knowledge that your capability is always lagging behind what is possible. This can be illustrated by, for instance, the current differential availability of broadband and narrowband technologies, or the problems of web designers who have to design alternatives into their sites to cope with differently abled machines. The idea that we will all, globally or even just in terms of the rich countries of the world, at some point be equally technologically able is based on some notion that this 'upgrade culture' will at some point stop and we will all be able to 'catch up'. A cyberpunk future seems more likely, in which the 'digital divide' between the technology rich and the technology poor is only bridged by adaptation and recycling, on the one hand, and a range of social entrepreneurship initiatives on the other (2003:180).

The digital divide is the negative side of the upgrade culture; it is an integral part of the technology itself, and will always influence the ways it can be used.

The Internet is currently one of the main media platforms (but not the only one) where the relationship between mainstream and alternative media is played out. The Internet and its convergent media technologies offer various communication activities and spaces for different forms of action. Mark Poster (1997) describes the kind of public sphere created by these networked sites and activities as a mediated and mediating space, a space of communication flows. That these communication flows constitute a mediated and mediating space is crucial in order to understand that the Internet or any form of (new) public sphere is not created by a technology, but by the processes of the production and uses of, and access to, a technology.

The question of the democratic potential of the Internet and other media technologies needs to be considered in the context of the concerns over the potential negative aspects of new media. The enthusiastic perspective on the Internet as a new and more democratic public sphere often treats it and the cyberspace it creates as something that is separate from the real world. This separation is not the case. Liza Tsaliki (2000:400) points out that this perspective ignores the fact that the technologies that enable the Internet, cyberspace and virtuality have been developed for specific purposes within military, educational and commercial contexts. The Internet and media technologies are therefore directly linked with government policy-making and commercial interests. One of the tasks of media studies is therefore to analyse and describe these direct links between new media technologies and their political and economic contexts.

Brian McNair (2006) has suggested that there are three conditions necessary for a public sphere to work: accessibility, independence and influence. The Internet potentially enables all three of these. However, it also limits them. When it comes to the question of accessibility, for example, the Internet, because of its technology, can allow for an equality of participation and information access. More and more information is circulated and possibly freely available. At the same time, however, there are information access inequalities. Broadband development and access is not the same in all countries; and the technological infrastructure varies (broadband or not, for example, free Internet access or not). Independence is similarly limited by the tension between positives and negatives. It allows for alternative cultures and uses, but at the same time there is an increasing commercialisation and 'colonisation' of the

Internet by market forces (Dahlberg 2005; Golding 1999). For many corporations, the Internet is yet another mass enterprise (Papacharissi 2002:19). This tension between the revolutionary potential and the commercial and hegemonic (that is political) uses of the Internet then comes to a head on the question of influence, the extent to which the public sphere and the various actions within it will and can actually matter politically. The Internet is not a virtual space of an idealised public space, but a highly regulated space. There are issues of equity, freedom of speech, intellectual property, privacy and security, to name just a few (Flew 2005:218–19).

There are many incidents that exemplify the two-sidedness of the Internet and its technologies. One such example, which reminds us of the political realities of the Internet, is China and its use of Internet censorship. The Chinese Internet is an intranet. Users need special software to access international websites and break through the government's firewalls. The Chinese media specialist Erping Zhang talks about there being only about three gateways between world cyberspace and the 'Chinese Internet' (*Lateline* 2008). An even stronger example of the vulnerability of Internet-based technologies and of an hegemonic use of the Internet comes from the 2007 Myanmar (Burma) 'Saffron Uprising'. After sudden rises in prices of everyday goods such as food and fuel oil in Myanmar, many people (and most notably Buddhist monks) began protesting against the junta regime. The growing demonstrations were met by the regime's brutal crackdowns. Everyday people turned into bloggers, posting images on weblogs. These became crucial sources of information for the outside world. Only few foreign journalists are posted in Myanmar, and they are forced to work largely undercover. A Japanese photographer, Kenji Nagai, was shot dead during a demonstration as he was trying to photograph soldiers charging at marching monks. A blogger who posted a photograph of a demonstration was arrested, questioned and had her computer seized. It is possible to identify a dissident's name and address through his or her registered accounts. In Myanmar, the government controls every aspect of online culture, from licensing computers to issuing accounts, through the government-monitored Internet service providers. The regime blocked individual Burmese blogs during the Saffron Uprising. But because images and blogs kept leaking into the global Internet and into international media, the regime switched off the Internet altogether.

■ Democratic communication and alternative media production

Let us now move from the question of the Internet as a means of facilitating democracy to the related question of how media technologies might provide tools for democratising media production. In this section we discuss the claims that new media technologies have led to a revival of the participatory nature of the public sphere. We suggested that the central imperative of alternative media is to provide diverse and multiple perspectives that go beyond what is available in the mainstream media. One site of alternative media production that has become influential for its open publishing system and philosophy is Indymedia.

Indymedia describes itself as a democratic media outlet. It is a collective of independent media and grassroots organisations that provides both news coverage and a network of print, satellite TV, video, and radio links; all of this content is user-generated, see <www.indymedia.org>. The Indymedia network is not government- or corporate-owned, and funds itself through donations. The network was founded in the context of the 1999 Seattle protests against the World Trade Organization meeting. During the 'Battle for Seattle', media activists set up independent media centres to provide up-to-date news, audio and visual coverage from the protest locations. There are now local **independent media centres (IMCs)** in many countries and in several languages. The core idea behind these media centres is to 'empower people to become the media' (Indymedia.org). The original mission statement from the Seattle Independent Media Center expresses the political vision behind their uses of media technologies:

> The Independent Media centre is a grassroots organization committed to using media production and distribution as a tool for promoting social and economic justice. It is our goal to further the self-determination of people under-represented in media production and content, and to illuminate and analyze local and global issues that impact ecosystems, communities and individuals. We seek to generate alternatives to the biases inherent in the corporate media controlled by profit, and to identify and create positive models for a sustainable and equitable society (Seattle Indymedia Center).

Independent media centres (IMCs) Grassroots organisations committed to using media production and distribution as a tool for promoting social and economic justice.

To this end, Indymedia use an open-publishing system. Anyone can post and contribute, and the editing and filtering are transparent. Open publishing, and the development of open source models in a free software movement from the late 1990s onwards, have been crucial elements in the development of alternative media. Key to open publishing is that the processes of production are open and transparent. Users can see the material posted on a site, as well as editorial and filtering decisions.

The Aotearoa Independent Media Centre (2008), for example, explains how its site works, how to post material, and what material ends up on the main site and why. The newswire consists of articles uploaded by users that are instantly displayed on the site. This function gives space to material and voices that might be ignored by the mainstream media. In addition, the newswire enables comments. There is, however, some editing. The editorial collective (membership is open) can remove articles if there is a violation of the editorial policy (Aotearoa Independent Media Centre 2008). The second part of the editorial process is a user-rating system. These ratings of articles determine the prominence an article receives in the display on the site. Articles that fail to reach a certain rating are moved into a 'hidden articles' section, which is still available for viewing. Furthermore, the Aotearoa Independent Media Centre takes on a networking function by providing links to local news resources, such as community radio.

To get an idea of the kind of imperatives that drive alternative media, consider how the Aotearoa Independent Media Centre articulates its 'mission statement':

> The Aotearoa Independent Media Centre (AIM) ethos:
>
> ■ we AIM to provide a decentralised Internet media forum for voices and viewpoints currently suppressed or distorted by the commercial imperatives of corporate and government-backed media

- we AIM to create 'virtual' and real-life networks between grass roots community groups and non-profit NGOs
- we AIM to open access to media technology so all groups can speak for themselves
- we AIM to promote the participation of citizens in social, environmental and political issues that affect communities at local, national and global levels
- we take AIM at profit-driven media and its manipulation of the public mind
- we believe that people taking back their voices is both vital to empowering individuals to define themselves as citizens rather than consumers, and creating sustainable communities (2008).

This constitutes the expression and performance of an attempt to transform community and society by using media technologies. Raymond Williams once highlighted three aspects of democratic communication: decapitalisation, deprofessionalisation and deinstitutionalisation (1980). Indymedia incorporates all three aspects into their media production.

The mission statement of the Aotearoa Independent Media Centre also shows what the terms 'alternative' and 'mainstream' media mean. **Mainstream media** are seen as something that need countering, because they are seen as being controlled or influenced by commercial interests, dominant groups, government and, more generally, the political and social status quo. **Alternative media**, on the other hand, are seen in opposition to something: specifically both established forms of power and the field of the media itself. Alternative media have political objectives, and often want to intervene in specifically defined contexts (as during the Seattle protests against the WTO in the case of Indymedia). Alternative media can, in this sense, be seen as a form of political activism. They involve formal and stylistic strategies, including strategies about actively reaching out for audiences. The media production of alternative media is characterised by low production costs, targeted circulation and distribution, representation of minority perspectives (including political or even militant voices) and a close interaction between producer and receiver (for an introductory overview of alternative media, see Atton 2002).

■ The blogosphere

Indymedia, and its forms of media production, is an example of the do-it-yourself ethic of alternative media production. Another new media practice that emerged around this ethic can be found with weblogs. A **blog (weblog)** is software that enables regular entries on a website, as well as links to other blogs or websites. Blogs range from personal diaries or journals to sophisticated social commentary or news coverage. From the late 1990s, the number of blogs has expanded so rapidly that the phenomenon began to be described as the **blogosphere**. Part of their popularity stems from the ease and user-friendliness with which blogs allow people to go online. Blogs provide a tool for what Marshall calls 'the will to produce' (2004:52). Blog software enables people with access to a computer and the Internet to participate in media production. Many blogs produce what is now seen as a form of journalism, referred to as **citizen journalism**, or web journalism. This kind

Mainstream media In the present climate, mainstream media are seen as a force that needs countering, because they are seen as being controlled or influenced by commercial interests, dominant groups, governments and the political and social status quo.

Alternative media
A variety of media forms and practices of media production; generally, any media that are outside the mainstream media.

Blog (weblog) Software that enable regular entries on a website, as well as links to other blogs or websites.

Blogosphere
The phenomenon of the rapidly expanding practice and popularity of blogging. The blogosphere also refers to the network of debate, dialogue and commentary that influences and transforms traditional media practices (most obviously journalism).

Citizen journalism
The activity of non-professional journalists, who act independently from major media outlets to gather and spread information, usually through direct eyewitness accounts.

of do-it-yourself media production is also evident in the development of YouTube, which allows users to post videos, blog style. The gatekeeping processes that are part of traditional print and broadcast platforms are removed in the blogosphere. Therefore, many have heralded the blogosphere as a democratisation of the public sphere; not least because it can give a public voice to non-mainstream interest groups (McNair 2006:124).

The popularity and the sheer amount of media production in the blogosphere has begun to influence traditional media practices, particularly news and journalism. In this context, the blogosphere is an important part and form of alternative media. Blogs practise both interpretation and dissemination of alternative—or oppositional—information. Many **bloggers** are technoactivists who perform global media critique and journalistic sociopolitical intervention. One of the most famous examples of this is the 'Baghdad Blogger', Salam Pax. During the 2003 invasion of Iraq, he provided coverage from Baghdad, which quickly found a wide readership in the absence of a substantial news corps on the ground. Later, Salam Pax was taken on by the *Guardian* newspaper as a columnist, and a collection of his posts was published in book form. The blogosphere constitutes a 'dynamic network of ongoing debate, dialogue and commentary' (Kahn & Kellner 2005:88).

Blogger Someone who maintains a blog (weblog), in the form of either a personal diary, journal, or social commentary and news coverage.

What becomes crucial in the success of a blog is the value of the information it makes available, and the capacity to reveal information that is not in the mainstream media (McNair 2006:127). In the case of the Baghdad Blogger, his presence in the Iraqi capital during the invasion gave him an advantage and his posts a newsworthiness. Similarly, bloggers at location in the wake of the Boxing Day Tsunami gave insight into the events, before journalists had even arrived at the scene. This proved to be crucial in the development of the blogosphere as a vehicle for citizen journalism (McNair 2006:129). These blogs (including visuals provided by digital cameras) produced by eyewitnesses, provided coverage of a massive natural disaster to a global audience. Another moment in this evolution of the blogosphere was the spreading of amateur news from the 2005 London bombings. The mainstream news media were more than one step behind, and quickly picked up images taken by mobile phone cameras.

Brian McNair (2006) suggests that there are three main characteristics of blogs: subjectivity, interactivity and connectivity. The development of new and user-friendly software encouraged these characteristics. What is really striking about this is that the blogosphere, as with **cyberspace** generally (websites, chat rooms and so forth), invites media production in highly personalised and intimate forms. The practice of blogging, as the use of digital media technologies generally, negotiates questions of identity and reflects a desire for intimacy: with oneself, but also to share with the wider world, as the move from personal blogs to news blogs (or also the many blurred forms) show. Constructing one's identity online easily turns into constructing one's role in the world, and into participating in the world. The best examples of this are the many emerging forms of do-it-yourself media services, such as grassroots journalism, citizen journalism or web journalism, such as Indymedia. These forms represent a shift in how we consume and make the news. New media

Cyberspace This term was originally coined by the science fiction author William Gibson in his novel *Neuromancer* (1984). It is now used generally to refer to the spaces and networks created by both the digital technologies and our uses of them (the World Wide Web, for example).

technologies also enable shifts in how we make and consume knowledge, as the enormous success of the open source encyclopedia *Wikipedia* shows. Many other initiatives, such as the BBC's iCan project or Greenpeace's website, try to make use of new media's capability to produce, exhibit and distribute content and connect people.

Cyberspace is a public and a private space. The fluid boundaries between public and private spaces, which have been increasing with the advancement of new digital media technologies, are now an essential element of media production. These new technologies have given us, at least theoretically, an extension of the access to media: we can talk back to and become the media. Material and voices find their way into the public domain that might otherwise be filtered out from the mainstream media. This 'We Media' element has huge potential for empowerment and, as Williams has put it, for the 'production of new means (new forces and new relations) of production' (1980:63).

What gives the blogosphere its appeal—its characteristics of independence, interactivity and intimacy—at the same time constitutes its weak points. The sheer volume of unfiltered material raises important questions of quality control in the blogging world. Plagiarism, inaccuracy and deliberate fabrication are issues. So is the problem of the willingness or capability required to plough through, and the literacy needed to differentiate between, vast amounts of information. Traditional journalism, for example, did not just filter, but also summarised, explained and contextualised its information and stories. In this context, it is maybe less surprising that the blogosphere also has its forms of gatekeeping. Glenn Reynold's Instapundit is an example of the need for gatekeeping and quality control. It sifts through blogs and guides the reader to the shortest route to relevant information (McNair 2006:128).

Along with the problem of dealing with the sheer volume of material comes the question as to whether the blogosphere and other digital media help create a new, globalised public sphere, or whether they are rather just a source of entertainment and self-indulgent noise. With more and more information available online, it becomes increasingly difficult to evaluate the quality of that information. McNair describes the globalised public sphere as crowded and noisy, and reiterates the need for 'gatekeepers and sense-makers' (2006:154).

The rise of PR and advocacy in the media

The role of communication in the transformation of society and politics needs to be examined in the context of a crowded media landscape, with its potential cacophony of voices and a high degree of personalised communication. The Internet and digital media have not just provided new media for personalised communication, but also for other interested communication. The Internet has also provided a medium for, and platform of, political communication for 'use by governments and official agencies, party organisations, non-governmental organisations, lobby groups and all forms of political collectivity, including terrorist organisations and insurgent armies' (McNair 2006:133). Terranova describes the dilemma this causes for media studies:

> It has become impossible to ignore the way in which much communication is not simply about access to information and public debate, but is also about manipulation by way of positive (spin, propaganda, hegemony) and negative tactics (censorship, exclusion, distortion, etc.). The impossible task of the public sphere thus becomes that of returning communication to an older, purer function by combating the corrupting influence of manipulation, censorship, propaganda and spin (2004:133).

We have already mentioned that the political economy of the media—and the fact that the media have become a huge industry that is currently characterised by a concentration of global media ownership and deregulation—impacts both media content and media production. The media are influenced by, and mobilised for, the special interests of the powers behind them.

Alongside the expansion of mass media in the twentieth century has come the proliferation of opportunities for political actors (from politics, business, the military and think tanks) to intervene in the media (McNair 2006:61; Beder 2002). A considerable part of media use is managed. One of the main techniques for media management is public relations (PR). Public relations is the term for a range of activities and techniques that first emerged early in the twentieth century (Beder 2002:107; see also chapter 5). There are many reasons for the growing importance of PR, such as 'selling' wars or promoting government policies. Public relations is experiencing a rise in institutionalisation in governments, through press secretaries, ministerial media advisers and public affairs departments. The marketing of government activities, to promote either policies or politicians, is now a central activity within governments and political parties, to such an extent that several critics talk about 'PR states' (Ward 2003). The increasing political influence and activity of **spin doctors**, or PR professionals, makes it more difficult to distinguish whether material on specific issues is public information or political party propaganda.

Public relations has also become a structural aspect of how the media work today (Turner 2002:220). PR influences media through a variety of strategies, such as direct political action or intervention through lobbying politicians or media executives (Beder 2002:118–21). One of the main and oldest tools, however, is still the press release. Press releases, press conferences, press tours, photo opportunities and pre-arranged interviews are all aimed at providing reportable events for the media. 'The art of PR is to "create news"', writes Sharon Beder (2002), 'to turn what are essentially advertisements into a form that fits news coverage and makes a journalist's job easier while at the same time promoting the interests of the client' (113). Press, or news releases, go either directly to newspapers and media offices, or to wire services, which makes it even easier for a news release to be picked up and become a legitimate news story (114).

Spin doctors A public relations professional who 'spins'; that is, offers his or her own interpretation of terms, facts, events or campaigns in order to favour the interests of an organisation or individual.

PR is criticised by many media analysts and practitioners for having a negative influence on the public sphere and public debate, as well as having an impact upon the media's function as the fourth estate (Pilger 2004; Beder 2002; Franklin 1997). Others, however, make the point that it needs to be acknowledged and analysed as being part of media production (Turner 2002; McNair 2006:61–5). In any case, the increasing capacity for commercial imperatives to control, or at least strongly influence, the news agenda and the flow of information, and the fact that the interests of major media proprietors and corporations may not be in the public interest, needs to be noted (Turner 2002:224–5).

All of this leads us back to the questions we began with: Why does thinking about the public sphere matter? What are the relationships between political action and the role of media? The promise of transforming a society by using new and more democratic media technologies, in order to create a more inclusive public sphere, also raises problems. Ultimately, the question becomes whether online tactics are a useful and functional form of political activism—or mere ineffectual desktop activism.

One of the more widely read blogs is George Monbiot's online archive of his weekly columns for the *Guardian* newspaper (Monbiot.com). Monbiot has worked as an investigative journalist and is an activist. In 1995, Nelson Mandela presented him with a United Nations Global 500 Award for outstanding environmental achievement. In his book *Heat: How to Stop the Planet from Burning* (2006) Monbiot explains how the necessary cut in carbon emissions can be made through quick and comprehensive policy regulations. He also makes a case for the importance of climate change campaigning and environmental advocacy. In the book, he discusses social action and the role of the media. Thinking about the potential reasons for why there is such a slow change in reducing carbon emissions, he writes:

> But I also blame that tool of empowerment, the Internet. Of course it is marvelously useful, allows us to exchange information, find the facts we need, alert each other to the coming dangers and all the rest of it. But it also creates a false impression of action. It allows us to believe that we can change the world without leaving our chairs. WE are being heard! Our voices resonate around the world, provoking commentary and debate, inspiring some, enraging others. Something is happening! A movement is building! But by itself, as I know to my cost, writing, reading, debate and dissent change nothing. They are of value only if they inspire action. Action means moving your legs (Monbiot 2006:214–15).

As Castells makes clear in *The Network Society* (1997), the media form the public space of our time. However, as environmental challenges demonstrate, the world is not only a virtual space within which texts and ideas (and white plastic wristbands) float around. There is a reality behind all of this. Is all the fashionable (media) discourse about social activism and social action really part of bringing about social change? Or, is it merely a production and circulation of more and more texts about activism, 'courses of inaction that give the impression that something is being done'?

Part of the current enthusiasm over the kind of citizenship enabled by media and emerging technologies is the idea that you can make a difference by 'becoming the media' (Indymedia.org). In other words, you can change the world simply by interacting with the media, through 'Have Your Say' functions, or through purchasing related products. George Monbiot's reminder that action involves moving your legs is a criticism of this claim that you can rescue the world through media campaigns. An example of the ironies of this view is the 2005 Make Poverty History campaign (<www.makepovertyhistory.org>; Nash 2008). Self-proclaimed celebrity world saviours such as Bono and Bob Geldof encouraged people to buy a white wristband—the symbol of the campaign—and by doing so to 'join the celebrities by wearing a white band and help end poverty for ever' (*Mirror* 2005).

Castells (1997) argues that social life now takes place in the **space of flows**. The Make Poverty History campaign and the business of the white wristbands provide examples of the kinds of flows Castells talks about. The Make Poverty History campaign was intended to put pressure on the political leaders of rich countries to achieve the Millenium Development Goals they had signed (Nash 2008:167). By itself, buying fashion accessories will change nothing. So, is there potential in these flows and networks created by our communication and the tools (or gadgets) we use? Castells conceptualises the public sphere in the context of the network society, new technologies and why networks matter. He says that technology does not determine society, but without specific technologies some social structures could not develop. For example, industrial society could not have emerged without electricity and the electrical engine. Today's public sphere is a network of public spheres, a network of many spaces and many activities. However, there is a distance between the normative assumptions of public sphere theory and the practical manifestations of the Internet. As Lyon points out in *The Information Society: Issues and Illusions* (1988), dreams of electronic democracy must be tempered with recognition of technological and political realities.

Space of flows Virtual terrains created by webs of electronic information.

Decreased citizen involvement, and a disillusion and growing cynicism with politics, has been put at the heart of conceptualisations of the public sphere. Decreased citizen participation, however, is only one of the problems facing today's political systems. The current focus on a capitalist mode of production also compromises democratic ideals, such the ideal of equality (Papacharissi 2002:22). But still, in the face of many political challenges, the problem of democracy is one of the loss of sociospatial practice: face-to-face civic engagement and direct action. The forms of citizen involvement and the spaces and sites for political action and the production of political agency are important.

Conclusion

The media are not simply the new public sphere. There are other sites that are part of where we inform ourselves and shape our actions in everyday life, both private and public. Although the traditional spaces of interaction (such as the street, the village church, coffee houses and taverns) have been less significant, the importance of everyday conversation and direct face-to-face contact in social spaces remains. The public sphere not just exists of networks of subspheres and flows of communication, but also of many various and everchanging adaptive practices.

Many media critics have pointed out that it is not a specific technology that makes something (Williams 1980; Papacharissi 2002). To understand the nature of media technologies requires the skills to grasp their processes and institutional and economic structures. Internet-based technologies in themselves do not make a more democratic world. It is our skilled use, based on our ideas and vision of their power, that creates realities (Papacharissi 2002).

When it comes to understanding politics and action, Hannah Arendt made a crucial point in her still influential book *The Human Condition*: that human beings have inherent political capacities because they are human beings—they are plural and each of them is capable of new perspectives and new actions. And therefore, humans will not fit into tidy, predictable models. They would only fit into such models if their political capacities were crushed. This observation gave the book a lot of power, and, not surprisingly, during the 1960s it was seen as a 'textbook of participatory democracy' (1998:xvi).

This point about the inherent political capacities—the capacity for new actions because of a plurality of perspectives—is useful for thinking through media technologies and conceptualising the public sphere. As we have shown in this chapter, the ongoing development of new media technologies means that the public sphere today is a network of various public spheres, in and through which many different people and ideas can potentially connect. As such, the public sphere has the means to both foster and deal with the untidiness and unpredictability Arendt describes as so crucial to change.

In the next chapter, we discuss an alternative perspective to the relation between the media and the public sphere. Instead of considering the media as a tool of public debate, we look at how the media facilitate a generalised process of commodification: what Debord (2006) describes as the society of the spectacle.

Additional reading

Introductory

Coyer, K., Dowmunt, T. and Fountain, A. (2007). *The Alternative Media Handbook.* London: Routledge.
This introductory handbook is useful for its combination of theoretical and practical information about alternative media and alternative media production.

Habermas, J. (2006). 'The Public Sphere: An Encyclopedia Article'. In M. Durham and D. Kellner (eds). *Media and Cultural Studies: Keywords.* London: Routledge.
This article is useful because it is a brief but comprehensive formulation of Habermas's concept of the public sphere.

Advanced

Habermas, J. (1989). *The Structural Transformation of the Public Sphere.* Cambridge, MA: MIT Press.
Habermas's original description of the public sphere and his subsequent refinements of the concept form the basis of work on the public sphere within media studies, sociology, political science, law and philosophy.

Thompson, J. B. (1990). *Ideology and Modern Culture: Critical Social Theory in the Era of Mass Communication.* Cambridge: Polity Press.
A comprehensive and readable critique of Habermas's concept of the public sphere, particularly in regards to the role of media technology.

THE MEDIA AS SPECTACLE

Introduction

In this chapter we consider, first, the historical antecedents of the spectacle; second, Guy Debord's influential notion of the society of the spectacle (Debord 2006); and third, the extent to which the characteristics and functions of the spectacle have been modified or shaped by the field, logics, imperatives, practices and changing technologies of the media. We will address questions such as: What does the notion of the spectacle mean in the twenty-first century? What kind of work does it perform? How does it address mass media audiences?

The ancient Roman spectacle

There are a number of well-known intertextual references that we associate with the spectacle. The first of these, historically speaking, and in some ways the template for all those that follow, is derived from the Roman Empire. Most of us are familiar, from history books, Hollywood films (*Ben Hur, Gladiator*), television series (*I, Claudius, Rome*) and various computer games (*Circus Maximus: Chariot Wars, Colosseum: Road to Freedom*) with the notion of the Roman spectacle. We think of the Colosseum filled with water to allow fleets to replicate sea battles; 250 000 people packing the Circus Maximus and cheering passionately for or against the Greens, Blues and other chariot teams; or the processional triumphs of the Imperial family and successful generals through crowd-lined streets, with seemingly endless lines of soldiers and slaves in chains, and a triumphant and larger-than-life figure (such as Caesar, Augustus or Trajan) riding in a gold chariot.

These examples of the **Roman spectacle** seem curiously close to the contemporary world, largely because Western culture has inherited and strongly incorporated both the notion of, and the sociocultural functions associated with, the Roman spectacle. The cultural field of sport, for instance, is a modern phenomenon: codified rules, the quantification of distances, equipment, parameters and fan attachment to teams only came into existence slightly after the middle of the nineteenth century (Schirato 2007). When the field of sport did start to articulate itself—identifying its ethos, values and imperatives—it drew heavily (indeed modelled itself) on the ideas and history of ancient Greek athletics, and in particular the games held at Olympus. These games were seen as embodying all that was noble in Greek culture (such as the idea of overcoming adversity, the aesthetics of physical activity, the virtues of learning and developing self-discipline and spirituality). On the other hand, the connections with Roman circuses and spectacles were largely disavowed, mainly because they seemed crass, vulgar, unpleasant, violent and brutish in comparison with Olympian ideals:

> The Romans differed from the Greeks in their attitude to games, which they viewed as a form of popular entertainment designed to amuse (and in some cases, divert or assuage the disaffections or discontents of) the people … The popularity and continuity of the Roman games gave rise to a level of professionalism, specialization and bureaucratization that, along with their strongly secular nature, enables them to match up quite well with … modern sport. And to some extent the Roman concept of spectatorship, the bureaucratic transformation of athletics into a form of entertainment, and the culture of mass identification with athletes and teams is as close to modern sport as anything derived from Greece (Schirato 2007:30–1).

As well as providing the people with entertainments and diversions, and demonstrating the power and generosity of the emperor, Roman spectacles were also occasions when the people manifested a certain communal or group identity, either as partisans of one of the colour factions, or as an antagonistic mob driven by a shared grievance (high corn prices), sense of injustice (corruption unpunished) or object of hatred (such as a recently arrived ethnic group, a new religious sect or an unpopular official).

Spectacle
The commodification of society as a whole. It is a certain way of presenting cultural forms and texts; its main function is to arouse passion and excitement, manage the viewer's attention, and organise what and how we can see.

Go online

The Roman spectacle

Characteristics of the popular spectacle

To get an idea of the way in which the Roman spectacle has been translated into contemporary popular culture, consider the famous chariot race in the 1959 Hollywood film *Ben Hur*. The scene is a chariot race in one of the massive Roman circus venues, with the hero racing against numerous opponents. As with all spectacles, this is bigger than life: the crowd is huge, and the architecture is massive and imposing. There are two other related features that command our attention.

First, this is an occasion of constant drama, excitement, violence, speed and excess. Our attention is caught and maintained by the spills (chariots overturned, drivers trampled), tension (Will Ben Hur catch up and win? Will fallen charioteers avoid being killed by other chariots?), and the antagonistic and competitive nature of the race (drivers overturning and whipping and snarling at each other). The event—the chariot race–film as spectacle—piles one dramatic incident on top of another, each one outdoing what has gone before. If the action of 12 chariots racing past and colliding with one another is not enough, Ben Hur and his chariot have to jump over a crashed driver and chariot, almost toppling over in the process, and so forth. In other words, we are presented with non-stop **hyperbole**: whatever drama has occurred, you can be sure that in a few seconds something bigger, more spectacular and dramatic will take its place.

Hyperbole Extravagant statement, for effect; not meant to be taken at face value.

Second, the scene in the film and the content being represented work not just to procure the attention of the audience; they also work to produce a passionate identification with, or rejection of, the actors (such as the charioteers, crowd or soldiers). The film works hard to get a strong emotional response from us. The camera continuously pans to the crowd and to individual spectators, and we see numerous shots of concentrated and committed faces and tense bodies; so in a sense the race audience is used to cue and encourage the film audience. Moreover, it is made easy to identify with certain characters and against others. Charlton Heston as Ben Hur moves skilfully and bravely through the field, never initiates contact with other chariots and never abuses his (white) horses. His main Roman opponent, played by Stephen Boyd, snarls a lot, cheats and deliberately wrecks other chariots, and maniacally and brutally whips his (black) horses. It is clear, too, that the Roman authorities identify with the brutal charioteer, while the ordinary people in the crowd cheer for and support Ben Hur; so once again, as an audience of film watchers, we are meant to take our cues from the crowd.

Society of the spectacle

To this point we have referred briefly to the characteristics and historical antecedents of the spectacle, and identified its main features. It is designed to do the following: impose its authority on audiences; get and hold our attention; dispose us to identify with or against protagonists; and arouse passion and excitement. We are now going to consider theories about the contemporary media-as-spectacle, starting with the influential *Society of the Spectacle*, written by the French Marxist **Guy Debord** and first published in 1967. Debord opens the book by making a series of quite remarkable claims:

Go online

Guy Debord and the
Society of the Spectacle

> The whole life of those societies in which modern conditions of production prevail presents itself as an immense accumulation of spectacles. All that once was directly lived has become mere representation … The Spectacle appears

at once as society itself, as a part of society and a means of unification. As a part of society, it is that sector where all attention, all consciousness, converges … The Spectacle … is a social relationship between people that is mediated by images (2006:12).

Debord is making two closely interrelated points here. First, and most profoundly, he is asserting that human lived experience—that is, our 'authentic' sensory and intellectual engagement with the world—has been lost. In its place we have media representations that pretend to deliver up the world—in a continuously dramatic and hyperbolised manner. Second, he presumes that the functions of the social field—even society itself—have been taken over by the field of the media: the 'between us' of the social is now played out, more or less exclusively, through media simulations, discourses and sites.

For Debord, the mass media are both synonymous with, and a critical extension of, capitalism and its drive to commoditise everything and reduce all activity—including social interaction—to forms of commodity consumption. The media are critical to this enterprise because they provide the sites, technologies and images through which people are seduced away from the supposed realities of the world. The capitalist strategy is, from this perspective, to privilege sight—and the kinds of enhanced vision that is derived from media technology—as the natural and most reliable sensory means of engaging with the world; and then, for the commercial media to produce images and representations that are superior (more dramatic, over the top and seductive) to the world, and that effectively make it redundant. Put simply, media-as-spectacle 'manifests itself as … out of reach and beyond dispute. All it says is: "Everything that appears is good; whatever is good will appear"' (2006:15).

Critiques of the notion of the spectacle

Debord's ideas and arguments have been highly influential, if only because they have helped draw attention to the ways in which media technology and media as popular culture were increasingly involved (in some areas almost monopolising) in social and public sphere roles and functions. There has been considerable debate, however, about what these changes actually mean. Debord was in no doubt: 'In the course of this development all community and critical awareness have ceased to be' (2006:21). Other cultural theorists have taken a different position. Michel Foucault, for instance, is critical to the point of being dismissive. 'Our society', he writes in *Discipline and Punish*, 'is not one of spectacle, but of surveillance … We are neither in the amphitheatre, nor on the stage, but in the panoptic machine' (Foucault 1995:217). For Foucault, the society of the spectacle, with its grand public displays of power and punishment, is an anachronism. He opens *Discipline and Punish* with a description of one such spectacle, the torture and execution of the regicide Damiens in Paris in 1757, and explains how this kind of dramatic display had to go simply because it was often counterproductive. The Damiens affair is handled in a clumsy and ineffectual manner (for example, there are not enough horses to tear the body apart), and in the end power (the King, the State, justice) looks ridiculous and the crowd sympathises with the victim. Foucault argues that the society of the spectacle starts to disappear after the eighteenth century, and that power is increasingly exercised through mechanisms such as the panopticon, a tower situated in the centre of a prison that concealed the guards, but provided them with complete visual access to all the prisoners. In other words, inmates were potentially subject to constant surveillance, and they had to take this into account whenever they did anything. Foucault's point is that eventually whole populations become trained to act as if they are being watched. As a first year university student explained in a lecture, with regard to the practical aspects of (potentially) being under surveillance: 'See that computer on the desk? I'm aware that cameras are monitoring this room, and so I don't even think about stealing the computer—I'm a good citizen. But take away that sign, and you won't find a computer here in the morning.'

This culture of surveillance has been applied, literally and metaphorically, to populations from the nineteenth century up to the present. Moreover, Foucault's examples of the prison, the military academy, the school and the workplace as initial and obvious examples of disciplinary society can be succeeded, without much difficulty, by the notion of mass media and popular culture as sites of surveillance and self-surveillance. American television sitcoms of the 1950s and 1960s, such as *The Nelsons*, *Leave it to Beaver* and *Father Knows Best*, contained exemplary narratives (do your duty and you will be rewarded; authority figures do know best) and subjects (the understanding father, the self-sacrificing mother) that functioned as a kind of constant pastoral gaze directed at general viewers, who incorporated and redirected it specifically upon themselves.

While Foucault criticises Debord's ideas and narratives for being historically out of date, for the culture theorist John Frow (1997) they constitute 'a narrative teleology that relegates real history and the time of lived experience to a time before representation and the mass-mediated spectacle'(1997:8); in other words, it is not history so much as a fiction about a lost ideal that can only be restored in a utopia. There are plenty of examples, in popular, artistic and scholarly cultures, of a similar narrative of and longing for an organic world that has been lost through a variety of causes. In his book *Homo Ludens*, which is concerned with the notion of play, the Dutch historian Johan Huizinga suggests that 'real play' disappears after the Industrial Revolution. The wastefulness of play gets 'disappeared', in this account, by the logics and culture of business and industry (Huizinga 1966).

Both the English fantasy writer J. R. R. Tolkien and the New Zealand film director Peter Jackson subscribe to a similar narrative in the written and filmic versions of *Lord of the Rings*. Middle Earth is a world where the links between the different groups and sections of society (such as wizards, kings, aristocracy and peasants) are set in stone and completely natural. Nobody questions the authority of (good) wizards or kings. The aristocracy are born leaders. Peasants are jovial, plucky and salt-of-the-earth Celtic types who know their place. A racial narrative is also evident in the film: the 'good' groups are either Nordic or Celtic, while the savage Orcs are played by predominantly dark skinned Māori or Pacific Islanders. Middle Earth is a pre-capitalist, pre-scientific, semi-feudal white utopia threatened by hordes of dark-skinned peoples—which may or may not be Peter Jackson's nostalgic take on contemporary New Zealand. In *The Matrix*, new media technology has more or less 'done a Debord' and rendered society compliant or comatose. Finally, television has, from the 1990s onward, produced a wave of shows (such as *Ballykissangel, Northern Exposure, SeaChange, Hamish MacBeth* and *Monarch of the Glen*) set in organic semi-rural or isolated communities that are more or less sequestered from the evils of modern life (such as capitalism, technology, class politics, alienated youth and religious differences), and where real lived experience is facilitated and guaranteed by pre-modern traditions, ideas, values and structures.

Spectacle and the management of attention

There have been other, more positive, critical responses to Debord's notion of society-as-spectacle: responses that look beyond the problems identified by Foucault and Frow. The first we will consider is that of Jonathan Crary. His book *Techniques of the Observer* (1998) deals with the relationship between modernity, technology, visual representation and ways of seeing (see chapter 2). This explains his interest in, and reappropriation of, the notion of the spectacle, despite the fact that his account of historical changes to vision is heavily influenced by Foucault's work on disciplinarity and surveillance. Crary imagines 'Foucault's disdain, as he wrote one of the greatest meditations on modernity and power, for any facile … use of "spectacle" for an explanation of how the masses are … "duped" by media images' (1998:18), but he points out that:

> Foucault's opposition of surveillance and spectacle seems to overlook how the effects of these two regimes of power can coincide. Using Bentham's panopticon as a primary theoretical object, Foucault relentlessly emphasizes the ways in which human subjects become objects of observation … but he neglects the new forms by which vision itself became a kind of discipline or mode of work … nineteenth-century optical devices … no less than the panopticon, involved arrangements of bodies in space, regulations of activity, and the deployment of individual bodies, which codified and normalized the observer within rigidly defined systems of visual consumption. They were techniques for the management of attention … The organization of mass culture … was fully embedded within the same transformations Foucault outlines (18).

Crary identifies four main aspects of the society of the spectacle. The first, and by far the most significant, concerns the task of attention management. Precisely because modern subjects have so many media and texts, visual and otherwise, addressing and attempting to engage them (such as audiovisual and poster advertising, radio jingles, computer emails, cell phone messages, digital sports scores, CD covers, book blurbs and covers, magazine photographs, newspaper headlines and government and municipal signs), their attention span will necessarily be relatively brief. Spectacle and its sites and texts encourage this visual wanderlust ('never stop looking'), but at the same time it needs to get results: the subject must be attentive enough for long enough to consume or comply. This is the second, related aspect of spectacle: 'vision is arranged, organised and disposed within various … visual regimes, the most influential and pervasive of which is capitalism' (Schirato 2007:104). Third, every part and activity of sociocultural life are made available for consumption and promoted as commodities. They includes both 'hard' (breasts and erections, replacement body parts, partners) and more affective commodity forms, which are effectively rolled into one (if you want to experience passion and identify with a group of people, buy a ticket to or watch a football game). Fourth, subjects experience and understand the world and themselves more or less exclusively through commodities and acts of consumption. At one level this can be as straightforward as moving from one medium of information and entertainment to another to another ad infinitum: in the morning I read an online newspaper, get the weather and traffic forecasts from the radio, log into my computer at work, go home and watch television all night. A more extreme version involves people 'disappearing' into alternative electronic worlds such as *Second Life*, and wandering around imaginary landscapes, buying digital property and upgrading to more fashionable or exotic avatars, and rarely surfacing back in the 'real world'.

Go online

The 1936 Berlin
Oympic Games

The fascist spectacle

Fascism A political ideology and system of government in which individual fate and actions are subordinated to the interest of the state embodied in the figure of an authoritarian leader. Relies on a strong sense of a common, and usually racial, identity to the exclusion of others to the point of violence, destruction and even genocide. Example: Nazism in Germany (1933–1945).

Nazi Party The National Socialist German Workers Party, which controlled Germany from 1933 until 1945, ruled by the dictator Adolf Hitler.

Crary suggests that the spectacle, 'as Debord uses the term, probably does not effectively take shape until several decades into the twentieth century' (Crary 1998:18), and he cites the use of mass media techniques by the **fascist** government in **Nazi** Germany during the 1930s and 1940s. Television and audiovisual synchronisation in film were concurrent with this development. **The Berlin Olympic Games of 1936** constituted the first great international spectacle. Goebbels and Hitler understood, earlier than most, the potential power of the mass media, and they were in a position to do something about this power. Goebbels had pioneered the use of phonograph records, magazines and films during the German election of 1932, but the extent and coordination of media and other communication technologies, used to promote the games while demonstrating the legitimacy and power of the Nazi Reich, was not to be matched for several decades (Fest 1977:473). By the mid-1930s Goebbels' propaganda committee:

> was providing 24,000 copies of its newsletter worldwide … This included 3,075 foreign newspapers and journals … the press service was enlarged and … translated and printed in fourteen languages … Olympic placards were distributed complete with logo in nineteen languages and a total press run of 156,000 copies … leaflets were distributed in fourteen languages and a press run

of 2.4 million. The ten days of the torch run from Olympia to Berlin received the full attention of every aspect of the German media ... In terms of participating journalists, these were by far the most successful games until 1964 (with) ... 700 foreign journalists from 593 foreign media ... 41 radio stations ... reached an estimated 300 million radio listeners (Kruger 2004:44–5).

The Berlin Olympics-as-spectacle can be compared to the Roman circuses we referred to at the beginning of this chapter. If you watch any number of versions of the opening ceremony in the Berlin Olympic stadium, you will probably be struck with the similarities to the triumphal procession from the BBC television series *Rome* (first screened in 2005). There is a huge arena filled by a massive (120 000) noisy, enthusiastic and focused crowd. All of this is meant to overwhelm and carry off individual members of the audience, and to motivate them to engage and identify with, and contribute to, what is happening. In other words, each person watching is meant to think, feel, react and behave via the spectacle. This establishment of a 'between us' at the opening emerges from a series of interconnected visual trajectories. The audience watches, cheers and gives an extended-arm Nazi salute to the athletes (and less formally, to Hitler). The athletes, disciplined and ordered, march past and (mostly) acknowledge Hitler with the same Nazi salute. Hitler, proud and imperious, watches and takes in this adoration, and returns acknowledgment through a very brief and undemonstrative raised-hand version of the Nazi salute. 'The unification of the social', to use Debord's expression, comes about through these visual exchanges. Hyperbole and **monumentality** give rise to excitement and shared ecstasy-as-community. The figure who initiates, encompasses, guarantees and embodies this process, standing high above the crowd and the athletes, is Adolf Hitler; and what is manifested at this moment is a celebration and demonstration of Aryan supremacy, the triumph of the will and Hitler as the nation.

> **Monumentality** Giving the impression of being enormous, imposing or historically important.

What differentiates the Berlin Olympics from the Roman circuses—or at least the representations of them we see in *Rome*—is to be found in two of Crary's observations regarding Debord's work. First, that spectacle can and does function, in modern society, as a means of surveillance and discipline; and second, that it also needs to be understood as a form of architecture (Crary 1999:75). With regard to the first point: in the Berlin Olympics, and in scenes from the Nuremberg rally recorded in Leni Riefenstahl's film *Triumph of the Will* (1935), what is compelling is how the sheer precision, power, grandeur and immensity of the event is linked and transferred to the prestige and person of Hitler—what we have is 'power clearly visible and up on stage', to paraphrase Foucault. But what we also have is a series of social, political and cultural stories continuously articulated by Hitler and other leading Nazis—not just 'Hitler is Germany's destiny', but racist narratives about Aryan supremacy and the inhumanity of Gypsies, Jews, Negroes and Slavs, which derive their authority largely from the superhuman figure of the Führer. These narratives are circulated throughout the social, become naturalised and normalised, and quickly both inform the identification, categorisation and evaluation of others (my neighbour is not really human), while just as easily being turned upon the self (if I feel sympathy or pity for the Gypsies, something is wrong with me).

Crary's second point is also applicable to the spectacles of Nazi Germany. The Nuremberg rallies, for instance, are not just sites and times when Germany spontaneously (and joyously) comes into being—they and other similar occasions are more or less prescribed and managed as the only means through which individual-as-communal identity is 'authentically' manifested. This is what Crary (1999) means when he suggests that spectacle is not 'an optics of power but an architecture' (75). It is architectural in the sense that it channels, orientates and contains subjects within a particular set of configurations. In order to recognise oneself as a patriot, a parent, a worker or a citizen, an 'authentic' German subject was required to metaphorically take certain paths (I think and perform as a good national socialist; I submit my will to that of the Führer; I act as if I believe that it is the destiny of Aryans to rule over others).

In a sense Nazi spectacles and their accompanying ideologies and narratives functioned very much like Foucault's panopticon: citizens were always potentially under surveillance, not just in a conventional sense, from the Party and its apparatuses (such as informers and the secret police, state departments and Nazi-dominated professional bodies), but also at Nuremberg rallies or the Berlin games or any other occasions where certain types of normative performances (giving the salute, becoming one with the passionate crowd, demonstrably 'losing' yourself to the Führer) were required. The spectacles of Nazi Germany are clearly differentiable from those of ancient Rome, precisely because they incorporate this culture of an architecture-of-surveillance.

Go online

Walter Benjamin

Go online

Jean Baudrillard

Modernity and media affects

Affect A sensory and emotional response to stimulation. In media studies, the attitudes or emotions produced as part of textual interaction. Hardt and Negri (2001) refer to the 'affect industries', especially the media and advertising. The 'politics of affect' refers to the media practice of producing all events and issues in such a way as to elicit an immediate, unconsidered emotional reaction.

Two other significant events that Crary (1998) identifies as markers of the modern spectacle are the advent of mass television and synchronised sound in movies, both of which follow on from and accentuate the changes arising from the development of photography in the nineteenth century (18). For Crary, and other cultural theorists such as **Walter Benjamin** and **Jean Baudrillard**, the photograph more or less facilitates the emergence of modern consumer and commodity-driven society. How does this happen? Before the modern period very few voices, positions, opinions, arguments, worldviews or experiences were given any kind of public exposure. Consequently representations and explanations of the world, events and ideas, and the meanings that were associated with words, images, narratives, social categories and various sign systems (such as clothing, bodies, architecture and painting) tended to be set in stone or delimited by authorised literate cultural elites (such as the aristocracy, the Church and the legal profession). New techniques for the reproduction of objects, images and texts, however, challenged this 'monopoly and control of signs' (Crary 1998:12).

As we suggested in chapters 1 and 2, mechanical reproduction took objects and signs out of a regime of exclusivity and control, so that they circulated more or less freely and widely. Moreover, decisions about their production, circulation and consumption are increasingly inflected by the rhythms, values and logics of fashion. From this point on, meaning and value cease to be an aristocratic privilege, but instead are technologised, democratised and thrown into the marketplace:

> Photography and money become homologous forms of social power in the nineteenth century. They are equally totalising systems for binding and unifying all subjects with a single global network of valuation and desire. As Marx said of money, photography is also a great leveller, a democratizer … a fiction 'sanctioned by the so-called universal consent of mankind'. Both are magical forms that establish a new set of abstract relations between individuals and things and impose those relations as the real (Crary 1998:13).

Television and sound-synchronised film are even more effective and 'magical' in producing such effects, for a variety of reasons. For a start, moving images (enhanced by special effects, animation, editing, camera angles, close-ups, music and noise-as-narrative) are far more capable of hyperbolising the world. Think of the representations of spectacles that we referred to earlier: *Ben Hur*, *Triumph of the Will* and *Rome* abound with continuous and insistent series of images of massive stadiums and buildings (often viewed from below to enhance their size and power), huge passionate crowds, exciting, dramatic or portentous events, martial or stirring music and larger-than-life characters, all of which accentuate the grandeur and monumentality of the spectacle, 'it's enormous positivity, out-of-reach and beyond dispute', to use Debord's words (2006:15).

Next, television and film offer up much more obvious and accessible narratives, which help both to garner and maintain attention, and heighten levels of fantastic identification and involvement. Again, music and more generally sound play a significant role here, signalling and alerting audiences to where things are going or how to respond to images (be afraid; this is a crucial decision; he is evil; this is funny). In Michel Chion's (1994) words, sound in film and television places spectators 'in a specific perceptual mode of reception' (xxv). To get an idea of just how transformational and affectively involving sound can be, think of any scene of a couple engaged in some form of sexual activity. Soaring violins or soft, muted cellos can dispose an audience to read and respond to embraces or kisses as if they were something much more than physical, beyond time and flesh and routine human desires and urges. Run the same images, this time accompanied by a repetitive and featureless horn or organ background punctuated with loud groans, grunts, screams and cries of 'yes, yes, yes': immediately the ethereal disappears, and the fantasy of timeless attachment gives way to the here-and-now of slobbering bodily lust.

Finally, film and television allow for and in fact dispose audiences to identify with stars and characters; and such fantastic attachments sometimes come to replace reality. Actors in television soaps, for instance, often complain about the way in which fans presume a continuation, from screen to the everyday, of character traits, proclivities and forms of expertise. One of the best representation-as-examples of this phenomenon can be found in the 1999 film *Galaxy Quest*, a parody both of the *Star Trek* television series and the delusional behaviour of its geeky fans. The cast, now reduced to attending fans' conventions and dressing up in character to sign autographs and repeat famous, dramatic utterances ('By Thor's hammer, you shall be avenged'), are visited by a group of aliens who have been watching earth television in the belief that it was factual ('So you think the marooned crew on *Gilligan's Island* …' muses one of the characters, to which an alien replies 'Ah, those poor people'). The aliens want the heroes to fight and defeat the evil empire that is oppressing them, as happens frequently in the television series. Naturally enough, and to their own surprise, the crew do exactly that. The point we are concerned with, however, is the way an audience can form a fantastic attachment to a television program-as-milieu, and channel its hopes, beliefs, and aspirations through the style, achievements and ethos of fictionalised characters. The alien community is periodically called into being via a series of individuated gazes directed towards, and confirmed by and returned from, the heroes of the Starship *Enterprise*.

Crary (1998) suggests that what Debord describes as the spectacle had effectively taken shape by the late 1920s (18). Certainly the two sets of examples (the Nazi spectacle, film and television) we have referred to indicate, at an incipient level, where spectacle was heading. There are significant points of differentiation, however, between the spectacle of the first half of the twentieth century (both the **totalitarian** and democratic capitalist versions), and what we are familiar with in the new millennium. Debord's account of spectacle is largely focused on capitalist society, although it does acknowledge totalitarian variations and the 'contributions' they make to the modern society of the spectacle. Fascism's use of the mass media and communications to revive and naturalise ancient blood and race myths (Debord characterised it as 'a cult of the archaic completely fitted out by modern technology'), on the other hand, is clearly a 'factor in the formation of the modern spectacle' (Debord 2006:77). For Debord, however, the society of the spectacle is ultimately about the replacement of society by the market. From this perspective, the *Triumph of the Will*-style spectacle, based on a cult of leadership and exclusivist narratives, is a historical dead end. Fascism offered spectacle without the pervasive commoditisation of everyday life. In democratic capitalism, the technological and ideological preconditions for society of the spectacle are present, as Crary makes clear, from the late 1920s. However it is not until late in the twentieth century that the society of the spectacle fully assumes its specialised role of 'spokesman for all other activities … the source of the only discourse that society allows itself to hear' (Debord 2006:18–19). There are two persuasive and influential accounts of how this came about, the first derived from the work of the Marxist Claude Lefort, and the second from Pierre Bourdieu.

Totalitarian A type of centralised government that allows no dissenting opinions within society.

Spectacle and the performance of communication

In *The Political Forms of Modern Society* (1986), Claude Lefort observes that totalitarian ideology (fascism, communism) 'denies all oppositions'; most particularly it 'effaces the opposition between the state and civil society' (215). Put simply, and very much in keeping with the totalitarian spectacle, it foregrounds itself, and concentrates all social narratives and categories within the master narrative, such as the Führer as embodiment of Aryan destiny. In the Western democracies of our time, on the other hand, ideology moves in the opposite direction, attempting to make itself and the workings of power invisible. For Lefort, the capitalist class achieves this through their strategic use of the mass media. He refers mainly to television and radio, but post-digital technology is perhaps even more relevant here, since it is more effective in simulating 'the illusion of choice and interactivity' (Crary 1999: 75), which effectively comes to replace, monopolise and facilitate all social and public sphere activity.

> **Capitalised ideas** A term taken from the work of Claude Lefort, referring to certain concepts (such as democracy, freedom and childhood) that have taken on a particular significance and value.

The media address subjects, simultaneously, as both individuals and as members of sociocultural communities and categories (citizens, patriots, parents) that are characterised and animated by normative principles and **capitalised ideas** (such as the nation, freedom, democracy, the family, progress or civilisation). These capitalised ideas have little or no specific content, or, more correctly, their content is always subject to change and variation. We know that in the name of freedom, for instance, the United States invaded Afghanistan and Iraq, slaughtered hundreds of thousands of their inhabitants, kept political prisoners in jail without trial and engaged in widespread acts of torture and assassination. Moreover, there was a general acceptance, in Western media reports, discussions and analysis of these actions and policies, that they were justified because their goal was to bring or protect 'freedom'. However, Lefort's point is not simply that the media take on the task of circulating and reinforcing an association between capitalised ideas and certain meanings (the United States always works to spread freedom; political freedom is synonymous with freedom of the market). Rather, the advent of the mass media as a de facto public sphere creates an entirely new form of politics, predicated on continuous performances of communication as sociopolitical activity.

In this scenario, the real and potential antagonisms of sociopolitical life (at the level of class, race, gender and sexuality) give way to, and are dissolved by, the imperative to communicate. Every topic must be discussed and analysed, every issue and problem to be brought to light and every group must be represented and speak. In most media, facilitated performance of communication, sociopolitical differences and antagonisms simply disappear. Lefort refers to the 'constant staging of public discussions turned into spectacles, encompassing all aspects of economic, political and cultural life … dissolved into the ceremony of communication' (Lefort 1986:226).

In *On Television and Journalism* (1998a), Bourdieu provides a specific, technical analysis of television debates in France as a form of this 'ceremony of communication':

> First of all, these are debates that are entirely bogus, and immediately recognizable as such. A television talk show with Alain Minc and Guy Sorman, or Luc Ferry and Alain Finkielkraut … is a clear example, where you know commentators are birds of a feather … In the U.S., some people earn their living going from campus to campus in duets like these … These people know each other, lunch together, have dinner together. Guillaume Durand once did

> a program about elites. They were all on hand: Attali, Sarkozy, Minc ... At one
> point, Attali was talking to Sarkozy and said, 'Nicholas ... Sarkozy', with a pause
> between the first and last name. If he'd stopped after the first name, it would
> have been obvious to the French viewer that they were cronies, whereas they
> are called on to represent opposite sides of the political fence (30).

As is the case with all forms of media spectacle, such debates and discussions, and the circulation of ideas, opinions and positions, are 'produced ostentatiously' (Lefort 1986:227), and in vast quantities. As Lefort writes: 'In no other period has so much been said: the discourse on the social, facilitated by modern means of transmission, natters on; it is overcome by a dizzying infatuation with itself' (227). At the same time, the ostentation and vastness of information dispersal, opinion sharing and other forms of communication are produced and mediated in such a way as to fulfil the main imperative of spectacle, which is to gain, hold and manage the viewer's attention. The media always addresses 'only me'; in other words, the screen (of the television, computer or digital phone) is, first and foremost, the site of a 'between us' where an intimacy, a shared familiarity, a mutual interest, a relationship of service, all unfolds. Even when a subject is being called up as a member of a wider community (the nation, professional women, children), membership of that community is only brought into being, and facilitated, via the media interface and its texts and genres (such as advertising, news broadcast or coverage of a sporting event).

The contemporary spectacle: Time and effect

Once the subject has been integrated into this network of media technologies and texts, the various ongoing forms of address and media content necessarily partake of the logic of spectacle. Why? It is largely a question of the relation between attention management and practices and logics of consumption. As we noted earlier in this chapter, spectacle needs to capture the wandering eye of the spectator and hold his or her attention; however, it also needs to do something more, which is to incite an affective response—a manufactured desire—that will translate into the consumption of commodities. This is particularly obvious in media commercials, where the spectator is offered what Baudrillard (2003) describes as a fantasmagoria; that is to say, a set of fantasies and desires built on nothing (147). Baudrillard cites the example of an advertisement for Gillette 'showing two velvety females lips framed by a razor blade', and makes the point that:

> it can only be viewed because it does not really express the—unbearable—
> fantasy of the castrating vagina to which it 'alludes', and because it is simply
> content to combine together signs emptied of their syntax, isolated signs,
> itemized signs, which trigger no unconscious associations ... This is a Madam
> Tussaud's of symbols, a petrified forest of fantasies/signs (148).

The same logic applies, however, to other, apparently more serious and substantial, media genres, such as news reporting, current affairs programs and documentaries. Bourdieu argues that the field of commercial television, for instance, is dominated by the twin constraints of time and effect (Bourdieu 1998a). The fact that every television news program is competing with other channels, as well as alternative new media sources (such as independent and professional blogs, the web pages of all the major international newspapers, and informational updates on news, sport and weather received on digital phones) means that it has to make its news bigger, more dramatic and exciting, more trustworthy and authentic, more up to the minute. Moreover, the imperative is to cover the relevant story in a short space of time—two minutes for an international disaster with thousands of deaths and graphic footage; thirty seconds for a story without dramatic content. If a story has been running for too long, however, it does not really matter how many bodies are involved; think of the way the international media coverage of events in Afghanistan and Iraq trailed off, and eventually more or less disappeared, even though the slaughter continued. What sometimes returns media attention to 'old stories' is a particularly dramatic piece of footage (a gruesome decapitation captured on film, or the **Abu Ghraib** footage of torture and humiliation being inflicted on prisoners), or some 'personalised' dimension (a movie star visits a famine site; a former football star is killed by 'friendly fire').

One of the effects of the constraints of time and effect on the media is that all stories—whether disasters, hard political news, sport, the weather or scandals—are effectively interchangeable. Categorisation and evaluation (how much time is given to a story; whether visuals accompany it; where it comes in the order of presentation) are predicated more or less entirely in terms of commodity value and status. This is why news stories are predominantly played out and focused through visuals complemented by hyperbolised commentary ('A human tragedy of epic proportions'; 'Madmen motivated by insane hatred'; 'Nothing can quench their taste for freedom'): it not just allows for but demands an immediate, affective response (such as pity, joy anger or revulsion). Film of someone being chased and beaten to death by an angry mob, a missile zeroing in and destroying a village or emaciated bodies with their hollowed-out eyes staring into the camera, seem to take the viewer to the heart of the story. In fact, the story and its contexts (political, social and economic) are not so much accessed or explained as dissolved. The next disaster, famine or bomb will be infinitely more attractive and newsworthy—that is to say, a more valuable commodity—and therefore more worthy of media and spectator attention.

Go online

Abu Ghraib

September 11 and the War on Terror

Go online

September 11

Perhaps the best contemporary example of the media-as-spectacle was the group of events of September 11—the highjacking of four airliners, and the destruction of the two World Trade Centre buildings and a section of the Pentagon—and the way these were covered, represented and narrated in the global media. The best way of understanding how spectacle works, however, is not to concentrate on those events, which were indeed easy enough to produce as a spectacle; rather, we will look at what did not happen after September 11, and consider how the media were able to apply the logics and techniques of spectacle to all the things that did not happen.

In *Welcome to the Desert of the Real* (2002), Slavoj Zizek writes that:

> For the great majority of the public, the WTC explosions were events on the TV screen, and when we reached the oft-repeated shots of frightened people running towards the cameras ahead of the giant cloud of dust from the collapsing tower, was not the framing of the shot itself reminiscent of spectacular shots in catastrophe movies ... the 'terrorists' themselves did not do it primarily to provoke real material damage, but for the spectacular effect of it (11).

The cultural theorists Jean Baudrillard and Paul Virilio, who also wrote books on or about September 11, place a similar emphasis on the destruction of the World Trade Centre (WTC) as a media event and a form of entertainment. Baudrillard (2002) writes that 'At a pinch, we can say that they did it, but we wished for it' (5); and Virilio (2002) refers to it as 'a global super-production in which reality ... tip(s) over once and for all into electronic nothingness' (6).

These readings are derived from the manner in which the global media applied the logics of spectacle to their coverage of the event. For a brief period immediately after the event, as news arrived in of terrible events—heroism, tragedies, people being lucky or cruelly unlucky regarding where they were, widespread panic, turmoil, death and destruction—it must have seemed to the media that, in Debord's terms, 'Everything that appears is good; whatever is good will appear' (2006:15). When after a week or so nothing much more had happened, this itself was extraordinary news, and accordingly it was written large and loud and threatening ('Nothing Happens!') on a Melbourne newspaper billboard, and spoken of, in sombre but excited tones, from CNN to the BBC, and on local television and radio news show around the world. That nothing happened was huge, stupendous and the stuff of hyperbole, for if something had happened then we would simply have had more of the same (bombings, deaths and tragedies). The logic of spectacle, as we know, cannot tolerate what appears to be 'the nothing new'; cannot accept that the next thing to happen will not be more dramatic, more intense and more spectacular. It does not tolerate it because it cannot afford to tolerate it: spectacle makes something into nothing, but it is always the most hyperbolised, extravagant, exciting nothing. So nothing happening, as it did after September 11, meant that *something was happening and we did not know about it*—which was both something new and exciting and indeed very serious; or that something was welling up, and forces were being directed and prepared, that might unleash something that would make September 11 seem insignificant in comparison.

As the excitement and melodrama about nothing happening gradually developed into a suspicion, on the part of publics, that perhaps really nothing was happening, the 'Coalition of the Willing' and the Western media were able to segue into the war on terror by making use of a combination of techniques associated with spectacle (produce everything as extravagant and dramatic) and the horror and slasher film genre (**hystericise** everything as unfamiliar, discordant and potentially threatening). Once familiarity and certainty were abolished or put on hold, then everything and everyone has to be watched carefully and mistrusted, just in case. This played out, most obviously, in the way in which governments and the media in Australia, Britain, New Zealand and the United States demonised 'the usual suspects': not just Osama bin Laden, al-Qaeda, Hamas, the Palestinians, the Taliban, Saddam Hussein, Syria and Iran, but more generally Moslems, Arabs and, as in the case of **Jean Charles de Menezes**, anyone who could not be identified and categorised, quickly and unambiguously, as 'one of us'. Menezes was the unfortunate Brazilian who, in 2005, was shot eight times and killed—effectively executed—by British undercover police who mistook him for a terrorist. The security forces originally claimed that Menezes had an out-of-date visa, was Arab-looking, refused to stop when verbally challenged, and jumped a barrier at a Tube station in order to effect an escape—all of which was reported in and more or less accepted by the media, and none of which turned out to be true. Within the context of the War on Terror as spectacle, however, it both rang true and needed to be true—or at least believed. Moreover, executing an innocent man for no particular reason other than his skin colour did not appear to be an overreaction, given the climate of fear and overwhelming impending disaster that the War on Terror produced. The British Prime Minister Tony Blair more or less sanctioned the action by infamously declaring that the police 'would have been criticised had the suspect turned out to be a terrorist and they had failed to take action' (BBC News Website 2005).

If the two main features of spectacle are attention management and the arrangement of vision, then the War on Terror clearly fulfilled those functions. But what of the other main characteristics: commoditise everything, and ensure that every significant form of identification is orientated through the spectacle? The hysteria and anxiety produced by and through the media translated into a necessary hysterical and anxious consumption of media texts and images. In a sense, this simply mirrored the situation immediately after events of September 11, when viewers sat glued to CNN as it replayed, every few minutes, the planes crashing into the WTC; and then produced a seemingly unending flow of panels of experts, interviews with victims or their relatives, accounts of heroism and tragedy and projections about who was involved and what would happen next. The same arrangements applied to the period of the War on Terror, only now the events to be represented and analysed were in the future and about to happen. As with all examples of the spectacle, from Roman circuses to the Berlin Olympics and on to *Ben Hur*, identification is, as is the case with a professional wrestling match, straightforward (we know who is good and who is evil) and very much demanded of us (you must take sides; if you are not passionately for us you must be against us). To perform ambivalence, or to caution care and distance, is the equivalent of 'giving comfort to the enemy'. As Judith Butler (2004) wrote regarding the commentary on the war in Afghanistan:

> The Left's response ... ran into serious problems, in part because of the explanations that the Left had provided to the question 'Why do they hate us so much?' were dismissed as so many exonerations of the acts of terror themselves ... moralistic anti-intellectual trends ... produced a situation in which our very

Hysteria, hystericise An intense, over-excited and uncontrollable state of mind brought about by panic and/or an overreaction to events and stimulations, which the subject sees as immediately threatening. The threat is misplaced, or even imaginary, but the response produces a regime of excess and slippages. In Baudrillard, the general condition of media hyperbole.

Go online

Jean Charles de Menezes

capacity to think about the grounds and causes of the current global conflict is considered impermissible. The cry that 'there is no excuse for September 11' has become a means by which to stifle any serious public discussion of how US foreign policy has helped to create a world in which such acts of terror are possible. We see this most dramatically in the suspension of any attempt to offer balanced reporting on the ... conflict, the refusal to include important critiques of the US military effort by Arundhati Roy and Noam Chomsky, for instance, within the mainstream US press. This takes place in tandem with the unprecedented suspension of civil liberties for illegal immigrants and suspected terrorists, and the use of the flag as an ambiguous sign of solidarity with those lost on September 11 and with the current war, as if the sympathy with one translates ... into support for the latter (3).

How and why, then, did the War on Terror play itself out, to some extent? More generally, what are the conditions under which the media spectacle (everything from the moral panic over the corruption of Miley Cyrus and other children to the War on Terror, the Iraq war, September 11, the refugee crisis in Australia and the Tuhoe 'terrorist raids' in New Zealand) ceases to gain and hold our attention, or exercise an influence over subject identification and other forms of behaviour? Media and cultural studies scholars have two generic responses to this question. The first, articulated by the sociologist Manuel Castells (1997a) among others, takes the line that media interactivity and digitalised communication networks are characterised by an 'inclusiveness and comprehensiveness of all cultural expressions'. His point is that the electronically based communication system is potentially 'able to embrace and integrate all forms of expression, as well as a diversity of interests, values, and imaginations' (1997a:374). In other words, it has the potential to function as a genuine public sphere.

There is a second and complementary explanation, derived from the field of cultural studies, which suggests that, contrary to both Debord and the old Frankfurt School ideas about media audiences being passive consumers of cultural texts, viewers and readers are highly literate with regard to, and sceptical about, media extravaganzas, hype, authority, credibility, representations and explanations. The argument runs that, no matter how convincingly texts try to give the impression that they are merely showing what is there (conveying the evident truth), and that they offer an authoritative account of events (you can trust us), media audiences understand that the world is mediated by institutions with their own specific interests, imperatives and biases. Texts—including the various sites of the media-as-spectacle—always reveal their textuality. That is to say, they cannot conceal how what looks like a 'slice of the real' (news footage of a war or a natural disaster) is always a version of the real produced (filmed, read, written, viewed) from a particular perspective. The credibility of the war-on-terror finally ran out, the argument would go, because in the end there were too many loose ends, unconvincing explanations, and unfulfilled expectations arising from the media coverage. In short, audiences were no longer willing to commit to a willing suspension of disbelief.

There is a third and perhaps less attractive version of the cause of the eventual 'failure of spectacle' to be found in the work of Jean Baudrillard. It is predicated on the assumptions that, in emptying out all meaning and significance from the world, and replacing it with a hysteria for the new, the strange, the dramatic and the hyperbolic, spectacle simply:

> exhausts itself in the act of staging ... communication; instead of producing meaning, it exhausts itself in the staging of meaning ... The non-directed interview, speech, listeners who telephone in, participation at all levels ... More and more information is invaded by this sort of phantom content ... Immense energies are deployed in order to keep this simulacra standing upright, and to avoid the brutal ... obvious reality of a radical loss of meaning (Baudrillard 2007:101).

Baudrillard (2007) suggests that audiences seem to 'go along with the game', to continue to accept the myth that the media-as-spectacle does what it claims (they watch, listen, discuss, enjoy or even take it seriously). However:

> One both believes and doesn't believe. The question is simply not posed. 'I know very well, but all the same ...' To the tautology of the system the masses have responded with ambivalence; to dissuasion they have responded with disaffection ... The myth exists, but one must guard against thinking that people believe in it (102).

For Baudrillard, our engagement both with the sites and texts of spectacle, and the subject positions derived from it, are no longer characterised by seriousness or passion, but rather by a sense of the ludic, or play. In other words, while we mimic or perform as if we care about a flood in Bangladesh, the slaughter in Iraq or a sex scandal involving the forced prostitution of migrant women, these stories and images soon give way to other combinations of images and narratives competing for our attention. Baudrillard compares this situation to someone playing a pinball machine:

> The player becomes absorbed in the machine's noise, jolts and flashing lights. He is playing with electricity. As he presses the controls, he has a sense of unleashing impulses and currents through a world of multi-coloured wires as complex as a nervous system. There is in his play an effect of magical participation ... The relation of man to object is strictly magical, which is to say that it is bewitched and manipulatory. This ludic activity may give the appearance of being a passion. But it never is. It is consumption—in this case, abstract manipulation of lights, 'flippers' and electrical reaction time, in other cases, the abstract manipulation of marks of prestige in the variants of fashion. Consumption ... is exclusive of passion (2003:114).

This last explanation is not attractive to many cultural critics and theorists, who are more comfortable with the idea of literate audiences subverting media texts with their sceptical, against-the-grain readings. Baudrillard's explanation has to be taken seriously, however, if only because it offers an account both of how and why the media-as-spectacle manage to do so much dramatically successful work, but also how they eventually lose the attention of their audiences.

Conclusion

In the beginning of this chapter we looked at the idea of the Roman spectacle, with its circuses and military processions, and identified its main feature, which was the authorisation and reiteration of the power and prestige of ruling elites (the Emperor, the aristocracy) by way of the provision of dramatic and extravagant events that entertained and distracted the people. We moved on to look at how Hitler's Germany took this principle and added another dimension: all identity, all consciousness of self and community were now restricted to the site of spectacle, understood as a manifestation of the figure of the Führer and the narratives of the Nazis (Germany's historical destiny; the supremacy of the Aryan race). Our next step was to consider Guy Debord's Marxist account of the media-as-spectacle, which presumes that the functions of the social field—even society itself—have been taken over by the field of the media: the 'between us' of the social is now played out, more or less exclusively, through media simulations, discourses and sites. Our relation to everyday life is mediated by 'an immense accumulation of spectacles … where all attention, all consciousness, converges' (2006:12). The crucial distinction between the Nuremberg rallies and the contemporary spectacle, for Debord, is that the mass media facilitate capitalism and its drive to reduce all activity to forms of commodity consumption. The media provide the sites, technologies and representations through which we engage with, experience and consume the world as a series of commodities. These representations-as-commodities are superior (more dramatic and hyperbolised) to the world, and effectively make it redundant. Media-as-spectacle, in Debord's words 'manifests itself as an enormous positivity, out of reach and beyond dispute. All it says is: "Everything that appears is good; whatever is good will appear"' (2006:15).

Finally, and following Baudrillard, we have suggested that our willing suspension of disbelief regarding the media is at best ambivalent, and in the end events such as the slaughter of the Iraq war is unable to maintain the interest of audiences any more than the 'nothing is happening' of the War on Terror. This is, for Baudrillard (2007), the reality of the 'resistance of the masses' to spectacle (108). To a system that would make everything dramatic, exciting and meaningful, strategic resistance occurs via a kind of boredom on the part of the audience, an eventual refusal of all meaning, all belief, all attention. Spectacle always lives on borrowed time.

In the next chapter, the advent of the network society will be our main focus. This will provide us with an alternative account of the rise and omnipresence of media and information technologies in capitalistic societies, and the forms of economic and social organisation which ensue.

Additional reading

Introductory

Featherstone, M. (1993). *Consumer Culture and Postmodernism.* London: Sage.
    Sociological work on contemporary consumer society and the media.

Schirato, T. and Webb, J. (2004). *Reading the Visual.* Sydney: Allen & Unwin.
    Deals with the relation between visuality, normalisation and spectacle.

Advanced

Baudrillard, J. (2003). *The Consumer Society.* London: Sage.
    Excellent account of logics and practices of consumerism and media culture.

Debord, G. (2006). *The Society of the Spectacle.* New York: Zone Books.
    Influential work on the characteristics of spectacle.

8

NETWORKS AND DATA

Introduction

In chapter 1, we discussed the historical rise of the mass media, and their relation to the development of technologies, democracy and capitalism. In chapter 6 we saw how public debate, public opinion and the public sphere are intertwined with, and dependent upon, media technologies to the extent that the media constitute the public sphere. These discussions are related to the advent of mass media and their constitutive networks as the centrepiece of communication. In this chapter, we discuss the media's relations to the logic of networks. We will show how their recent changes both extend developments that have been unfolding since the Industrial Revolution, and shape an increasing number of daily activities. This chapter takes the logics of network as its focal point. This emphasis reflects one of the most significant and recent developments of the academic field of media studies, in the form of a consideration of systems of connection, database and software, as opposed to the more traditional analysis of media texts in the form of magazines, television programs and films.

We will first discuss the advent of network society and the writings of two key thinkers, Manuel Castells and Armand Mattelart. Both connect network society to historical processes and to major transformations in contemporary culture, despite having contrasting analyses. We will then explore how the transformation of information into digital data facilitates the logics of networks, especially through interface, software and databases. Finally, we will look at how the flow of information through networks operates through mechanisms of navigation, management and control and raise the spectre of surveillance.

The premise of this chapter is that networks and the management of information do not simply extend the life of objects into digital environments, but they also alter their forms and functions. Think, for instance, of the contemporary experience of music. A song encoded in the form of an mp3 file has been rendered into data, and therefore can now be downloaded, uploaded, stored, copied, altered, sampled, remixed and shared. It has changed the structures of the music industry, because access to music does not require a physical support, such as a CD-ROM. Music as data is now increasingly sold and delivered through the Internet. It is also much more susceptible to piracy. This has also changed our relation with, and our experience of, music. The song as data is arguably less about the performance of the musicians, than it is about the malleability and networked potential of the mp3 file.

Similarly, our notion of what a community is has been altered by the constitution of online communities, at least to the extent that individuals and groups connect with each other in instantaneous ways, from remote and distant locations. These developments do not simply improve or facilitate our experiences of music or communities or substitute themselves to the real world; they change them. But the logic of networks has other effects, which we will also discuss. The transformation of information into data has expanded the reaches of control and management of citizens, and produced a more invisible relationship with power and authority. It has also altered our relation with information.

Network society

Go online

Network society

The term **network** describes a system of interconnected machines, computers, means of communication, places and/or people. The term is used to denote a system of remote, channelled, organised, structured, expandable and more or less instantaneous and multidirectional connections. What is most important in a network is the **connectivity**. The information or data that is carried through takes its functions and significance from the fact that it is transported through the network. Instantaneity is of course relative. When railways and telegraph networks were introduced in the nineteenth century, contemporary commentators spoke of the transformation of social life because of the instantaneity of these new means of transport and communication. What these comments reflect is the perception that transport and movement of information change our ways of thinking of ourselves in the world, and in relation to other parts of society and the world. The network connects, but it also produces relations that are not necessarily in the content and form of the information.

One aspect of the logic of the network is to remind us of the network itself. After the events of September 11, which saw the hijacking of four airplanes, the destruction of the World Trade Centre, and substantial damages to the Pentagon, television channels around the world, and especially news channels, made it a

Network A system of interconnected machines, computers, means of communication, places and/or people. The term is used to denote a system of remote, channelled, organised, structured, expandable and more or less instantaneous and multidirectional connections.

Connectivity The means and potential for connections on the communication networks to be implemented and activated.

regular fixture to have a scroll with news headlines, recaps and/or quotations running at the bottom of the frame. The scroll is a longstanding convention of financial news delivery, especially for the stock market. In the aftermath of the terrorist attacks, television channels provided uninterrupted news coverage and in the moment of panic, hysteria (as we discussed in chapter 7), intensity and shock, they responded by escalating the mass of information they delivered to viewers. The frame was consequently divided in different parts, including the scrolling news at the bottom. The scroll has not gone away. It is now a regular fixture of news channels, and is often accompanied with flashing signs ('News Alert', 'Breaking Story'), even though the announcements rarely justify the intrusion on the screen. The point is that no matter how insignificant the information in the scroll, it reminds the viewers of the instantaneous and far-reaching capabilities of the channel. The scroll represents, illustrates and advertises the channel's access to a vast network of information-gathering resources. The scroll is less significant for the content of the news than for what it says about the channel. Networks often function like this: they produce a relation with the activities, reaches and connections above and beyond whatever information and data they carry.

Networks are a major part of our interactions with each other and the world. As we will see later, one of the driving forces in the advent of networks is the circulation of finances. One the most banal yet telling examples of networks is the omnipresence around the world of automated teller machines (ATMs), or bank machines, in front of many banks, inside many commercial and public spaces, and even in mobile and portable units in vehicles. The terminal itself is a node, that is, a device capable of interacting with the network, by sending and receiving information. In this case, it provides access to the global network of banks and financial institutions, without requiring physical access to a bank. An individual card with a strip and a security pin allow for an individual financial transaction.

Until recently, when talking about network in the context of the media, one would have thought about the American use of the term: a television broadcaster with multiple affiliates across the country. This implied a series of contractual agreements between local television stations and parent company, the reliance on programs (especially news items) coming to and from all these affiliates and a strong corporate structure. With the advent of telecommunication satellites, Internet, cell phones and other electronic communication devices, we are much more likely to think of networks as systems of communication that are created because of extensive technological infrastructures (such as undersea cables, satellites, transmission towers and fibre-optics cables).

What characterises contemporary communication networks is that they do not simply carry data and information, but generate their own forms of information and actions. In the stock market crash throughout the world in September and October 2008, the responses of world markets were entirely dependent upon the hyperactive circulation of information about stocks around the world as evidence of trends, forewarnings or aftershocks. When the New Zealand stock market opened on Monday mornings during that period (the first market in the world to open after weekend closures), international news channels, which would normally not carry any news about the New Zealand market, discussed its results and trends. The news channels also engaged in extensive interpretation as to whether the movements on the New Zealand market demonstrated its reaction to the previous Friday's markets that had stayed open after New Zealand's, or whether it announced what would happen later on other international markets. This example demonstrates that the communication networks allow for the circulation of detailed financial information, which in turn makes all financial movements connected to each other. Less evident but just as important, the access to information generates its own forms of responses, interpretation and analysis. The intense scrutiny to all forms of minute financial information exacerbated the sense of crisis. After a few days, expert commentators abandoned making any kind of predictions about the possible return to stability. The intensification of financial information produced a dominant discourse about the scope of the financial crisis, and an accumulation of evidence about its severity. That accumulation produces a new set of responses and reactions, which are entirely predicated upon the instantaneity of the response.

■ Production and circulation of information: Castells

Networks are an integral part of financial and media systems. Two main authors offer us grounding work for this discussion of networks: Manuel Castells and Armand Mattelart. Castells looks at recent developments in networks, especially as they relate to the advent of digital technologies. Castells sees the advent of networks as indicating a major shift from an economic order based on the production of material goods to that of the production and circulation of information (1997a). Mattelart (2000) historicises the development of networks and associates them with the spread of capitalism. He sees continuities between the advent of networks in the late eighteenth century, and the advocacy of globalisation as progress and emancipation. If Mattelart insists on never disconnecting networks from a critique of capitalism, Castells is more sympathetic towards, and positive about, network society.

In *The Rise of the Network Society* (1997a), Castells offers an analysis of networks in the age of the Internet, digital technology and the interdependency of economic interests and corporate structures. Castells describes changes in the last few decades as the advent of an 'information technology revolution', what he also calls **informationalism**, which he sees as starting in the early 1970s. He compares the impact of the current revolution with that of the Industrial Revolution of the eighteenth century, which saw the advent of industries, manufacturing and production, as well as entire economic, social and political structures. He argues that something on a similar scale has happened in the present 'information technology revolution'.

The new economic, social and political system he sees emerging is based on a shift away from manufacturing processes and industry, to the production, management and circulation of information. Castells writes that:

Informationalism The use of processes, technologies and social and administrative structures to facilitate 'the accumulation of knowledge and towards higher levels of complexity in information processing' (Castells 1996:17).

> In the new, informational mode of development, the source of productivity lies in the technology of knowledge generation, information processing, and symbol communication … What is specific to the informational mode of development is the action of knowledge upon knowledge itself as the main source of productivity (1997a:17).

In this new configuration, the driving engine of industry is the development of further information technology in order to generate new connectivities and forms of information-gathering mechanisms, and increase productivity and demand for more information. Information, for Castells, is both the dominant source and outcome of the new economy. Therefore information technology is a means of improving many sectors of industry and social life, but it is also an end in itself. One of the challenges facing Internet commerce, for instance, is the ways in which patterns of behaviour of the customer as they are recorded in databases can be transformed into useful information. Sites such as Amazon and iTunes collect information about browsing and purchase habits, and try to translate individual patterns and choices into suggestions to users. This has lead to increasingly sophisticated ways of analysing the information, and presenting the surfing customer with recommendations for and predictions about purchases. The development of tools to analyse patterns of behavior is one of the most guarded and competitive areas of the information technology industry. This information, in the form of a collected database, is a commodity, which can be used to make further profits, or can be sold to other business interests. One further objective for those companies collecting consumer data is to try to entice the customer into more areas, and find ways to construct increasingly precise profiles and prediction tools.

In addition to this intense focus on the collection and analysis of information, Castells sees the new informationalism as taking place within a global context:

> the activities of production, consumption, and circulation, as well as their components (capital, labor, raw materials, management, information, technology, markets) are organised on a global scale (1997a:66).

Through the availability of communications networks, and especially the Internet, the drive of information industries has to been to increase all forms of connections, and develop ever-expanding dependencies. Both of these characteristics, informationalism and globalisation, have reshaped our economies and redrawn the map of financial, cultural, social and political flows.

■ Informationalism and new developments

Network enterprise
According to Castells, a business structure characterised by the flexibility of its production context: a company might have branches in many parts of the world, but still have a high degree of interdependence.

We have seen the advent of transnational corporations, which Castells calls network enterprises. The **network enterprise** is characterised by the flexibility of its production context: a company might have branches in many parts of the world, but still have a high degree of interdependency. Manufacturing might be performed in one place, development in another, marketing and promotion in a third and distribution somewhere else. Also, the network enterprise relies on an extensive set of alliances around common interests. This means that there might be partnerships driven by shared ownership, or simply through alliances. To return to the ATM machine, banks must collaborate to facilitate the use of their facilities and to share in the profits.

The labour force has been transformed. There has been a shift away from manufacturing to service industries, computing and data jobs and communications.

Many permanent positions are giving way to temporary, project-based and contracted positions. Castells notes that 'the ability to assemble and disperse labor on specific projects and tasks anywhere' (1997a:278) has resulted in 'labor [losing] institutional protection and [becoming] increasingly dependent on individual bargaining conditions in a constantly changing labor market' (278). The idea of organised and unionised labour has given way to individual bargaining and contracts. Contemporary labour is increasingly resembling the precarious conditions of creative industries workers (such as artists, musicians, game developers and independent filmmakers) who trade job security and wealth for cultural capital and lifestyle.

Because of our daily experience of the logic of network, our relation with space and time has changed. Castells sees a rising tension between geographical location, culture and identity, and the production of flows in the global and networked economy. We saw earlier how the 2008 stock market crash unfolded in all parts of the world economy as a linear sequence around the clock, and with no respite and no interruption. Geographical boundaries and datelines were secondary to the 'now' and the ever-present of the financial crisis. These new forms of relation with time and space, Castells argues, have facilitated the development of three new entities.

There are networked global cities 'where corporate headquarters and advanced financial firms can find both the suppliers and the highly skilled, specialized labor they require' (1997:384). Global cities such as Bangkok, New York, London, Tokyo, Los Angeles, Shanghai and Mexico City have transformed and produced themselves as entry points into the networked economy. They are financial, business and cultural centres, which compete, while constructing strong links, with each other. They exist in specific geographical locations, but they are geared towards transnational and transcultural flows.

Furthermore, new industrial spaces, such as the **technopoles** (1997a:390) of Silicon Valley in the USA or Bangalore in India, have become areas of technological and research concentration, often thanks to favorable economic and regulatory policies. Countries strive to participate and enter into the new economy, and construct places with favorable tax policies. This is the case of Dubai Media City in the United Arab Emirates, which was first established with telecommunications infrastructures, including fibre-optics cables, a tax-free policy and with relaxed visa requirements. This has attracted major media companies, such as broadcasters, news agencies, publishers, advertisers, media production companies and other related businesses, and their multinational staff. These technopoles have been strategically constructed as major contributors to network economies and in geographical locations where policies and rules are altered if not suspended (Castells & Hall 1996). These strategic centres attract a new form of labour: highly skilled workers and managers from many parts of the world who accept geographical displacement in exchange for highly paid jobs.

> **Technopole** Area of technological and research concentration, often made possible by favorable economic and regulatory policies.

Consequently, a new 'managerial elite' has emerged (Castells 1997a:415). Its members are mobile, internationally orientated and share in the ethos of connectivity, individuality and enterprise. This elite distinguishes itself by constituting 'symbolically secluded communities', and by '[creating] a lifestyle and to design spatial forms aimed at unifying the symbolic environment of the elite around the world, thus superseding the historical specificity of each locale' (1997a: 416–17). Castells sees this elite as sharing an increasingly homogeneous set of values and lifestyle expectations. This social group's defining characteristics and ethos are those contributing to the development of informational society: flexibility, technological and informational literacies, and adaptability.

The advent of the information revolution is not a break from capitalism, the driving economic philosophy of the Western world since the advent of the Industrial Revolution. Rather, it announces a new stage of capitalism, where information has become the source of economic production, exchange and consumption. It is sometimes hard to tell whether Castells is describing the information society as something that has already been achieved, or whether it is in the process of actualising itself. In any case, his analysis provides one of the most sophisticated ways of understanding the impact of networks.

■ Mattelart's historical accounts of networks

Another key author who has written about networks is Armand Mattelart. In *Networking the World: 1794–2000* (2000), Mattelart uses the term network, as signifying a logic of communication, transport and control that took hold of many countries in the nineteenth century. Mattelart sees in the advent of the French Revolution the spread of ideals of the Enlightenment (including knowledge, democracy, science and universal principles), and free-market capitalism, as attempts at establishing a new world order. The creation of commerce and trade between countries, standardisation of technological and industrial practices, the rapid spread of the telegraph, electricity and railways, all generated systems of interdependencies which have provided the foundations of today's electronic and media networks. These interdependencies extended to the field of economics, with the advent of international credit, banks and financial institutions. What made these developments potent, and their transformation into deeply entrenched ideological principles, are their justifications in terms of utopian desires to overcome conflicts and exploitation.

Mattelart sees, in the egalitarian aspirations of the late-nineteenth century, the ambition to create a sense of transnational connection. The advocates of global and universal networks, such as Saint-Simon, argued that the idealistic principles of progress and peace through commerce and exchanges could be achieved by creating strong economic and communication networks across borders (2000:15). The development of networks is therefore not solely the outcome of technological innovation, but is also the materialisation of aspirations, of beliefs and of an ideology of progress, which would see its actualisation in the creation of universal social bonds. As Mattelart states:

> The communication network is an eternal promise symbolizing a world that is better because it is united. From road and rail to information highways, this belief has been revived with each technological generation, yet networks have never ceased to be at the center of struggles for control in the world (2000:viii).

For Mattelart the necessity to study and understand the history of networks is linked to the analysis of the principles and beliefs underlying their developments.

What Armand Mattelart teaches us is that there is history in the ideologising of communication technology and social change:

> Numerous public and private actors have played a part in shaping the topography of networks and systems on a global scale. They have done so in the name of a wide variety of ideals and have been motivated by a broad range of interests: the universalism of a predestined civilisation, the ecumenism of a religion, the interdependency of nations based on mutual security, the pragmatism of the corporation, or the categorical imperatives of the international division of labour, or the community of struggle against oppression. Networks, a leading symbol of progress, have also made their incursion into utopian thinking. The communication network is an eternal promise symbolizing a world that is better because it is united (2000:vii–viii).

This, he argues, remains true today. Contrary to Castells, Mattelart sees the current developments of digital networks as an extension of these idealistic principles of eighteenth- and nineteenth-century revolutionaries. The difference, and this is a major departure, is that the search for universalism as a form of social reconciliation and harmony has been transformed into a means of maintaining capitalism's constant search for new forms of industry and profit: 'The ideal of the universalism of values promoted by the great social utopias drifted into the corporate techno-utopia of globalization' (2000:120). For Mattelart, the egalitarian underpinnings of the logics of network, the aspirations of universal cooperation, bonds and interdependencies, have been recuperated by the anonymous and invisible transnational corporations that have tried to take control of the networks. The effect is the marginalisation of those who do not have access to the networks, in the form of what is the called the **digital divide** (see chapter 1).

Digital divide The technological inequalities between those who can and those who cannot afford computer technologies (hardware and software) and broadband access.

As a conclusion to this section, here are some means of characterising networks. These points do not summarise Mattelart and Castells nor try to reconcile their positions. They are, however, a useful reminder of the central points and issues. Networks are automotised, far-reaching, expandable and multidirectional series of connections. Networks exist as a logic, in the sense that they can perform function without direct human interventions. They may have localised entries through terminals or nodes, but their power relies on the possibility of their vast systems of connections, some of them self-generated. Networks shape social relations and our relation with information, even if no communication takes place. They provide 'a constant illusion of a between us … The certainty of communication may, ultimately, be sufficient in itself' (Lefort 1986:228). Networks are expressions of administrative organisations that are related to corporate structures. They lead to the creation of systems of economic interdependencies. They also provide the impetus for the development of global corporations and cities, and the rise of an economic elite. The resulting economic structures have altered the nature of labour. Networks can be expanded and they also drive to a high degree of technological convergence (the hardware and software compatibility of new technologies). Finally, networks are driven by a universalising logic that finds its origins in the utopian program of late eighteenth-century revolutions.

Interfaces, databases and software

Go online

Interfaces, databases
and software

Interface A point of connection between two distinct components of a communication process. This can be a user accessing a network through a computer terminal.

Database Information, facts and details that are collected and stored on a computer system. It is accessible, and can retrieve and organise information using programmed commands.

Software The programming that enables a person to control the operations of a computer, as opposed to hardware, which is the machine being programmed. By extension, the means by which actions and information can circulate and be translated in a simple and immediate way.

Binary code A coding system that translates information and instructions with two possible values. The Morse code is a binary code using dots and dashes. Computing uses a two-digit number system (0 and 1) which controls processors.

As we saw earlier, the ATM terminal provides one of the most common interactions with financial networks for an individual from a networked country. The network is omnipresent. It is characterised by its wide reach, both in terms of geographical spaces and its potential to service multiple customers. It does not require any form of interaction with another human being, yet it behaves as an interlocutor who responds to (simple) questions and requests. To the customer, the location and origins of the information is much less important than the ability to access money. The interaction with the ATM machine illustrates some of the key characteristics of our relation with networks. They require some form of **interface**, here in the form of a terminal or node, with a screen and touchpad. It provides access to a **database** which keeps track of personal details such as balance, overdraft and credit facilities, and can respond to requests and keeps records of our actions. The database in itself is not money, but rather the electronic and codified trace and record of transactions. No bank holds our money somewhere safely in a vault. The data adding and subtracting monetary values going in and out of the account is where, or rather how, our financial worth resides. It has no material existence. The access to database is of course limited to information that relates to the identified customer, who identifies himself or herself with a card and a password. However, the network does not know who the customer is, apart form the fact that he or she has a card and a password that the database recognises. All of this is based on our acceptance and dependence of the principles of networks: it is a logic of relation and connectivity rather than one of material objects and subjects.

What renders the interaction with the ATM possible is **software**. Software is the means by which actions and information can circulate and be translated in a simple and immediate way. Software is a form of automative and computing programming that is used to perform anything from simple tasks to extremely complex ones. At the basis of all computers and microchips, there is a **binary code** (a series of 0s and 1s) in which all information is encoded. The software makes the hardware perform calculations in order to do anything from constructing a three-dimensional figure and animating it, to translating music into a mp3 file. In the case of the ATM, software translates requests into the semblance of control of a personal account, and delivers cash out of the machine. This one is rather simple in its use, but that is precisely what makes the ATM such a ubiquitous machine. It was, after all, one of the earliest computing machines made available for everyday use (the first ATM was installed in 1967).

Software controls and translates the information contained in the database. As Lev Manovich (2002) suggests, the management and use of database is one of the more useful analogies for considering how subjectivity, information and power are articulated in contemporary culture. In *The Language of New Media* (2002), Lev Manovich identifies five key characteristics of media information in the digital environment. They are numerical representation; modularity; automation; variability; and transcoding. He uses the analysis of these five characteristics to extrapolate and analyse the status of media objects and information.

1 *Numerical representation implies that all information can be stored as binary code* 'using a mathematical function' (27). A picture, for instance, can be transformed or produced by dividing the space of the frame into a grid of singular points, called **pixels**. Each pixel can take on a different color based on the numerical value it has been assigned. The more precise the picture, the more pixels in the frame, and the more numerical values can be assigned to each pixel. This applies to all forms of information and the consequence of this is that 'media becomes programmable', and can be altered (27). The effects of this can be uncanny. At the end of Michael Jackson's video 'Black or White', a continuous series of morphing images translate the faces of people of different genders, ages, and ethnicities in a seamlessly and ever-changing human face. This is less remarkable for the rather simplistic message of universal understanding and connection, than it is for the technology's ability to erase differences we assume intractable. In other words, the malleability of digital technology challenges us to rethink what we assume are stable categories.

2 **Modularity** *signifies that a media object made of distinct elements can allow for all these objects to be altered and controlled separately.* Manovich gives the example of an Internet page that combines text, graphics, pictures and animation (31). Not only can all these elements be controlled separately, but they can be located and stored in different places. This is why, for instance, blogs can contain Youtube videos or any other media that can be embedded in the page.

3 **Automation** *is the consequence of numerical coding and modulation.* A media object can be transformed by the automised functions of software in ways which do not require intervention or choice. At the most basic level, Microsoft Word allows users to use templates to present their information without having to decide each of the individual components on the page, such as margins, indentations, font sizes and titles (32). In a more much more sophisticated way, this is what special effects can do for filmmaking and computer games. Peter Jackson's Weta Digital has created a piece of software called Massive, which can generate crowds in a shot and produce the move of each of the crowd members, without programmers having to manipulate each one of the characters.

4 *Variability reflects the fact that once the information has been stored in a database, it can be presented, exported and organised in a multiplicity of ways.* A digital image can be automatically adjusted to fit the context into which it can be exported. For instance, an image can be automatically transformed into an icon, which makes the image discernible without opening the full-size file and launching a viewing application, or automatically resized to be posted on a website. Manovich extrapolates from the variability of media objects by equating their capacities with the logic of postindustrial society (what Castells would have called the 'information society'):

> The principle of variability exemplifies how, historically, changes in media technologies are correlated with social change. If the logic of old media corresponded to the logic of industrial mass society, the logic of new media fits the logic of the postindustrial society, which values individuality over conformity (41).

Pixel Every digital image is rendered on a two-dimensional grid made of individual points called pixels. The more precise the picture, the more pixels in the frame, and the more numerical values can be assigned to each pixel.

Modularity A media object made of distinct elements can allow for all these objects to be altered and controlled separately.

Automation The way in which a media object can be transformed by the automised functions of software in ways which do not require intervention or choice.

5 **Transcoding** *refers to the fact that when information is stored in digital form (such as an image translated in the computer's memory as binary code), it takes on characteristics that originate from the computer.* In some cases this is intended, such as in the production of house music, when an original song can be layered with beats and samples from other songs and remixed, and becomes something that keeps the feel and the sound of computerised and digitally altered music. In the Michael Jackson video we mentioned above, we know that the morphing of human faces is the product of digital technologies; the enchantment, which results from the experience of seeing this sequence, is related to our knowing it is technologically produced, not that it could 'really' happen. But Manovich goes further: it is not simply a tool in the arsenal of musicians, or special effects specialists. It radically alters the nature of media itself.

Transcoding The fact that when information is stored in digital form (such as an image translated in the computer's memory as binary code), it takes on characteristics that originate from the computer.

The implications of Manovich's ideas about digital information and data complement our previous discussion of networks. While networks are systems of flexible connectivity, digital data allow for a wide range of information to be shared, altered, transformed and, ultimately, not be bound to location. In the remaining section of this chapter, we discuss specific but contrasting implications of the development of network society and the role of data and software. First we will look at the navigational and management logic of data management. Second, we will discuss the tensions between the potential mobility and the ever-present surveillance.

Go online

Navigation, control and surveillance

Navigation, control and surveillance

■ Navigation

As we saw from Lev Manovich's analysis of digital culture, media objects have a capacity to be altered, reshaped, and re-formed. When interacting with networks, this means that information can be transmitted and can travel, and be stored and shared, in many different ways. Computer, network and Internet users have had to acquire skills and literacies in order to navigate the digital environment. One of the most common terms to provide an analogy for the interaction with the Internet is **surfing**. The implications are that following hyperlinks through web pages is a form of recreational activity with neither economically productive objective nor preconceived itinerary. It emphasises the randomness of following links as they appear on pages. Surfing also suggests the experience of pleasure, immersion and absorption. Therefore the emphasis is on the experience, rather than the outcomes or the logic of the connections. Other terms that have been used include **browsing**, with its reference to the randomness and focus of the consumer casually exploring shops. The analogy has extended to an emblematic figure of the nineteenth-century, the flâneur (Manovich 2002:268–74; Friedberg 1993). The flâneur is an urban explorer and meanderer whose walk through the city, its streets, its shops and its back alleys constitutes a form of sensory immersion

Surfing the Internet, or web surfing Navigating the Internet by following the hyperlinks through web pages. Often considered a form of recreational activity with neither economically productive objective nor preconceived itinerary.

Browsing the Internet Navigating the Internet in the way a consumer casually explores shops.

in the logic consumer culture even if the flâneur does not see him- or herself as a direct participant. The city is rendered as a spectacle, with its activities, spaces, movements, and individuals and crowds on display for the observer. Manovich and others (2002:271) equate the activities of the **flâneur** with that of the surfer and the computer game player, because of his or her ability to transform the interface into an immersive and subjective encounter. The experience of digital space and architecture is seemingly open to and available for exploration: 'the virtual flâneur is happiest on the move, clicking from one object to another, traversing room after room, level after level, data volume after data volume' (274). For Manovich, this makes the experience enriching, subjective and empowering.

> **Flâneur** An urban explorer and meanderer whose walk through a city, its streets, its shops, and its back alleys, constitutes a form of sensory immersion in the logic of consumer culture. The flâneur does not see himself or herself as a direct participant.

■ Navigation and the performance of the self

The ubiquity of the network and the digital interface has generated new forms of communication and social practices. The feeling, potential and availability of connectivity is an experience and expectation of networked societies. Many people in industrialised countries, especially teenagers and young adults, engage in communication and exchanges in a variety of ways. These include emailing; text messaging while going about everyday activities; participating in online social networks such as Myspace, Bebo and Facebook; online chatting through messaging services such as Yahoo or MSN; blogging about one's personal life or interests; and micro-blogging with services such as Twitter. Contacts and exchanges are made through a series of conventions and codes that require literacies and an understanding of the terms of communication. For instance, knowing the difference between Myspace and Facebook or Bebo (many have profiles on two of these but for different reasons) constitutes one of these literacies. Myspace tends to be a more public space—a promotional space for musicians, for instance—whereas either Facebook or Bebo invite closer connections with people the user is likely to know.

As we stated earlier, and especially in chapter 8, communication and connectivity are important for the presentation and production of the self. In a context in which participation in communication is a social expectation, the performance of the self on the network is both the motivation to participate, and the outcome. Social networks do not substitute themselves for other forms of social connections. Rather, they intensify the need and/or requirement to perform, and to engage the self in networks. This engagement might be done on a voluntary basis; but as we saw earlier, it also corresponds to the requirement of informationalism and the new economy, and the logic of the spectacle.

■ Navigation as management of data

The possibility of navigating, communicating and storing information has required networked individuals to become managers of their data banks, which contain music, pictures, films, spreadsheets, texts, addresses and messages. This implies that users must store data on their computers or external drive. Computer software provides the means of performing such tasks. An operating system such as Mac OS X or Windows is a means of visualising the user's intersection with the hardware and the data. One of the best-known softwares that works as a management program is iTunes. It provides an interface with one's music and video library, allows for the construction of playlists, can automatically generate lists from one's library, can extract music from CD ROMs, burn CDs, play radio stations available on the internet, give access to podcasts, and extend to a music, film and television store. Of course the data management functions of iTunes are tied to commercial extensions (the online purchase of music) and the interdependence and convergence of hardware in the form of iPods or iPhones. In this and other contexts, the user can rely on software to organise material, or on the operating system to place the file in a pre-selected folder on the hard drive ('My files' and 'My pictures' on a PC, for instance). Many users like, and even enjoy, the capacity to manage their data, and to collect, search and store files.

Digital archiving The storage and preservation of material in digital form.

Despite the impression that digitised data can survive indefinitely, **digital archiving** is becoming a significant issue. Data might not physically deteriorate the way a book might, but it can be lost, damaged, filed in a way which makes it impossible to find, rendered obsolete or incompatible with new operating systems and, for public institutions and businesses, bare no trace of copyright and ownership and therefore be rendered unusable. All forms of data collection and management imply a form of control. Even iTunes, has many in-built limitations to ensure copyright protection. A playlist from another user on a local network might be visible on iTunes and be played by multiple users, but the mp3 files themselves cannot be downloaded onto other users' hard drives. Similarly, iPods are designed so that no music files can be extracted and downloaded onto a computer. These examples demonstrate that, as much as the interface with data and the network encourages some forms of individual choices and management, the network and computing capacities are subjected to control.

■ Control

Despite the image of the navigation of the network as surfing or flânerie, as spaces of communication or as data management processes, networks are subjected to a substantial degree of control. This might be in the forms of commercial and proprietary limitations and political censorship. We will focus on three issues: copyright, censorship and network neutrality.

■ Copyright

Go online

Copyright

We saw that iTunes encourages individual management, collecting and organisation of music. But the activities are not without some forms of limitation. Users can purchase music, films and televisions programs in the iTunes store. To prevent unlimited circulation of copyright material, Apple inserts a digital rights management (DRM) function in all its purchased files. This means that the file can be shared with a limited number of computers. Such copyright systems apply to other online rental and sales services, such as movies. As of mid-2009, Apple has decided to remove its DRM system from purchased music, and allow for sharing of these files. Apple has been compelled to do this because other competitors, such as Amazon, are selling music without copy protection. The challenge is that artists and musicians expect, rightfully, to get some financial returns from their creative labour. This is increasingly difficult, especially since the advent of peer-to-peer networks (p2p) and file sharing (such as Limewire, Gnutella and Freenet), where large amounts of copyrighted material is made freely accessible from one user's hard drive to another. The result has been increasing pressures on internet service providers (ISPs) to police their customers' access to p2p networks, and for media companies to enforce copyrights strictly. This has been the case recently of Google after it purchased YouTube. The company was compelled by major film studios and television networks and music companies to look for, and remove, material that breached copyright.

Conversely, as copyright practices are restricting the use of media material, Creative Commons, a non-profit organisation dedicated to expanding the use of media content, is organising support and providing the legal framework for making material available in the public domain. Creative Commons' licences make it possible for media producers to waive their proprietary rights allowing other creators to access and use their material.

Censorship is the most obvious form of control of networks. It might take the form of an office network or intranet making access to websites impossible. Some of the most commonly blocked websites are online auction facilities (for instance, Trademe.co.nz). But this can extend further to the systematic filtering and blockage of information circulating on the Internet at the scale of an entire country. China is the most obvious example. Censorship is applied to external sites with information that is deemed against the national interest, and to local postings on blogs and chat rooms (see chapter 6).

Western countries can often be complacent about access to the Internet, especially since their citizens would never imagine that political censorship would be applied. However, another form of control of the Internet has been the object of much debate. Proponents of unimpeded access to Internet have been advocating for the policy and legal recognition of the principle of **network neutrality**. This has been especially true in North America, but has implications in other parts of the world. In the last few years, large telecommunications companies have argued that they should be allowed to sell preferential access and speed to the Internet to clients willing to purchase those. Proponents of network neutrality insist that there should be no distinction in terms of treatment of customers while companies want to be able to package and provide differential services. Those who defend the principle of network neutrality insist on the public nature of Internet access and communication.

■ Surveillance

Networks and data are not simply potentially or actually subjected to some form of control. The ubiquity of networks, and the capacity for information for being intercepted and analysed, raises the prospect of surveillance. We discussed surveillance extensively in chapters 3 and 7. In this section, we want to look at its implications in the context of networks. **Surveillance** is the process by which data and information are potentially systematically collected, and later used for policing, commercial, censorship and/or harassment purposes. When browsing

Go online

Censorship

Network neutrality
The principle, currently under debate in many parts of the world, that would guarantee, if it became regulation, that broadband networks do not favour or use the control of information flow as a means of discriminating between service subscribers.

Go online

Surveillance

Surveillance A technological, architectural and political form of observation and monitoring of people and their activities in public spaces, on the Internet and/or through the accumulation of information.

the Internet for instance, sites people visit, searches they perform and forms they fill in can be, and often are collected. The recording of activity does not simply take place on the user's computer, but can be done by external sites. As we saw earlier, this information is important in developing knowledge of consumer habits, and can be sold as a commodity to other commercial interests. With the prospect of other forms of activities, such as credit card purchases, library loans, banking transactions and participation in social networking being centrally collected, stored and analysed, Internet users leave behind them a very substantial **digital footprint**. Often they do this consciously by filling out forms, signing up for services or by leaving names and passwords. They do this with the misconceived expectation that nobody is entitled to track our activities. The New Zealand Privacy Commissioner website provides a list of some of the means of recording which might take place:

Your browser sends information as part of its request for a web page. Details sent include the web page you arrive from, the web page you request, the IP address your ISP gives your PC, the name and version of your browser, and the software that runs your PC.

Web bugs, third party advertising and cookies add to this data.

Web bugs (in web pages) can track the pages on a website that you request.

Advertisers can track you if web pages you request contain their advertisements.

A cookie sent by a website and stored by your web browser can identify the PC and browser in the future.

Cookies can show if you have visited before.

Cookies can store personal information e.g. your name, address and other identifying information.

If you give information that identifies you to a website, a cookie can identify you in the future.

Bugs, advertisements and cookies can track you across more than one website.

When searching a website, the search terms you submit are collected.

Search websites, such as Google, also collect search terms. They may also set cookies and collect data about search results and advertisements clicked on by users.

Websites may ask that you create an account with a username and password. They may ask that you provide an email address for further contact. A username and password, or an email address may not identify you, but allows the site to recognise you and to track your browsing habits (New Zealand Privacy Commissioner 2009).

Internet sites and businesses declare that they enforce strong privacy protection policies and systems. However, slippages happen, sometimes on a major scale, such as when American Online, a global Internet company, accidentally released a compressed text file containing the results of over 20 million searches of site that were performed by 650 000 users. By looking at search fields, many of these users were identified and details of their private lives revealed publicly. The simple fact that such material can be collected and later used has been a major source of legal debate. Despite the fact that Google successfully resisted providing data from its search engine after it had been subpoenaed by the American Department of Justice, there are fears that third parties (such as government, police, corporations and other groups) will find ways to access this information. Google itself has been extensively implicated in methods of surveillance and control, especially because of its collaboration with the Chinese government's censorship of the Internet.

In a context in which governments have already rendered modes of surveillance a matter of daily life (including closed captioned television monitoring—CCTV— in public spaces), and have used the threat of terrorism as a means of reducing civil liberties, there is much concern about how digital footprints will be collected and used in the future. What we know for sure is that any attempt at collecting data ultimately results in abuse. This has been the case with the *Patriot Act* in the USA, and anti-terrorism legislation implemented after September 11, which gave the FBI and CIA extended surveillance powers. Despite the fact that this was a clear breach of the law, extensive numbers of phone conversations and electronic communications performed by American citizens, including journalists, intellectuals and academics, have been collected. In New Zealand, anti-terrorism legislation has seen the police spy on organisations such as Greenpeace (the only group victim of a terrorist attack in New Zealand and performed French government's spies in 1985) and the Green Party, when clearly there could be no justification for such activities. With the reality of much of our network activities being monitored, we face the constant prospect of surveillance; moreover, the prospect of being observed acts, as we saw in chapter 8, as a self-deterrent and as a self-monitoring mechanism.

Conclusion

In this chapter we discussed one of the most common and invisible forms of media: the network. We tend to think of media technologies as those bringing television programs, movies and music. However, a substantial part of our lives are spent connecting, communicating and responding to information transferred through communication networks such as computers and phone. We saw that the rise of network society is the outcome of historical processes that have transformed modern capitalistic societies into post-industrial societies driven by the production and circulation of information. In the next chapter, we will see how these developments have lead to new forms of literacies, which constitute requirements to work, play and communicate with each other, but are also foundations for the critical engagement with the media.

Additional reading

Introductory

Barney, D. (2004). *The Network Society*. Cambridge: Polity Press.
   An introduction to the impact of networks on all aspects of society, including technology, economics, politics and identity.

Mattelart, A. (2000). *Networking the World: 1794–2000*. (L. Carey-Libbrecht and J. Cohen trans.) Minneapolis: University of Minnesota Press.
   Provides an historical, sociological and critical analysis of the interaction of communication technology, capitalism and culture.

Advanced

Castells, M. (1997a). *The Rise of the Network Society*. Oxford: Blackwell.
   A detailed study of the advent of informationalism, networks and new forms of economic, social and corporate structures.

Manovich, L. (2002). *The Language of New Media*. Cambridge: MIT Press.
   This books reflects on the transformations of information and moving image culture brought about by digital technologies.

MEDIA LITERACY AND EVERYDAY LIFE

Introduction

The notion and significance of media literacies needs to be related to, and contextualised in terms of, the various technological, social, political, economic and cultural changes that have been occurring since the 1980s. Manuel Castells, in *The Informational City* (1989), elaborates on the nature of these changes. He refers to 'a historically situated complex of transformations that concerns, simultaneously, capitalism as a social system, informationalism as a mode of development, and information technology as a powerful working instrument' (1989:3). The main characteristics of these economic, cultural, social and technological changes have been identified by Castells (1997a) as: globalisation of the economy, production and finance; the emergence and diffusion of new information technologies; the growth of the 'knowledge economy'; a shift away from production of goods to services delivery; the globalisation of the media; the erosion of national sovereignty, for instance, with regard to the ability to control information flows across national borders; and the internationalisation of culture.

There is a line of argument that suggests that these changes are so radical and pervasive that they have produced a kind of 'crisis of literacy' in Western culture.

Allen Luke and Pam Gilbert (1993) argue that:

> There is indeed an educational 'crisis' in literacy in Western nation-states. But it is not the crisis over allegedly declining standards and skill-levels heralded in the press. Nor is it the crisis over which pedagogical approach to literacy is the most efficient or correct. These ... debates are but symptomatic of a larger concern: the reorganization and control of the modes of information and representation in what some have called 'late capitalist' societies (1).

Some of the consequences of this crisis have been in the progressive displacement of familiar and everyday activities into the context of networks, and especially the Internet. What would have been called customer service, for example, has been displaced back onto the customer, and people now have to acquire new skills to engage with networked services. The most obvious example of how this displacement has required major individual adjustments is at the level of interaction with technology. Financial transactions that used to be performed between a bank teller and a customer have moved to the realm of Internet banking. Consequently, bank branches have disappeared from many neighbourhoods and towns. For many people this is a practical, useful, flexible way of controlling and managing their accounts. But for many who are not familiar with the technology, this constitutes a major obstacle that points out their lack of skills and literacies, and isolates them from the flow of information. Such forms of marginalisation take place at levels of groups and communities, but also between countries.

This chapter takes these processes and changes as the departure point and context for a consideration of three important interrelated questions. First, what do or can we mean when we extend the notion of literacy outside its popular or conventional meaning (that is, as a reference to the ability to read and write), and use it with regard to the field, texts and practices of the media? Second, what is it about the place and function of the media in the contemporary world that requires us (say, as citizens, educators or audiences) to be media literate? Third, what changes are occurring within that field to which we particularly need to attend?

Go online

Cultural and media literacy

Cultural and media literacy

Every day we experience a flow of images and information—via television, newspapers, radio, film, computers and digital technology—that is far greater than was the case a generation ago. Moreover, the ubiquitous and seemingly uninterruptible nature of this flow means that most, if not all, cultural fields are consistently in communication with, influenced by, and exposed to, the media. Regardless of the field or fields to which we belong, we are required to negotiate, and be literate with regard to, different technologies, genres, discourses and modalities; and be able to read, relate and contextualise visual images and other media texts. In other words, we are required to possess a wide cultural literacy.

Cultural literacy can be defined as a familiarity with, and an ability to read and make use of, the meaning systems and their concomitant practices, technologies

> **Cultural literacy** A familiarity with, and an ability to read and make use of, the various meaning systems that characterise the cultural fields of a society.

and social relations that characterise a society and its cultures. Media literacy, by extension, refers to the meaning systems and practices specific to, or associated with, the field of the media. This seems a straightforward enough definition, seemingly in keeping with the account of **media literacy** found in textbooks such as W. James Potter's *Media Literacy*. He defines media literacy as:

> a perspective that we actually use when exposing ourselves to the media in order to interpret the meaning of the messages we encounter. We build our perspective from knowledge structures. To build our knowledge structures, we need tools and raw materials. The tools are skills. Active use means that we are aware of the message and are consciously interacting with them (2001:4).

Media literacy Extends the conventional meaning of literacy (the ability to read and write) to the field, texts and practices of the media. It refers to the ability to read and make use of the meaning systems and practices specific to the media.

There are, however, three important differences that distinguish how we understand media literacy from Potter's perspective. We will use this chapter to qualify this definition and offer alternative considerations. Our position is guided by the premise that media literacy is not simply a matter of learning better and new skills, something that is implied in Potter's definition.

First, Potter's definition misses out the crucial point that what constitutes knowledge and understanding is not an individual or personalised process, but rather something effectively based on, and determined by, our specific cultural affiliations and contexts. In other words, Potter's definition presumes that the viewer is an individual making individual readings and decisions: we sit in front of the television watching the news, exposed to images and words, and what happens is just 'between us' (the viewer and television story). But as Bourdieu (2000) writes, everything we think and see and do comes about because we are 'open to the world, and therefore exposed to the world, shaped by the material and cultural conditions of existence … with the singularity of the "self" being fashioned in and by social relations' (133–4). As we saw in chapter 3, subjectivity is increasingly created, maintained and authorised via our relation with the media. What we do with the media is not simply a matter of self-possessed awareness.

This leads to our second qualification of Potter's definition. Our engagement with the media is not simply in the terms of decoding messages. There are of course codes, discourses, genres, modes of address, conventions and structures of signification that qualify the ways in which we make sense of the media. We discussed many of these in chapter 2. However, as we have seen throughout this book, and especially in relation to discussions of spectacle, public sphere and networks, the media do not address us as if we were autonomous and free agents. We do not simply interpret messages: our relation with the media involves activities, time and emotions. Our relations are always qualified by what the media want from us, and what we want from them (or what we think we want from them). There is an economy at play in our daily use, immersion, affective connection and playful encounters with technology. This economy involves complex literacies. We will discuss this economy in relation to the tension between media, work and play.

Our third point of difference with Potter's definition is that individual cultural fields not only dispose subjects to see things in a particular way, but they also close down the possibility of seeing otherwise. So if we are watching television, the images and words that are presented to us are not simply available to be decoded providing we have access to the appropriate cues (violins denoting sadness, piccolos indicating the comic or the quirky). Rather, we see and respond to cues, signs and stories in terms of what we know, what we expect and what we are familiar with. If a culture has consistently represented a set of signs or markers (such as skin colour, nationality, religion and dress) as commensurate with, say, terrorism, then it is very difficult for media audiences to see and understand that group of people sympathetically, or to have any empathy with their situation. A telling example of this can be found in a documentary called *One Land Two People* (Royal 1996). The film focuses on a Treaty of Waitangi claim for a piece of land that had been dispossessed from Māori and had been in the hands of Pākehā (non-Māori New Zealanders) for several generations. When contemplating the fact that the local inhabitants of European descent had been unaware of the deep sense of grievance and pain in the local indigenous population, the voiceover concedes that it is not that the white population did not pay attention to this, but rather that they could not see. The sense of pain and loss experienced by Māori just could not be registered by Pākehā.

What is missing in Potter's definition is what Bourdieu calls **disposition**, the forms of understanding and conceptualisation that are produced by authorised practices and perceptions. In Bourdieu's (1990) terms these are:

Disposition
Forms of understanding, conceptualisation and behaviour that we are inclined towards, as a result of our habitus and membership of a field. Dispositions are forms of literacy.

> structured structures predisposed to function as structuring structures, that is, principles which generate and organise practices and representations that can be objectively adapted to their outcomes without presupposing a conscious aiming at ends or an express mastery of the operations necessary in order to attain them (53).

Dispositions are forms of literacy. They frame our understanding, naturalise our beliefs and at times conceal the obvious, but they also give us the tools to negotiate the relation between the everyday and the media. In the last section of this chapter, we will look at the politics of the relation between the everyday and the media.

How can we apply the notion of cultural literacy to the field of the media? First, the media can be considered as a cultural field (see chapters 2 and 4): they have their own discourses, imperatives, values, logics, technologies and forms of cultural capital that influence and dispose the practices of subjects within the field. They also have specific relationships with, or are influenced by, other fields (such as government policies and regulations or the workings of the stock exchange). This is where we differ from media theorists such as Marshall McLuhan and Neil Postman, who presume that the media are relatively autonomous. We insist that the texts, images and meanings that are disseminated by the media are always tied up with, and influenced by, the wider world and its configurations of power and influence.

It is particularly important, when considering the issue of media literacy, to appreciate that the question of technology needs to be contextualised in these wider social, cultural and political contexts. One of Marshall McLuhan's legacies, for instance, has been a disproportionate weight given (within media theory) to 'the properties of and actions exerted upon ourselves by technologies and media and artefacts' (McLuhan & McLuhan 1988:98). For McLuhan, the question of the relationship between media, meaning and technology is largely a technical and an empirical, rather than a political, issue. Even acute theorists such as Neil Postman fall into the trap of explaining the poverty or inadequacy of the media (for instance, its lack of competent analysis of newsworthy and socially and politically relevant events) in terms of the limitations of (predominantly visual) technologies. Postman (1998) writes, for instance, that:

> The whole problem with news on television comes down to this: all the words uttered in an hour of news coverage could be printed on one page of a newspaper. Of course, there is a compensation: television offers pictures, and the pictures move ... But the language of pictures differs radically from oral and written language, and the differences are crucial for understanding television news. To begin with, the grammar of pictures is weak in communicating past-ness and present-ness ... Without the help of the written word, film and video cannot portray temporal dimensions with any precision (72–3).

What distinguishes Bourdieu from Postman is that for Bourdieu 'Technologies are socially shaped along with their meanings, functions, and domains and uses' (Sterne 2003:373).

When we are considering media technologies and their uses, we need to understand the cultural politics that underpin the apparently easy and pervasive assimilation and naturalisation of media technologies with regard to everyday life. Castells argues (1997a) that the advent of the network society has transformed the economy, the workplace and the forms of social interaction. He also suggests that it has changed the forms of actions and types of engagement of individuals. In other words, the transformation of society by the media and their networks and technologies has, at the same time, brought about a transformation of subjects.

The economy of media, work and play

This transformation of subjects does not originate simply from the way we receive media messages (one of our objections to Potter's definition). It starts from the exchange that constantly takes place between our attention, technology and activities. This is what we call an economy, an interconnected loop between what technologies do to us and what we do to them. When we walk, go for a run or take the bus, we often also take our iPod (or another mp3 player); we do not just walk or run or sit in the bus. Work similarly is closely connected with media. Many jobs include working with a computer, and many of us effortlessly sneak in checking Facebook or Bebo, or fantasy ice hockey results, into our daily work routines: we do not just work at work, we also play.

Go online

The economy of media, work and play

But whether working or playing, what we do above all else, is communicate:

> Communication now occupies a central place in strategies whose object is to restructure our societies. Via electronic technologies, it is one of the master instruments in the conversion of the major industrialised countries. It accompanies the redeployment of powers (and counterpowers) in the home, the school, the factory, the office, the hospital, the neighborhood, the region, and the nation. And beyond this, it has become a key element in the internationalization of economies and cultures. It has thus become a stake in the relations between peoples, between nations, and between blocs (Mattelart & Mattelart 1992:xii).

Media technologies enable and direct our communication practices, and in doing so they facilitate both our participation in social and personal life and in politics, and the dissemination of knowledge and information. Particularly new media technologies, such as the Internet or mobile technologies (bluetooth, mp3s and other wireless and portable technologies), have become integral to our lifestyles, and to the ways in which we express our 'self' and form communities. As we saw in chapters 7 and 8, network society compels subjects to communicate and to engage with information technology. In return, this has substantial effects on the field of the media.

The practice currently changing the broadcast and publishing industries is **podcasting**, a word that combines 'iPod' with 'broadcasting'. Podcasting refers to the creation and distribution of multimedia files, such as audio programs or music videos, over the Internet for playback on mobile devices and computers. Rather than depending on program sites and schedules, members of the audience can listen to and watch what they want, when and where they want. This does not necessarily require the Apple iPod; any other mp3 player or computer will do. The name association of this new form of broadcasting with the iPod shows how successfully the iPod has been turned into a brand. The iPod and podcasting phenomenon also begins to influence education and learning. Many distance learning providers have begun to integrate podcasts, or 'profcasts', into their teaching packages: audio recordings of lectures, for example, that students can play back.

The implications about the transformation of subjects in the information society extend to how media immersion, especially gaming, allows for performances and construction of the self that are inscribed in an economy of play and labour. The fact that in many new forms of media communication and interaction there are no visual cues about gender, age, ethnicity or social status causes people to ask whether conventional markers of identity have become irrelevant, given that users cannot see each other. Sherry Turkle argues that the computer network as a communication media (the Internet, for example) challenges users' senses of identity. With regard to the refraction of identity through role play and interaction with other users, she writes that: 'There is an unparalleled opportunity to play with one's identity and to "try out" new ones' (Lister et al. 2003:248). Video games involve users in an interactive engagement: they invite 'the player to cross into the screen', as David Marshall has put it (2004:71). The various technologies—sound, images—have been developed to create a successful simulation and game environment that immerses the player in

Podcasting The creation and distribution of multimedia files, such as audio programs or music videos, over the Internet and for playback on mobile devices and computers.

the fictional world. They are designed to erase the boundary separating the player from the game world, to create a virtual reality and community—and a networked community at that. To borrow an analogy from popular culture:

> we are being 'Borged', as devotees of *Star Trek: The Next Generation* would have it—transformed into cyborgian hybrids of technology and biology through our ever-more-frequent interaction with machines, or with one another through technological interfaces (Lister et al. 2003:247).

New media critics working on games point out that because of this interactivity, digital games bring players into a production relationship with the text (Flew 2005:111) or, in a stronger line of argument, that '[t]he process of playing is a process of production' (Marshall 2004:72). Terry Flew (2005) writes that:

> The elements that tend to drive a game can be identified in terms of goals, cybernetic feedback loops … and performance. Juul … notes the difference in the relationship of the player to the game as compared with the reader to the text. He suggests that because of the goal-driven nature of games, the emotional engagement with the text comes, not from the engagement with characters and events, such as occurs in conventional narratives, but because the player is an actor in the game. The engagement comes because the player is the performer, and the game evaluates the performance and adapts to it (112).

The games texts referred to by Flew fall into two loose categories: linear and emergent. **Linear games** are highly structured, and the options offered to a player are limited. **Emergent games** (which are becoming highly popular) offer an environment and sets of rules, without deciding the direction in which a player must proceed. *EverQuest*, for example, is a role-playing game that provides a world for players to log into, and to play with each other. In the variety of player-created events unpredictable outcomes occur. This is a text that is added to and changed by the player, rather than completely finished by the developer (Flew 2005:112).

> **Linear games** Games structured in a linear way, with limited options for the player.
>
> **Emergent games** Games that offer an environment and sets of rules, without deciding the direction in which a player must proceed.

EverQuest is an extremely popular online game, with the total number of players estimated at two million (Marshall 2004:74). Such online game playing—usually called multiplayer online gaming (MMOG), or massive multi-player online role-playing game (MMORPG)—comes in many forms and styles, and currently represents the most significant development in gaming cultures. It is through them that players increasingly form themselves into online virtual communities. These virtual communities increasingly turn into face-to-face interactions, at gaming tournaments, for example.

There is a further dimension to the immersion into gaming cultures: play produces its own forms of technological transformations. Players may be engaged in competition with each other, but their playing constitutes a form of labour. This play loops back into the hardware and software component of the game and provides the feedback for manufacturers to change their products. In other words, players may purchase the right to play a game, but their playing constitutes a form of labour that benefits game manufacturers. The knowledge, skills and temporal investment that the players make contribute to the transformation of the technology. The emergence of video games and the gaming phenomenon have influenced the developments in and of new media technology, industry and culture. The relationships are tangled and complex. Games have popularised computer technology, and made it accessible through the development of software programming and more user-friendly interfaces. The implications of this economy of play and labour go beyond the game industry. Evidence of this connection between play and innovation can be found in the history of digital technology.

Playing with the design of games has historically been a part of the push forward in developing computer technologies. For example, experimenting with realtime computer interaction and animation through the design of games has been a crucial factor in establishing a new mode of computer use, which ultimately resulted in PC graphical user interfaces. Among the people who have first experimented with that were students at Massachusetts Institute of Technology (MIT) in the late 1950s. They challenged the official uses of the institution's mainframe computers—such as statistical analyses and scientific simulations—by playing around and tinkering with them. They developed non-instrumental ways of exploring the computers' potential. They played music on them, programmed the lights at the front of the machines, or experimented with the possibilities of artificial intelligence in chess programs. They were 'just seeing what the machine would do' (Lister et al. 2003:264).

The key aspect of how and why games influence the development of new media, and new media industries more widely, lies in their interactive and participatory character. Flew has explained the complex significance of interactive games to new media development in the following way:

> The convergence of continuous technological innovation, dynamic corporate marketing and branding practices, and the intensity of immersive play and interactive experiences associated with games, place this sector at the leading edge of both new media innovation (sic). It also links games to debates about the cultural appropriateness of digital content, gender identities, the experience of childhood, and intellectual property regimes. Moreover, the rise of games and gaming culture and particularly the development of massive multiplayer online games (MMOGs), where the players are increasingly the creators of the game's content, and form themselves into online virtual communities, brings to the fore a series of debates ... about whether interactive media would lead to 'de-massification' of media and the rise of the *pro-sumer*, as users increasingly became the creators, and not simply the consumers, of their own media (Flew 2005:102).

The emergence of user-led games development is central to this discussion: proponents see this trend as transforming media production and consumption. Henry Jenkins, for example, sees the new participatory culture between games producers, media companies and end users as lying at the intersection of several new media trends: the new media tools and technologies that enable consumers to archive, annotate, appropriate and recirculate media content; the rise of subcultures that promote do-it-yourself media production, which in turn shapes how consumers have deployed those technologies; and the growth of horizontally integrated media conglomerates, which add value to media content by encouraging the flow of images, ideas and narratives across multiple media channels and actively engage with media audiences and users (Flew 2005:107).

Media technology and everyday life

Go online

Media technology and everyday life

How do we live and work with media technologies? Which new media technologies are part of our everyday life, and what are the everyday uses of these media? What precisely do we mean when we refer to everyday life? To take the last question first, everyday life constitutes the social conditions within which the field of the media operates; and it is the main site of our productive and consumptive media activity. What we have seen from the examples above, however, is that technologies developed for one purpose are often used for another. As Armand and Michèle Mattelart (1992) write: 'the logic of the media is first of all a technique of action' (x). Media, both texts and technologies, need to be understood in terms of what their users do with them. When media critics began to actually look at the media practices of people, and the processes of their consumption, it became clear that, in Mattelart and Mattelart's words, 'social uses of the media do not necessarily reproduce the logics that emerge from the analysis of the structure of the media' (74).

One of the thinkers crucial to this development in media theory is Michel de Certeau. De Certeau was one of the first critics to consider what people do with things and places on an everyday basis. In *The Practice of Everyday Life* (1998), de Certeau sets himself the task of finding a way or method of describing and analysing the ordinary and everyday, without at the same time 'finishing it off' (5). De Certeau makes the point that theorists remove practices from the time and place of their use, in a sense turning them into museum pieces. He refers to the example of the Shelburne Museum in Vermont, in the United States: its faithful and exhaustive reconstruction of buildings, tools, toys and other aspects of nineteenth-century life never articulates, explains or captures the many uses to which those items could be (and were) put, and the everyday lives of which they were a part.

For de Certeau, everyday practices can only be understood in terms of their contexts; that is, of the ways in which places relate to practices. Theoretically, in a factory, workers arrive at a given hour, perform preassigned tasks as per instruction, produce a certain number of objects or products, and then leave. However, all places are 'inhabited' by practices that impose their own logic on the place, without making it too obvious. A different version of things would be that, in a factory, workers arrive late but cover for each other, spend a lot of time socialising and making idle conversation, and finish their Technical Certificate project in the afternoon. De Certeau calls this logic *la perruque* (in French 'the wig'), which refers to the worker's own work disguised as work done for employers (25). Whereas the official logic of a factory establishes the worker's role in the place of capitalist production, for the worker the factory is a space full of opportunities (and resources, mainly time), that can be utilised (illegally and quietly) to the worker's own ends.

How do we 'inhabit' new media technologies in ways that extend their conventional uses? We have already discussed how blogs have been used by activists to provide alternative versions of events that are missing or excluded from the mainstream media (see chapter 6). More generally, the easy connectivity of wireless technologies (such as cell phones, pagers, PDAs and laptops) has changed forms of activism and how we live and act as citizens. The success of the massive protests at the World Trade Organization summit in Seattle in 1999, which became famous as 'The Carnival against Global Capitalism', was made possible because of the new and fast networking, and organisational possibilities offered by mobile phones and laptop computers with wireless internet access. The WTO protests in Seattle became significant as an instance of the new possibilities for social organisation and action opened up by new and mobile communication technologies (Rheingold 2003). Seattle and the WTO protests also became significant for the study of media, not least because the alternative media network Indymedia was originally founded as a strategy to cover the protests and show the events that the mainstream media filtered out.

Cyberspace is another example of how new media technology is transforming communities and social practices. In their introduction to *Cyberkids: Children in the Information Age*, Sarah Holloway and Gill Valentine refer to cyberspace as:

> one of 'the zones that scripts the future' ... Information and Communication Technologies (ICT) are about to inflict far-reaching economic, social, cultural, and political changes upon the twenty-first century ... Most notably ... the transformation of work ... The opportunities that ICT offers users to access information and communicate with whom they want, freed from the material and social constraints of their bodies, identities, communities and geographies mean that these technologies are regarded as potentially liberating for those who are socially, materially or physically disadvantaged ... However, these opportunities also bring new risks. Most notably that those who lack technological skills to participate in the Information Age will be excluded from these activities and, unable to exercise their rights and responsibilities, will consequently be denied full citizenship (2003:1).

This suggests some of the potential risks these changes might bring. Rather than being liberated by these new technologies and their practices, we might be denied certain crucial rights if we lack the means or privileges—or the literacies—to participate in them fully. The question, therefore, is not which new media and new technologies we have, but how we use them.

Transformational culture

Go online

Transformational culture

We shape the technologies we use (MacKenzie & Wajcman 1999), but at the same time we are shaped, even transformed, by these technologies. What are the kinds of experiences, social interactions and identities that new media enable or invite?

One of the common ways of conceiving of this transformative relation between individuals and media technologies and networks is that of an interaction in the mode of a nervous system (van Dijk 2006:241). This image of the 'wired' individual, animated by the flows of data transfer through the network and responsive to sensory and **cognitive stimulation**, is used extensively especially in popular media, magazines and advertising. There is even a magazine dedicated to the information economy and to digital technologies called *Wired*.

In a book entitled *Business @ The Speed of Thought: Using a Digital Nervous System* (1999), Bill Gates calls for the reorganisation of corporate and management structures by instilling a reliance on a 'digital nervous system'. What Gates is promoting is a reliance on information technology and networked processes that allow for business to avoid hierarchical boundaries and the slowness of administrative structures, and can respond to stimulation (such as customer requests) faster and more effectively. He is articulating one of the common ideas associated with what Mattelart (2000) refers to as techo-utopian ideas. He comments:

> To function in the digital age, we have developed a new digital infrastructure. It's like the human nervous system. The biological nervous system triggers your reflexes so that you can react quickly to danger or need. It gives you the information you need as you ponder issues and make choices. You're alert to the most important things, and your nervous system blocks out the information that isn't important to you. Companies need to have that same kind of nervous system—the ability to run smoothly and efficiently, to respond quickly to emergencies and opportunities, to quickly get valuable information to the people in the company who need it, the ability to quickly make decisions and interact with customers (xvii–xviii).

Gates is proposing a reconception of the company in which the social, architectural and institutional spaces of the office have disappeared in favour of a networked and fluid digital organisation lubricated by a series of sensory triggers. In this configuration, the individual is invisible, but his or her capacity to respond and to channel the flow of information has become essential and his or her key to participating to the company. In this model, subjectivity is related to a capacity to sense, to experience and to respond. The individual's adaptation to this environment is measured by his or her capacity to experience and to contribute to the informational flow. The reward for the individual employee is the exhilaration brought about by the transformational experience. Apple's advertising campaign for iPod portrays a series of individuals in different but distinct styles animated by the intense but individual experience of music. There again the encounter with digital technology is portrayed in terms of a sensory experience.

Another example of this, also connected to Bill Gates, is an advertisement for the Microsoft XP operating system released in October 2001, entitled 'Soaring Anthem'. In this television commercial a series of individuals who log on to their computers, and connect to a wireless network, literally take flight with intense pleasure above a field, a library, an office, a street and a restaurant to the tune of Madonna's 'Ray of Light'. The ad is the enthusiastic celebration of the liberating potential of digital technologies advocated by Gates and other advertisers. What matters for the characters of this advertisement is not so much the capacity to perform tasks, but rather to experience intensities. The assumption underlying this and many other such commercials is that the more we experience, the more we can disconnect ourselves from the social world.

What this conception of subjectivity expresses is a dominant ideology that advertising often expresses, but also a common position among politicians and commentators. This position uncritically assumes that one must be excited and accepting of the liberating potentials of new media technologies.

Media literacy and the public sphere

In this book we argue that, rather than uncritically repeating this assumption, we must understand the stakes and contexts of such developments. With the advent of the so-called 'information revolution', and concomitant changes to the volume, speed and modalities of information flows, different kinds of literacies (particularly the ability to 'read', relate and contextualise visual images) are now demanded of us. These technological changes have altered the way we negotiate meanings. It follows that those processes and changes also inform the way we come to understand ourselves as members of different groups or communities—for instance, as citizens of democratic societies able and willing to contribute to public sphere debates (see chapter 6). The relationship between the public sphere and democracy, and the practices, institutions, fields and technologies associated with the media, are central to debates about, and evaluations of, the relation between media and society.

The media are the most important sites of public sphere debate and dissent, simply because they allow people and groups to reach and influence national and global audiences. This is why politicians and corporate executives, drilled by media professionals, have become particularly adept in dealing with and deflecting those sections of the media that do take their 'public sphere responsibilities' seriously. There are numerous examples of this that come to mind. General cases include the way in which George Bush, since September 11, managed to keep the media committed to the notion of a global 'War against Terrorism' campaign, despite the fact that their own policies and discourses (for instance, in relation to the Israel–Palestine conflict, or their designation of states such as Cuba and North Korea as 'terrorist sympathisers') were unilateralist, divisive and likely to exacerbate the conditions which bred widespread anti-American sentiments.

More specific examples of the way the media struggles to break down or challenge what Bourdieu (1998a) refers to as the doxa emanating from the field of power are to be found in any number of interviews or press conferences involving Bush, but in some ways it is more useful and productive to refer to examples of, say, politicians being interviewed about domestic matters. We will refer to two of these that occurred in the Australian media: the first on a public television current affairs show, and the second on public radio.

In the first case, the interviewer was questioning the Minister for Foreign Affairs about international legal challenges that were being threatened with regard to a state government's policy of mandatory detention for those convicted of three offences: a policy clearly directed at, and having an impact upon, the local Indigenous population. When pressed by the interviewer as to whether this was another example of covertly racist policies being promulgated to take advantage of right-wing populist sentiment, the minister replied such a notion was ridiculous: 'Australia was a democracy', he said, 'and democracies don't implement racist policies.' This effectively ended any further line of questioning on the issue.

The second example we refer to occurred when two companies involved in the pay television industry announced that they had come to an agreement to share programs and services. Consumer groups strongly opposed the move, suggesting that it was anti-competitive, and would allow the companies to eventually operate as a duopoly. A public radio journalist interviewed a media analyst from a large corporation as to what the effects of this 'cooperation' might be. The analyst stated that it was a 'win–win' situation, and dismissed the idea that there were public interest issues at stake. The journalist was initially taken aback, but then simply responded by saying that 'this was good news', and thanked the analyst for his time.

In the first example, the television interviewer was caught out by the media's dependence on the logic of 'time and effect'. The minister's sweeping generalisation could have been countered by specific examples to the contrary, but this would have required that the interview 'digress' (to the history of Australians' attitudes towards both their Indigenous population and migrants), and take on a level of detail (about specific policies within a wider historical frame). In the second example, the radio interviewer was clearly unfamiliar with the immediate issues, but also unaware that the media analyst was not speaking from a position of 'disinterestedness', but simply reproducing the party line emanating from multinational corporations (one of which was his employee) that what was good for big business was also good for the public.

There are three issues of media literacy at stake in this pair of examples. The first is that when the Minister attempted to deflect the line of questioning by resorting to a false generalisation ('democracies aren't racist'), the interviewer was either unfamiliar with the historical contexts that would have given the lie to this claim, or unable to bring that knowledge into the interview in a way that was commensurate with the imperatives of 'time and effect' under which the field operates. The radio interview exemplifies two related, but essentially separate, issues. Journalists and media practitioners are increasingly being asked to operate, at relatively short notice, across a variety of fields. Consequently they are forced to rely on experts to give them their stories, and to explicate or contextualise what is happening and why. The problem is that they are often unfamiliar with issues under discussion, and are forced to rely upon, and can be led by, whatever apparent expertise is at hand (such as a spokesperson, analyst or academics). As a corollary, they are also not in a position to identify whoever, within a field, has the appropriate expertise and is likely to comment from a relatively disinterested position. In a sense, the media are placed in an untenable position: they are required to comment on, analyse and ask questions about everything (that is, a variety of fields and practices), while knowing little or nothing (it is more or less illiterate with regard to those same fields and practices).

Conclusion

These examples point to the significance of, and the difficulties involved in, addressing the question of media literacy. The twin constraints of time and effect make it much easier for representatives of the field of power to deflect or avoid the kind of critical questioning and analysis, and demands for public disclosure that are essential to public sphere activity. Bourdieu himself addressed this problem (he wished to intervene in the public debate in France about issues such as the war in Algeria, globalisation and migration) both through writing a polemical book on television and journalism, and through two lectures he gave about television which were delivered on television, and were designed to get around the problems of trivialisation, sensationalism and the lack of time he associates with the media. Bourdieu gave his lectures via the audiovisual service of the Collège de France, and was not restricted with regard to time, topic or technical requirements. In his own words: 'I have a control of the instruments of production' (Bourdieu 1998a:13).

The book taken from the lectures was a bestseller in France, as was *The Weight of the World* (Bourdieu et al. 1999). These texts, along with *Acts of Resistance* (1998b), provoked widespread debates, particularly in the media, about issues such as the market's domination of the public sphere, racism, social inequality, globalisation and the erosion of the welfare state. Of course Bourdieu was able to make these kinds of interventions precisely because of the considerable cultural capital he carried, particularly in France. But he was (media) literate enough to understand that, although the media is dominated by commercial interests, and although its commitment to its own ethical imperatives and values (to serve the public interest, to act as a responsible public sphere) is an empty one, the existence of these values provides an opportunity for some kind of intervention in the media-inflected public sphere. And if we are to have a functioning public sphere, it will inevitably be because those individuals and groups who do wish to contribute to public sphere debates are at least as 'media literate' as are the representatives of the field of power.

Additional reading

Introductory

Schirato, T. and Yell, S. (2000). *Communication and Cultural Literacy*. Sydney: Allen & Unwin.
Useful introduction to the concept of cultural literacy.

Silverstone, R. (1994). *Television and Everyday Life*. London: Routledge.
Sociological account of the relation between television and everyday life.

Advanced

Certeau, M. de (1988). *The Practice of Everyday Life*. Berkeley: University of California Press.
A highly influential work on everyday life and the notion of cultural practice.

Lefebvre, H. (1990). *Everyday Life in the Modern World*. London: Transaction Publishers.
Important Marxist account of theories of everyday life.

GLOSSARY

active audience

Rather than being simply passive receivers of media texts, members of the audience engage with the media in a wide variety of ways.

affect

A sensory and emotional response to stimulation. In media studies, the attitudes or emotions produced as part of textual interaction. Hardt and Negri (2001) refer to the 'affect industries', especially the media and advertising. The 'politics of affect' refers to the media practice of producing all events and issues in such a way as to elicit an immediate, unconsidered emotional reaction.

alternative media

A variety of media forms and different practices of media production; generally, any media that are outside of the mainstream media.

audiovisual illusion

In film, television and other audio-visual texts, sound is used to naturalise, inflect or produce certain readings, meanings, narratives, responses and moods.

aura

In Walter Benjamin's writings, the quasi-religious and enchanting experience of encountering a unique art object. Absent from mass-media objects because they exist in multiple copies and are readily available.

automation

For Manovich, the way in which a media object can be transformed by the automised functions of software in ways that do not require intervention or choice.

binary code

A coding system which translates information and instructions with two possible values. The Morse code is a binary code using dots and dashes. Computing uses a two-digit number system (0 and 1) which controls processors.

biopower

In Foucault, the processes by which knowledge, power, administrative and political authorities effect and enforce standards of normality for subjects and serve the interest of the modern state.

blog (weblog)

Software that enables regular entries on a website, as well as links to other blogs or websites.

blogger

Someone who maintains a blog (weblog), in the form of either a personal diary, journal, or social commentary and news coverage.

blogosphere

The phenomenon of the rapidly expanding practice and popularity of blogging. The blogosphere also refers to the network of debate, dialogue and commentary that influences and transforms traditional media practices (most obviously journalism).

bricolage

The French word for 'the use of only the materials or tools at hand to achieve a purpose'; a term first used by anthropologist Claude Lévi-Strauss to describe the way in which everyday objects have their meaning transformed by a new kind of use.

browsing the Internet

Navigating the Internet in the way a consumer casually explores shops.

camera obscura

A device to capture accurate images. It is usually a darkened box with a tiny pinhole through which light can enter. As light passes through this opening, an upside-down image is projected on the wall opposite, with great detail.

capital (including social capital and cultural capital)

The accumulation of resources which constitute the basis for involvement in trading and exchange systems. In Marxism, capital, which is privately owned, provides the impetus for the creation of surplus, which adds to the original capital and reinforces power and social structures. For Bourdieu, social and cultural capital are the recognised expertise, status and power that a subject can acquire within a field and can use as leverage.

capitalised ideas

A term taken from the work of Claude Lefort, referring to certain concepts (such as democracy, freedom and childhood) that have taken on a particular significance and value.

capitalism

The dominant economic system in the West since the advent of the industrial revolution in the eighteenth century. Based on the ever-expanding logic of private ownership of capital, investment, production, the organisation and control of human labour, consumption, and the accumulation of more private capital.

citizen journalism

The activity of non-professional journalists, who act independently from major media outlets to gather and spread information usually through direct eye-witness accounts.

citizenship

The duties and rights associated with being a member of a community and country. Organises and structures relations between members of the shared community, and their individual relation with government and society.

commodity

Something which is the subject of a financial transaction. It can be objects (consumer electronics) but it can also be experiences (going to the movies). They exist in relation to the capitalistic system of economic exchange and as part of consumer culture.

commodification

The transformation of an object, text or experience into a commodity; something which can be integrated into the logic of consumer culture and can be purchased outside of its original context.

commoditisation

The process of producing something predominantly in terms of its exchangeability.

communication

The production, exchange and negotiation of meanings. The word originally referred to 'making common to many, imparting', but also refers to transport lines as 'lines of communication', and now also to the media and other forms used to disseminate information.

conglomerate

A large grouping of companies, which are connected through common ownership.

connectivity

The means and potential for connections on the communication networks to be implemented and activated.

consent (or consensus)

The processes of reaching an agreement of opinion. The term is important within media studies because consent can also mean an unconscious assent, which in turn can easily be used for the manipulative purposes of building a silent majority from which different opinions can be excluded.

context

The circumstances in which communication practices take place. The verbal, historical, cultural and social situations out of which a text takes meaning. Expression and communication are always linked to contextual signification.

copyright

The rights and obligations related to the ownership and use of intellectual property.

corporation, corporate

A business and legal entity which is owned by shareholders and usually conducts business across states and exerts significant influence on economies, and social and political institutions.

countertext

A text produced in relation to an original text as a way of celebrating, expanding or undermining the source text.

cultural capital (see also capital)

A term associated with the work of Pierre Bourdieu, which refers to anything deemed to be of value and exchangeable within a cultural field.

cultural field

A social system—with institutions, agents, subjects, discourses and practices—that structures and reproduces power relations within and without. The field's practices are organised and validated through the habitus.

cultural literacy

A familiarity with, and an ability to read and make use of, the various meaning systems that characterise the cultural fields of a society.

cultural trajectory

The subject's movement across various cultural fields that shapes the habitus.

culture

Communication practices, meanings and meaning systems considered as a totality or unit; shared practices, beliefs, values and meanings that form the basis of communal identities.

culture industry

In Adorno and Horkheimer, the way in which cultural products (films, music, etc.) are produced in mass form, much like an assembly line produces cars. For them what was significant was that cultural products produced on such a scale began to resemble one another, in that they were 'standardised,' but also in that they generate the same kind of responses.

culture jamming

The use of the media against themselves to point out their ideological intent; for example, the use of techniques such as graffiti on advertising texts to call attention to their particular bias and/or solicitation to buy a particular product.

cyberspace

This term was originally coined by the science-fiction author William Gibson in his novel *Neuromancer*. It is now used generally to refer to the spaces and networks created by both the digital technologies and our uses of them (the world wide web, for example).

database

A collection of information, facts and details that is collected and stored on a computer system. It is accessible and can retrieve and organise information using programmed commands.

digital archiving

The storage and preservation of material in digital form.

digital footprint

Within the Internet itself, the remains and traces of activities such as browsing, credit card purchases, library loans, banking transactions and participation in social networking.

digitalisation

The process whereby information is produced as a universal binary code, and is thus able to circulate more freely and at greater speed across communication technologies, and not just within them.

digital divide

This term refers to technological inequalities between those who can and those who cannot afford computer technologies (hardware and software), broadband access, etc.

discipline (also disciplinarity)

In Foucault, refers to a process in the late eighteenth and early nineteenth centuries, whereby people would be disposed to bring their behaviour, thinking and seeing into line with what the state and its various institutions considered to be normal, healthy and productive. This process was meant to train people to lead normal lives without the need to think or reflect on what they were doing.

discourse

In Foucault's writings, discourse does the work of both opening up and closing off the world. It disposes us to make sense of and see things from a field-specific perspective.

discursive regime

Forms of discourse regulated by a particular cultural field, group, or institution.

disposition

Forms of understanding, conceptualisation and behaviour that we are inclined towards, as a result of our habitus and membership of a field. Dispositions are forms of literacy.

dot com boom

The 1990s saw a surge in business interest in the Web. Thousands of start-up companies used the Web and the Internet as a business resource, with much speculation and venture capital invested in companies and individuals. By the end of the millennium most of them had collapsed.

doxa

A common and unquestioned statement that stands as self-evident truth.

emergent games

Games that offer an environment and sets of rules, without directing the way in which a player must proceed.

epistemology

The means by which we come to know and understand the world.

ethos

The fundamental disposition and beliefs in a field which guide and inform its participants' practices. This might not be codified in rules but it should be shared by all participants.

everyday life

Constitutes the social conditions within which the field of the media operates. Everyday life is also the main site of our productive and consumptive media activity.

fan fiction

A subgenre of writing wherein the readers of an established genre expand upon its possibilities, usually by writing new fiction about the characters within that genre.

fanzine

A small, often hand-printed magazine, dedicated to a specialised topic or cultural phenomenon.

fascism

A political ideology and system of government in which individual fate and actions are subordinated to the interest of the state embodied in the figure of an authoritarian leader. Relies on a strong sense of a common, and usually racial, identity to the exclusion of others to the point of violence, destruction, and even genocide. Example: Nazism in Germany (1933–1945).

field

See cultural field.

flâneur

An urban explorer and meanderer whose walk through a city, its streets, its shops, and its back alleys, constitutes a form of sensory immersion in the logic of consumer culture. The flâneur does not see himself or herself as a direct participant.

flash mob

Temporary gathering of people, called together for a collective prank, usually alerted through email or text messages.

fourth estate

Refers to the institutional status of the press. The first three estates are executive, legislative and judicial powers. The expression raises the status of the press to that of a pillar of democracy.

franchise

See media franchise.

Frankfurt School

Originally a group of German philosophers and social researchers brought together by an interest in the study of mass-culture, social organisation, capitalism and the prospect of radical social change. Usually associated with the work of Adorno, Horkheimer, Benjamin, and Habermas.

genre

The way texts are put together and read. A system of classification that uses categories of texts and communication practices. The use of genre creates and delimits meanings.

globalisation

Characterised by the contraction of time and space brought about by new communication technologies, and the free circulation of texts across conventional borders; the cultural, social, economic and political movements, and new technologies, that displace people and texts from local to global settings.

habitus

A concept based on the work of Pierre Bourdieu. Habitus is history naturalised. The values and dispositions gained from our cultural history are part of who we are, how we see the world, and how we do things.

hegemony

A term used to talk about political predominance, usually of one state over another. The use of the term in media studies has developed from the work of Antonio Gramsci, who showed that the ruling classes need the acceptance of their subordinates. To gain hegemony through an agreement of opinion is a struggle: a constant negotiation and renegotiation, organisation and reorganisation, of structuring experience and consciousness.

hyperbole

Extravagant statement, for effect; not meant to be taken at face value.

hypertext mark-up language (HTML)

A language with a set of annotations and instructions which provides the basis for the structure and behaviour of web pages.

hypodermic model

Refers to a conception of media effects, suggesting that people take in media texts without any kind of filter or critical reflection, just as a doctor gives a patient drugs. with a hypodermic syringe.

hysteria, hystericise

An intense, over-excited and uncontrollable state of mind brought about by panic and/or an over-reaction to events and stimulations, which the subject sees as immediately threatening. The threat is misplaced or even imaginary but the response produces a regime of excess and slippages. In Baudrillard, the general condition of media hyperbole.

ideology

Narrative about the forces that organises the world. It disposes people to see things and act in certain ways. It authorises or privileges one group over another. An ideology produces meanings that are naturalised or universalised.

imagined communities

In Anderson, refers to the sense of shared histories, values and narratives which allow for and produce a sense of common interest. The basis for this sense of community is an imaginary relation with others one has never met.

imbrication

An overlapping pattern, as of cultures or different types of media.

inalienable culture

Things, people, categories and practices considered intrinsic to the community and not subject to the market.

incorporation

Process whereby marginal and/or subcultural practices are brought back into the mainstream.

independent media centres (IMCs)

Grassroots organisations committed to using media production and distribution as a tool for promoting social and economic justice.

informationalism

The use of processes, technologies, and social and administrative structures to facilitate "the accumulation of knowledge and towards higher levels of complexity in information processing" (Castells 1996:17).

information society

The stage of capitalism where the production and consumption of information has become the driver of the economy as opposed to the production and consumption of goods in the industrial society.

information technologies (IT), also, information and communication technologies (ICT)

The use of computers, software and computing hardware to disseminate, collect, retrieve, store and organise information.

institutions (media)

Public or industry bodies which promote, defend, govern and regulate the industry.

interface

A point of connection between two distinct components of a communication process. This can be a user accessing a network through a computer terminal.

Internet

A vast regulated network composed of other networks, including military, business and personal networks.

interpellation

Interpellation produces subjects. It refers to the way institutions, texts and discourses call (or 'hail') and address subjects in order to 'recruit' them.

intertextuality

The process through which individual texts relate to other texts and, in part, draw their meaning from that relation. Implies the systems of visible or invisible references that shape an individual text. All texts refer to other text.

journalistic field

The rules, roles, institutions and practices relating to the journalism in all its forms.

knowledge

In Foucault, the systematic and disciplinary forms of information gathering which shape the consciousness of subjects and support the objectives and justify the powers of the state.

liberalism

A general distrust of, and opposition to, strong state intervention in society, particularly in economic matters.

linear games

Games structured in a linear way, offering limited options to the player.

literacy

See cultural literacy.

logic of practice

In Bourdieu, refers to the practical sense which provides the tools to understand how to function in a specific cultural field, including the various discourses, genres, written and unwritten rules within which we operate.

logo

A trademark or symbol that identifies a company or organisation.

mainstream media

In the present climate, mainstream media is seen as something that needs countering, because it is seen as being controlled or influenced by commercial interests, dominant groups, governments, and the political and social status quo.

manufacture of consent

The management of public opinion by propaganda and other strategies to reach an agreement of opinion.

Marxism

A political philosophy drawn from the work of Karl Marx (1818–1883), which provides an analysis and critique of capitalism. It draws its analysis of economics, politics and culture from the understanding that the subject's forms of consciousness and knowledge originate out of their material conditions and interests, and their relation with, and place within, social structures.

mashup

A musical collage made up of a vocal track from one song mixed with the instrumental portion of another.

mass media

Media with a wide target audience, and a broad appeal in terms of content.

meaning

The significance that is read into and from a sign.

media

The physical and technical means of communication.

media effects argument

Model suggesting that audience members ingest the media uncritically, often resulting in the simple equation, for example, that violence on screen begets violence off screen.

media franchise

The commercial exploitation of a media product as a brand, which involves licensing of all aspects of the media text (such as characters, costumes or imagery in a film) and the development of further products such a sequels, novels and computer games.

media institution

An official body involved in the promotion, defence, reproduction, governance and regulation of the industry. Media institutions define the sphere of influence of media industries, and defend their interests in relation to other fields. They enforce the self-imposed rules of media industries, and translate government laws and regulations into actions and rules. They also intervene to resolve conflicts and pass judgment on potential failures to follow rules and guidelines that are self-imposed or government-imposed.

media literacy (see also cultural literacy)

Extends the conventional meaning of literacy (the ability to read and write) to the field, texts and practices of the media. It refers to the ability to read and make use of the meaning systems and practices specific to the media.

mediation

The idea of a representation or medium of some kind that reproduces or gives us access to reality. There are many forms of mediation (such as paintings or photographs), with many technologies of representation (such as a brush or a camera).

media watchdogs

Organised groups which systematically monitor the activities of the media in order to highlight (perceived) biases or inaccurate reporting and practices. They are usually supported by independent foundations or advocacy groups.

medium is the message

Coined by Marshall McLuhan. Refers to notion of a range of discourses that surround appearance of a new technology.

micro media

Media, such as fanzines, targeted at audiences so highly specialised that they are not directed at audiences or markets, but only at highly focused interest groups.

modernity

The period in Western history dating from the Enlightenment, characterised by scientific rationality, democracy, urbanism, the rise of the mass media, the development of capitalism, and the extension of communication technologies to most facets of everyday life.

modularity

A media object made of distinct elements that can be altered and controlled separately.

monumentality

The quality of giving the impression of being enormous, imposing or historically important.

moral panic

A media response to events which may be construed as evidence of social problems. Their presentation in the media makes them appear to be spectacular events that the community/nation should be alarmed about.

narrative

The organisation of a a story into a sequence of causally and/or temporally connected elements.

Nazi Party

The National Socialist German Workers Party, which controlled Germany from 1933 until 1945, ruled by the dictator Adolf Hitler. *See also* fascism.

neo-liberalism (see liberalism)

network

A system of interconnected machines, computers, means of communication, places, and/ or people. The term is used to denote a system of remote, channeled, organised, structured, expandable and more or less instantaneous and multi-directional connections.

network enterprise

According to Castells, a business structure characterised by the flexibility of its production context; therefore, a company that might have branches in many parts of the world, but whose branches still have a high degree of interdependence.

network neutrality

The principle currently under debate in many parts of the world which would guarantee, if it became regulation, that broadband networks do not favor or use the control of information flow as a means of discriminating between service subscribers.

niche media

Media texts that target specific markets, based on demographic criteria such as age, sexuality and ethnicity.

normalisation

Taken from Foucault's work, referring to the means of managing populations by establishing norms (of behaviour, physicality etc.) against which people are measured.

open publishing

The process through which information can be accessed, posted, and edited by multiple participants with minimal editorial intervention. This especially applies to Internet websites where individuals can upload information for others to read and comment on.

palimpsest

The practice of scratching a text off a parchment (made of animal skins) and writing the new text over the top. This practice and the way in which the earlier text leaves a trace or residue are referred to as palimpsests.

panopticon

Jeremy Bentham's model for a prison with a central tower from which a guard could observe prisoners. Since the prisoners would never be able to know if they were being scrutinised, they would adjust their behaviour. Foucault, by extension, sees this as providing a model for the ways in which discipline operates in society.

pixel

The division of every digital image into a two-dimensional grid made of individual points called pixels. The more precise the picture, the more pixels in the frame, and the more numerical values can be assigned to each pixel.

podcasting

The creation and distribution of multimedia files, such as audio programs or music videos, over the Internet and for playback on mobile devices and computers.

postmodernity

Variously understood as a historical period, a way of thinking characterised by pastiche and relativism, a set of cultural practices and technologies, and a reaction against and a break with the culture of modernity.

propaganda

The use and presentation of information in such a way as to convince a large number of people of a particular belief, cause or idea. It implies manipulation and fabrication of material, deception, and the arousal of strong feelings and emotions.

pseudo-individuality

A termed coined by Theodor Adorno to explain the false sense that a mass media text offers its reader, viewer or listener of being addressed in a singular form; that is, being addressed as 'you'.

public opinion (and public debate)

What the people in a state want or think, the 'will of the people'. Public opinion, in the form of opinion polls, can have a political role in that policy makers use it to decide whether proposed policies will find approval, and politicians to determine voting intentions. Public debate is the process by which public opinion is formed.

public relations

The practices that mediate between an organisation or institution and the wider public, especially, the practice of gaining goodwill for companies, government organisations or individuals without paying for advertising.

public sphere

The public sphere is where, and how, we interact with society. It is a network of spaces and activities. The media is part of the public sphere, and provides the forms of transmission and distribution we need to participate in the political processes that affect our lives.

reasons of state

An expectation that governing and government is driven by human reason and rational decision-making.

reception theory

A theoretical model used to explore the way in which meaning in a text is generated through a reader's or viewer's experience of that text.

reflexivity

In Bourdieu's work, the set of dispositions that allow thought space outside 'the limitations of thought'; that is, it encourages us to look beyond the habitual frames through which we see the world.

regulation

The translation of government policy into legal and administrative requirements and constrains.

remix

The transformation of a musical or video text using various editing techniques.

representation

The system of signs, means and forms of expressions by which humans communicate. Also includes the ways in which they shape, produce, organise and make sense of the world in the acts and forms of communication.

sample

A small fraction of music, copied from another source, incorporated into a new piece of music.

self-surveillance

A social process by which subjects are disposed to make themselves the objects of their own gaze, constantly monitoring and evaluating their bodies, actions and feelings.

semiotics

The science of signs; a theoretical approach to the production and negotiation of meanings.

sign

Something that stands in for something else. Anything that is read or treated as if it were meaningful.

signification

The process of turning something into a sign.

society of the spectacle

Guy Debord's influential notion of society having turned into a spectacle. Debord asserts that human lived experience has been lost, and in its place are media representations. Society has been taken over by the field of the media, which means that the 'between us' of the social is not played out through media and media simulations.

software

The programming that enables a person to control the operations of a computer, as opposed to hardware, which is the machine being programmed. By extension, the means by which actions and information can circulate and be translated in a simple and immediate way.

space-biased media

In Innis, the limits specific to a particular medium in its ability to transcend space. Innis emphasises that the media are portable.

space of flows

Virtual terrains created by webs of electronic information.

spectacle

In media studies, spectacle refers to the commodification of society as a whole. It is a certain way of presenting cultural forms and texts. Its main functions are to arouse passion and excitement, to manage the viewer's attention, and to organise what and how we can see.

spin doctor

A public relations professional who 'spins'; that is, offers his or her own interpretation of terms, facts, events or campaigns in order to favour the interests of an organisation or individual.

subject

The notion of cultural identity produced through discourses and ideologies.

subjectivity

The forms and processes of individuation; that is, how humans are made subjects in relation to culture, place and power. Subjectivity is contextual in the sense that it relies on the forms of discipline, validation and authorisation in the specific cultural field to which the subject belongs.

surfing the Internet

Navigating the multiple possibilities of the Internet. The implication of the term is that following hyperlinks through web pages is a form of recreational activity with neither economically productive objective nor preconceived itinerary.

surveillance

A technological, architectural, and political form of observation and monitoring of people and their activities in public spaces, on the Internet and/or through the accumulation of information. In Foucault, it suggests a societal structure which disciplines and coerces subjects who internalise its logic and act accordingly even if nobody or nothing is monitoring them.

technology

1) tools that humans produce; 2) the ways in which humans manipulate and transform the world around them (the use of fire to keep them warm, to see, to prepare food, etc.); 3) the manner through which humans extend themselves into the world: various modes of communication (speech, art, etc.).

technopole

Area of technological and research concentration, often made possible by favourable economic and regulatory policies.

text

Refers to conventional cultural 'packages' such as books, films, television shows, music videos, CDs and the like: they signal, in a number of easily recognisable ways, that they should be read and treated as a collection or unit.

textual poaching

Taking source material from an original text and resituating it in a new text; a form of quotation.

time-biased media

Term used by Harold Innis to describe media used in civilisations which may have long life spans, but are not interested in territorial expansion. The media found here were marked by durability, such as clay tablets.

totalitarian

A type of centralised government that allows no dissenting opinions within society.

transcoding

According to Manovich, the fact that when information is stored in digital form (such as an image translated in the computer's memory as binary code), it takes on characteristics that originate from the computer.

uses and gratifications model

Model that attempts to explain the different kinds of interactions people have with media texts, as a way of explaining how certain individual and social needs may be met through an engagement with media texts.

vertical integration

An industrial structure where all of the stages of an industry are controlled by a single entity; for example, in film, the control of production, distribution and exhibition.

viral video

A video clip which spreads with such great speed that it becomes seen in many different contexts by many different people, and is thereby widely recognised.

visual culture

A term that describes the fact that our world is saturated with images. Visual culture is also a field of study; it studies the consumption of images. The study of visual culture is mainly concerned with the question of whether and what kind of new ways of seeing emerge with what kind of technology (think, for example, of the microscope).

visual regime

The way in which contemporary media and media technologies vision is arranged and organised. Vision is not just a biological function; it is also a cultural practice, with codes, conventions, and 'rules' (often specific to particular cultures).

World Wide Web

The hypertext and linked interface of the Internet. Whereas the Internet is the infrastructure supporting the web, the Web is one of its interfaces. It relies on web browsers (Firefox, Internet Explorer, Safari) and on HTML to create links.

BIBLIOGRAPHY

Achbar, M. and Wintonick, P. (1992). *Manufacturing Consent: Noam Chomsky and the Media.* Ottawa: Necessary Illusions Productions and National Film Board of Canada.

Acland, C. (ed.) (2007). *Residual Media.* Minneapolis: University of Minnesota Press.

Adas, M. (1990). *Machines as the Measure of Men.* Ithaca: Cornell University Press.

Adorno, T. (1990). *The Culture Industry: Selected Essays on Mass Culture.* New York: Routledge.

Althusser, L. (1977). *Lenin and Philosophy.* London: New Left Bookclub.

Altman, R. (dir.) (1992). *The Player.* Hollywood: Avenue Pictures Productions Guild Spelling Entertainment.

Anderson, B. (2006). *Imagined Communities.* London: Verso.

Ang, I. (1989). *Watching Dallas: Soap Opera and the Melodramatic Imagination.* London: Routledge.

Ang, I. (1991). *Desperately Seeking the Audience.* London and New York: Routledge.

Ang, I. (1996). *Living Room Wars: Rethinking Media Audiences for a Postmodern World.* London: Routledge.

Aotearoa Independent Media Centre (2008). 'Mission Statement'. <http://indymedia.org.nz/mod/info/display/mission/index.php>. Accessed 16 February 2009.

Appadurai, A. (1988). *The Social Life of Things.* Cambridge: Cambridge University Press.

Appadurai, A. (1997). *Modernity at Large.* Minneapolis: University of Minnesota Press.

Arendt, H. (1998). *The Human Condition.* Chicago: University of Chicago Press.

Atton, C. (2002). *Alternative Media.* London: Sage.

Bakhtin, M. (1986). *Speech Genres and Other Late Essays.* Austin: University of Texas Press.

Barney, D. (2004). *The Network Society.* Cambridge: Polity Press.

Baudrillard, J. (2002). *The Spirit of Terrorism: A Requiem for the Twin Towers.* London: Verso.

Baudrillard, J. (2003). *The Consumer Society.* London: Sage.

Baudrillard, J. (2007). *In the Shadow of the Silent Majorities.* Los Angeles: Semiotext(e).

BBC News (2005). 'Shot Man Not Connected to Bombing'. 23 July. <http://news.bbc.co.uk/2/hi/uk_news/4711021.stm>. Accessed 16 February 2009.

BBC News (2008). 'Full Text: Obama's Victory Speech'. 5 November. <http://news.bbc.co.uk/2/hi/americas/us_elections_2008/7710038.stm>. Accessed 16 February 2009.

Beder, S. (2002). *Global Spin: The Corporate Assault on Environmentalism.* Totnes: Green Books.

Benjamin, W. (1979). *Illuminations.* Glasgow: Fontana.

Bennett, T., Grossberg, L. and Morris, M. (eds) (2005). *New Keywords: A Revised Edition of Culture and Society.* Malden: Blackwell.

Bernays, E. (1929). *Propaganda.* New York: Horace Liveright.

Blumler, J. and Katz, E. (eds) (1974). *The Uses of Mass Communications.* Beverley Hills: Sage.

Bourdieu, P. (1989). *Distinction.* London: Routledge.

Bourdieu, P. (1990). *The Logic of Practice.* Cambridge: Polity Press.

Bourdieu, P. (1993). *The Field of Cultural Production.* New York: Columbia University Press.

Bourdieu, P. (1998a). *On Television and Journalism.* London: Pluto Press.

Bourdieu, P. (1998b). *Acts of Resistance.* Cambridge: Polity Press.

Bourdieu, P. (2000). *Pascalian Meditations.* Cambridge: Polity Press.

Bourdieu, P. (2008). *Political Interventions: Social Science and Political Action.* London: Verso.

Bourdieu, P., Accardo, A. and Ferguson, P. (1999). *Weight of the World.* Stanford: Stanford University Press.

Bourdieu, P. and Wacquant, L. (1992). *An Invitation to Reflexive Sociology.* Chicago: University of Chicago Press.

Briggs, A. and Burke, P. (2007). *A Social History of the Media: From Gutenberg to the Internet.* Cambridge: Polity Press.

Brooks, M. (dir.) (1974). *Blazing Saddles.* Hollywood: Warner Brothers.

Butler, J. (1993). *Bodies That Matter.* New York: Routledge.

Butler, J. (1997). *The Psychic Life of Power.* Stanford: Stanford University Press.

Butler, J. (2004). *Precarious Life.* London: Verso.

Caldwell, J. (2008). *Production Culture: Industrial Reflexivity and Critical Practice in Film and Television.* London: Duke University Press.

Carey, J. (1989). *Communication as Culture.* Boston: Unwin Hyman.

Caro, N. (dir.) (2002). *Whale Rider.* Wellington: South Pacific Pictures.

Castells, M. (1989). *The Informational City.* Oxford: Blackwell.

Castells, M. (1997a). *The Rise of the Network Society.* Oxford: Blackwell.

Castells, M. (1997b). *The Power of Identity.* Oxford: Blackwell.

Castells, M. (2001). *The Internet Galaxy.* London: Oxford University Press.

Castells, M. and Hall, P. (1996). *Technopoles of the World.* London: Routledge.

Certeau, M. de (1988). *The Practice of Everyday Life.* Berkeley: University of California Press.

Chambers, S. and Costain, A. (eds) (2000). *Deliberation, Democracy, and the Media.* Lanham: Rowman & Littlefield.

Chase, D. (prod.) (1999–2007). *The Sopranos.* New York: Home Box Office.

Chion, M. (1994). *Audio-Vision.* New York: Columbia University Press.

Coddington, D. (2006). 'Asian Angst: Is It Time to Send Some Back?'. *North and South,* December.

Cohen, S. (2002). *Folk Devils and Moral Panics: The Creation of the Mods and Rockers*. London: Routledge.

Coyer, K., Dowmunt, T. and Fountain, A. (2007). *The Alternative Media Handbook*. London: Routledge.

Crary, J. (1998). *Techniques of the Observer*. Cambridge: MIT Press.

Crary, J. (1999). *Suspensions of Perception*. Cambridge: MIT Press.

Dahlberg, L. (2005). 'The Internet as Public Sphere or Culture Industry? From Pessimism to Hope and Back'. *International Journal of Media and Cultural Politics*, 1 (1).

Danaher, G., Schirato, T. and Webb, J. (2000). *Understanding Foucault*. Sydney: Allen & Unwin.

'Dear Mr Obama'. <http://www.youtube.com/watch?v=TG4fe9GIWS8>. Accessed 16 February 2009.

Debord, G. (2006). *The Society of the Spectacle*. New York: Zone Books.

Democratic Audit of Australia (2008). 'Welcome to the Democratic Audit of Australia'. 18 December. <http://democratic.audit.anu.edu.au/index.htm?head=24>. Accessed 16 February 2009.

Derrida, J. (1980). 'The Law of Genre'. *Glyph* 7.

Dick, K. (2006). *This Film Is Not Rated Yet*. Independent Film Channel.

Dougherty, I. (1997). *Ham Sharks, Brass Pounders and Rag Chewers: A History of Amateur Radio in New Zealand*. Wellington: NZART.

Eisenstein, E. (1993). *The Printing Revolution in Early Modern Europe*. Oakleigh: Cambridge University Press.

Ellin, D. (prod.) (2004–2008). *Entourage*. New York: Home Box Office.

Eriksen, E. (2004). 'Conceptualising European Public Spheres'. Unpublished papers, One EU: Many Publics workshop. Stirling: Stirling University, 5–6 February.

Featherstone, M. (1993). *Consumer Culture and Postmodernism*. London: Sage.

Fest, J. (1977). *Hitler*. London: Penguin.

Fiske, J. (1987). *Television Culture*. London and New York: Methuen.

Flew, T. (2005). *New Media: An Introduction*. Oxford: Oxford University Press.

Flew, T. (2008). *New Media: An Introduction* (2nd edn). Oxford: Oxford University Press.

Foucault, M. (1973). *The Order of Things*. New York: Vintage.

Foucault, M. (1995). *Discipline and Punish*. New York: Vintage.

Foucault, M. (2003). *Abnormal: Lectures at the College De France, 1974–75*. New York: Picador.

Foucault, M. (2007). *Security, Territory, Population: Lectures at the College De France 1977–78*. London: Palgrave.

Foucault, M. (2008). *The History of Sexuality. Vol. 1: An Introduction*. London: Penguin.

Franklin, B. (1997). *Packaging Politics: Political Communications in Britain's Media Democracy*. London: Arnold.

Friedberg, A. (1992). *Window Shopping: Cinema and the Postmodern*. Berkeley: University of California Press.

Frow, J. (1997). *Time and Commodity Culture*. Oxford: Oxford University Press.

Frow, J. (2006). *Genre*. London: Routledge.

Gates, B. (1999). *Business @ the Speed of Thought: Using a Digital Nervous System*. New York: Warner Books.

Gauntlett, D. (ed.) (2000). *Web Studies: Rewiring Media Studies for the Digital Age*. London: Arnold.

Gauntlett, D. (2004). *Moving Experiences: Understanding Television's Influences and Effects*. Eastleigh: John Libbey.

Gilligan, V. (dir.). (2008). *Breaking Bad*. Hollywood: American Movie Classics.

Ginsborg, P. (2004). *Television, Power and Patrimony*. London: Verso.

Golding, P. (1999). 'Worldwide Wedge: Division and Contradiction in the Global Information Infrastructure'. In S. Marris and S. Thornham (eds). *Media Studies: A Reader*. Edinburgh: Edinburgh University Press.

Gramsci, A. (1971). *Selections from the Prison Notebooks*. New York: International Publishers.

Greenwald, R. (dir.) (2004). *Outfoxed: Rupert Murdoch's War on Journalism*. Carolina Productions.

Gregory, R. (1967). *Eye and Brain*. London: World University Library.

Guggenheim, D. (dir.) (2006). *An Inconvenient Truth*. Hollywood: Paramount.

Habermas, J. (1989). *The Structural Transformation of the Public Sphere*. Cambridge, MA: MIT Press.

Habermas, J. (2006). 'The Public Sphere: An Encyclopedia Article'. In M. Durham and D. Kellner (eds). *Media and Cultural Studies: Keyworks*. London: Routledge.

Hall, S. (2005). 'Encoding/Decoding'. In M. Durham and D. Kellner (eds). *Media and Cultural Studies: Keyworks*. New York: Routledge.

Hardt, M. and Negri, A. (2001). *Empire*. Cambridge: Harvard University Press.

Hawkes, T. (1977). *Structuralism and Semiotics*. London: Methuen.

Hearn, A. (2008). '"Meat, Mask, Burden": Probing the Contours of the Branded Self'. *Journal of Consumer Culture*, 8 (2).

Hebdige, D. (1979). *Subculture: The Meaning of Style*. London: Methuen.

Herman, E. and Chomsky, N. (1994). *Manufacturing Consent: The Political Economy of the Mass Media*. London: Vintage.

Hermes, J. and Dahlgren, P. (2006). 'Cultural Studies and Citizenship'. *European Journal of Cultural Studies*, 9 (3).

Hesmondhalgh, D. (2002). *The Cultural Industries*. Thousand Oaks, CA: Sage.

Holloway, S. L. and Valentine, G. (2003). *Cyberkids: Children in the Information Age*. London: Routledge.

Horkheimer, M. and Adorno, T. (1972). *Dialectic of Enlightenment*. New York: Herder & Herder.

Horrocks, R. (2004). 'The History of New Zealand Television: An Expensive Medium for a Small Country'. In R. Horrocks and N. Perry (eds). *Television in New Zealand: Programming the Nation*. New York: Oxford University Press.

Huizinga, J. (1966). *Homo Ludens*. Boston: Beacon Press.

Innis, H. (1950). *Empire and Communication*. Oxford: Clarendon Press.

Innis, H. (1951). *The Bias of Communication*. Toronto: University of Toronto Press.

Jackson, M. (2007). 'Back in the Mists of Fear: A Primer on the Terrorist Raids'. <http://www.arena.org.nz/terprimr.htm>. Accessed 16 February 2009.

Jackson, P. (dir.) (2001). *The Lord of the Rings: The Fellowship of the Ring*. Hollywood: New Line Cinema.

Jackson, P. (dir.) (2002). *The Lord of the Rings: The Two Towers*. Hollywood: New Line Cinema.

Jackson, P. (dir.) (2003). *The Lord of the Rings: The Return of the King*. Hollywood: New Line Cinema.

Jay, K. (2004). *More Than Just a Game*. New York: Columbia University Press.

Jenkins, H. (1992). *Textual Poachers: Television Fans and Participatory Culture*. New York: Routledge.

Jenkins, H. (1998). 'From Home(r) to the Holodeck: New Media and the Humanities'. *MIT Communications Forum*. 6 December. <http://web.mit.edu/comm-forum/papers/jenkins_fh.html>. Accessed 2 February 2006.

Jermyn, D. and Brooker, W. (eds) (2003). *The Audience Studies Reader*. London: Routledge.

Johnson, R. (2005). 'The Lawsuit of the Rings'. *New York Times*. 27 June. <http://www.nytimes.com/2005/06/27/business/media/27movie.html?ei=5087&en=db37ee5a99865c2f&ex=1122523200&mkt=bizphotocaption&pagewanted=print>. Accessed 16 February 2009.

Jonze, S. (dir.) (2002). *Adaptation*. Hollywood: Propaganda Films.

Kahn, R. and Kellner, D. (2005). 'Oppositional Politics and the Internet: A Critical/Reconstructive Approach'. *Cultural Politics*, 1 (1).

Kern, S. (2000). *The Culture of Time and Space (1880–1918)*. Cambridge: Harvard University Press.

Kruger, A. (2004). 'What's the Difference between Propaganda for Tourism or for a Political Regime?'. In J. Bale and M. Christensen (eds). *Post-Olympism*. Oxford: Berg.

Lasswell, H. (1938). *Propaganda Techniques in the World War*. London: Paul.

Lateline (2008). 'Tony Jones Interviews Erping Zhang'. 5 August. <http://www.abc.net.au/lateline/content/2008/s2325003.htm>. Accessed 16 February 2009.

Le Bon, G. (1903). *The Crowd: A Study of the Popular Mind*. London: Fisher Unwin.

Lefebvre, H. (1990). *Everyday Life in the Modern World*. London: Transaction Publishers.

Lefort, C. (1986). *The Political Forms of Modern Society*. Cambridge: MIT Press.

Legatt, R. (2000). *The Beginnings of Photography*. <http://www.rleggat.com/photohistory>. Accessed 16 February 2009.

Lewis, J. and Wahl-Jorgensen, K. (2005). 'Active Citizen or Couch Potato? Journalism and Public Opinion'. In S. Allan (ed.). *Journalism: Critical Issues*. Oxford: Oxford University Press.

Lewis, T. (2008). 'Transforming Citizens? Green Politics and Ethical Consumption on Lifestyle Television'. *Continuum: Journal of Media and Cultural Studies*, 22 (2)

Lippmann, W. (1997). *Public Opinion*. New York: Free Press.

Lister, M., Dovey, J., Giddings, S., Grant, I. and Kelly, K. (2003). *New Media: A Critical Introduction*. London: Routledge.

Livingston, K. (1996). *The Wired Nation Continent: The Communication Revolution and Federating Australia*. Melbourne: Oxford University Press.

Luke, A. and Gilbert, P. (eds) (1993). *Literacy in Contexts: Australian Perspectives and Issues*. St Leonards: Allen & Unwin.

Lyon, D. (1988). *The Information Society: Issues and Illusions*. Cambridge: Polity Press.

Lyotard, J. F. (1984). *The Postmodern Condition*. Minneapolis: University of Minnesota Press.

McKee, R. (1997). *Story: Substance, Structure, Style and The Principles of Screenwriting*. New York: HarperCollins.

McKee, R. (2009). 'Story Seminar'. <http://mckeestory.com/homepage.html>. Accessed 16 February 2009.

MacKenzie, D. and Wajcman, J. (eds) (1999). *The Social Shaping of Technology*. Buckingham: Open University Press.

McLeod, K. (2005). 'Confessions of an Intellectual (Property): Danger Mouse, Mickey Mouse, Sonny Bono and My Long and Winding Path as an Activist–Scholar'. *Journal of Popular Music and Society*, 28 (1).

McLuhan, M. (1962). *The Gutenberg Galaxy: The Making of Typographic Man*. Toronto: University of Toronto Press.

McLuhan, M. (1973). *Understanding Media*. Cambridge: MIT Press.

McLuhan, M. and McLuhan, E. (1988). *Laws of the Media*. Toronto: Toronto University Press.

McNair, B. (2006). *Cultural Chaos: Journalism, News and Power in a Globalised World*. London: Routledge.

Manovich, L. (2002). *The Language of New Media*. Cambridge: MIT Press.

Marshall, D. (2004). *New Media Cultures*. London: Arnold.

Marvin, C. (1988). *When Old Technologies Were New: Thinking about Technologies in the Late Nineteenth Century*. Oxford: Oxford University Press.

Mattelart, A. (1994). *Mapping World Communication*. Minneapolis: University of Minnesota Press.

Mattelart, A. (2000). *Networking the World: 1794–2000*. (L. Carey-Libbrecht and J. Cohen trans.). Minneapolis: University of Minnesota Press.

Mattelart, A. (2003). *The Information Society*. London: Sage.

Mattelart, A. and Mattelart, M. (1992). *Rethinking Media Theory*. Minneapolis: University of Minnesota Press.

Microsoft 'Soaring Anthem' (2001). House of Usher. <http://www.methodstudios.com>. Accessed 16 February 2009.

Miller, P. (2004). 'The Rise of Network Campaigning'. In H. McCarthy, R. Miller and P. Skidmore (eds). *Network Logic: Who Governs in an Interconnected World?* London: Demos.

Mirror (2005). '"White Band Aid" Historic Chance to End Poverty'. 2 February.

Monbiot, G. (2006). *Heat: How to Stop the Planet Burning.* Camberwell: Allen Lane.

Morley, D. (1980). *The 'Nationwide' Audience: Structure and Decoding.* London: British Film Institute.

Morris, M. and McCalman, I. (1999). 'Public Culture and Humanities Research in Australia: A Report'. *Public Culture,* 11 (2).

Mosco, V. (2004). *The Digital Sublime: Myth, Power and Cyberspace.* Cambridge: MIT Press.

Nash, K. (2008). 'Global Citizenship as Show Business: The Cultural Politics of Make Poverty History'. *Media, Culture and Society,* 30 (2).

New Zealand On Air (2009). 'About Us'. <http://www.nzonair.govt.nz/about_us.php>. Accessed 16 February 2009.

New Zealand Press Council (2007). 'Case Number: 1090 Tze Ming Mok and Others against *North & South*'. <http://www.presscouncil.org.nz/display_ruling. asp?casenumber=1090>. Accessed 16 February 2009.

New Zealand Press Council (2009). <http://www.presscouncil.org.nz/index.htm>. Accessed 16 February 2009.

New Zealand Privacy Commissioner (2009). 'Websites and Personal Information'. <http:// privacy.org.nz/websites-and-personal-information>, <http://www.methodstudios.com>. Accessed 16 February 2009.

Nye, D. (1996). *The Technological Sublime.* Cambridge: MIT Press.

Ong, W. (1988). *Orality and Literacy: The Technologizing of the Word.* New York: Methuen.

Papacharissi, Z. (2002). 'The Internet as a Public Sphere'. *New Media & Society,* 4 (1).

Pilger, J. (ed.) (2004). *Tell Me No Lies: Investigative Journalism and Its Triumphs.* London: Jonathan Cape.

Pilger, J. and Martin, C. (dirs) (2003). *Breaking the Silence: Truth and Lies in the War on Terror.* ITV.

Poster, M. (1995). 'Postmodern Virtualities'. In M. Featherstone and R. Burrows (eds). *Cyberspace/Cyberbodies/Cyberpunk.* London: Sage.

Poster, M. (1997). *Cultural History and Postmodernity: Disciplinary Readings and Challenges.* New York: Columbia University Press.

Postman, N. (1988). *Conscientious Objections.* New York: Knopf.

Potter, W. J. (2001). *Media Literacy.* Thousand Oaks, CA: Sage.

Raymond, J. (1996). *The Invention of the Newspaper.* Oxford: Clarendon Press.

Reuters (2008). 'will.i.am's "Yes We Can Song" Video Awarded Emmy(R) for New Approaches in Daytime Entertainment'. 16 June. <http://www.reuters.com/article/ pressRelease/idUS145884+16-Jun-2008+MW20080616>. Accessed 16 February 2009.

Rheingold, H. (2003). *Smart Mobs: The Next Social Revolution.* Cambridge: Basic Books.

Ricouer, P. (1984). *Time and Narrative. Vol. 1.* Chicago: University of Chicago Press.

Royal, H. (dir.) (1996). *One Land Two People*. Ninox Films.

Rush, M. (2006). 'Adult World Must Let Girls Be Girls'. *Sydney Morning Herald* (SMH). 10 October. <http://www.smh.com.au/news/opinion/adult-world-must-let-girls-be-girls/2006/10/09/1160246068431.html>. Accessed 16 February 2009.

Rushkoff, D. (1997). *Children of Chaos: Surviving the End of the World as We Know It*. London: HarperCollins.

Saussure, F. de (1989). *Course in General Linguistics*. London: Open Court.

Schirato, T. (1998). 'Meaning'. *Encyclopedia of Semiotics*. Oxford: Oxford University Press.

Schirato, T. (2005). 'Cultural Literacy, the Media and the Public Sphere'. In K. Kwansah-Aidoo (ed.). *Topical Issues in Communication and Media Research*. New York: Nova Science.

Schirato, T. (2007). *Understanding Sports Culture*. London: Sage.

Schirato, T. and Webb, J. (2004). *Reading the Visual*. Sydney: Allen & Unwin.

Schirato, T. and Yell, S. (2000). *Communication and Cultural Literacy*. Sydney: Allen & Unwin.

Schivelbusch, W. (1988). *Disenchanted Night*. Los Angeles: University of California Press.

Schudson, M. (1984). *Advertising: The Uneasy Persuasion*. Los Angeles: University of California Press.

Seattle Indymedia Center. <http://seattle.indymedia.org>.

Semetko, H. A. (2004). 'The Political Economy of Communications'. In D. H. Downing, D. McQuail, P. Schlesinger and E. Wartella (eds). *The SAGE Handbook of Media Studies*. Thousand Oaks, CA: Sage.

Silverstone, R. (1994). *Television and Everyday Life*. London: Routledge.

Simon, D. (prod.) (2002–2008). *The Wire*. New York: Home Box Office.

Soules, M. (2007). 'Harold Adams Innis: The Bias of Communications & Monopolies of Power'. <www.media-studies.ca/articles/innis.htm>. Accessed 22 May 2009.

Spielberg, S. (dir.) (1981). *Raiders of the Lost Ark*. Hollywood: Paramount.

Spigel, L. (1992). *Make Room for TV: Television and the Family Ideal in Postwar America*. Chicago: University of Chicago Press.

Standage, T. (1998). *The Victorian Internet*. New York: Walker and Co.

Sterne, J. (2003). 'Bourdieu, Technique and Technology'. *Cultural Studies*, 17 (3–4).

Stevens, G. (dir.) (1939). *Gunga Din*. Hollywood: RKO.

Straw, W. (2007). 'Embedded Memories'. In C. Acland (ed.). *Residual Media*. Minneapolis: University of Minnesota Press.

Terranova, T. (2004). *Networks Culture: Politics for the Information Age*. London: Pluto.

Thompson, J. B. (1990). *Ideology and Modern Culture: Critical Social Theory in the Era of Mass Communication*. Cambridge: Polity Press.

Thompson, P. (2003). 'Whale Rider'. 27 April. <http://sunday.ninemsn.com.au/sunday/film_reviews/article_1256.asp?s>. Accessed 16 February 2009.

Thornton, S. (1995). *Club Cultures*. Cambridge: Polity Press.

Todorov, T. (1981). *Introduction to Poetics*. Minneapolis: University of Minnesota Press.

Trotter, W. (1924). *Instincts of the Herd in Peace and War*. London: Unwin.

Tsaliki, L. (2000). 'The Internet as Public Sphere'. In D. Fleming (ed.). *Formations: A 21st Century Media Studies Textbook*. Manchester: Manchester University Press.

Turkle, S. (1995). *Life on the Screen: Identity in the Age of the Internet*. New York: Simon & Schuster.

Turner, G. (2002). 'Public Relations'. In S. Cunningham and G. Turner (eds). *The Media and Communications in Australia*. Crows Nest: Allen & Unwin.

Universal Declaration of Human Rights (2009). Article 19. United Nations. <http://www.un.org/Overview/rights.html>. Accessed 16 February 2009.

van Dijk, J. (2006). *The Network Society: Social Aspects of New Media*. Thousand Oaks, CA: Sage.

Virilio, P. (2002). *Ground Zero*. London: Verso.

Volosinov, V. (1986). *Marxism and the Philosophy of Language*. Cambridge: Harvard University Press.

Wasko, J. (2003). *How Hollywood Works*. Thousand Oaks, CA: Sage.

Webb, J., Schirato, T. and Danaher, G. (2002). *Understanding Bourdieu*. London: Sage.

Wertham, F. (1955). *Seduction of the Innocent*. London: Museum Press.

Williams, R. (1980). 'Means of Communication as Means of Production'. *Problems in Materialism and Culture: Selected Essays,* London: Verso.

Williams, R. (1982). *Dream Worlds*. Berkeley: University of California Press.

Williams, R. (1983). *Keywords*. London: Fontana.

Wilson, A. (1994). *Wire and Wireless: A History of Telecommunications in New Zealand, 1890–1987*. Palmerston: North Dunmore Press.

Zizek, S. (1992). *The Sublime Object of Ideology*. London: Verso.

Zizek, S. (2002). *Welcome to the Desert of the Real*. London: Verso.

INDEX